SAS OPERATIONS

GW00632269

SAS Operations

James D. Ladd

ROBERT HALE · LONDON

Robert Hale Limited
Clerkenwell House
Clerkenwell Green
London EC1R 0HT

British Library Cataloguing in Publication Data

Ladd, James
  SAS operations.
  1.Great Britain, *Special Air Service Regiment*
  —History   2. Great Britain—History—
  Military—20th century
  I. Title
  356'.167'0941   UA659.S67

  ISBN 0-7090-2372-3

Photoset by Rowland Phototypesetting Limited
Printed in Great Britain by
St Edmundsbury Press, Bury St Edmunds, Suffolk
Bound by Woolnough Bookbinding, Northants

Contents

List of Illustrations   ix
Author's Preface   xiii

1 CONCEIVED IN THE DESERT   1
   The first raid by L Detachment, November 1941 – David
   Stirling's innovations – Operations with the Long Range
   Desert Group – Jalo – L Detachment comes of age

2 'A BIT HERE, A BIT THERE'   21
   Raids in early 1942 – Frustrations in raids on ports – Life
   in the desert bases – Derna raid, June 1942 – New
   techniques – Sidi Haneish raid – Commando-style raids
   fail – Co-ordination with Eighth Army – Stirling captured,
   January 1943

3 ISLAND WARS AND MAINLAND RAIDS IN THE   45
   MEDITERRANEAN
   Jellicoe's Special Boat Squadron – Strategic raids on Crete,
   July 1943 – Diplomacy fails in the Dodecanese –
   Harassing Axis garrisons in the Aegean 1943–4 – Island
   of Simi captured, July 1944 – Anders Lassen VC – SAS
   units at Termoli, October 1943 – Landed 800km north of
   battle areas to cut rail links in northern Apennines,
   September 1943

4 TRIUMPH AND TRAGEDY IN NORTH-WEST
   EUROPE   68
   Formation of Brigade – Training in Scotland – Radio
   communications – Roles in Normandy, June 1944 –

'Titanic I and IV' – Bases deep in occupied France – 'Bulbasket' encircled, 3 July – 'Dingson' and other operations by French SAS – 'Gain' base opened at second attempt – SOE and other reception committees – The Orleans 'gap' – Parachuting jeeps – Railway sabotage – Road ambushes – 'Gain' compromised – German counter-measures – 'Houndsworth' – Value of military intelligence gained – 'Tombola' and heavy weapons (Italy) – Snatch operations – Anti-terrorism in 1945 – Operations in van of Allied advance – World War II casualties

5 NEW REGIMENTS, NEW ROLES   104
War Office report of 1946 – Formation of Territorial Volunteer Regiment – Malayan Scouts (SAS) – 'Tree' jumps – Belum valley, 1952 – Telok Anson, 1958 – Work with aborigines – Selection and training in 1950s – SOPs – Chain of Command

6 REFINEMENTS IN LOW-KEY TACTICS: BORNEO   118
   1962–6
Long distance radios – Borneo background – Confrontation on the border – Recce patrols and Long Jawai, March 1963 – G Squadron – The Border Scouts – Batu Hitan – Koemba River, February and May 1965 – Co-operation with Gurkha Regiments – Special patrols

7 TEACHING WAR AND WINNING THE PEACE   148
Oman background – Green Mountain, 1958 – Preventive action, 1969 – Dhofar background – 'Psyops' – Clinics – The *Firquats* – The decisive action at Mirbat, July 1972 – 'A gain of two'

8 INTERNAL SECURITY   166
Ireland, 1969 – South Armagh, 1976 – patrol targets – surveillance equipment – effective ideas – Counter-Revolutionary Warfare teams – Hostages rescued – Terrorism deterred

9   SOUTH ATLANTIC VICTORY   174
     South Georgia recaptured – Recces on East Falkland –
     Hides and observation – Offensive raids – Pebble Island –
     Diversion at Goose Green – Helicopter accident – Naval
     gunfire support – Surrender to persuasion – Raid on
     Stanley Harbour – Secret ventures

Appendix I   *Abbreviations*   191
Appendix II   *Summary of Operations*   193
Sources   209
Index   211

Illustrations

Between pages 50 and 51

1 L Detachment, the forerunner of the SAS, at Kabrit 1941
2 May 1945: 1 SAS enters Keel ahead of the Allied armoured columns
3 Desert patrols 1943: a jeep carrying twin K-guns at the front and a single at the rear
4 A jeep of the 2nd SAS Regiment near Tunisia fitted with Browning and K-guns
5 Patrol reaching Allied lines near Tripoli
6 Machine-gun team from No 3 Squadron, 2 SAS advancing towards the hills near Castino, Genoa
7 Major 'Sandy' Scratchly
8 Lt-Col Blondeel receiving the DSO from Maj-Gen G. Surtees
9 Celle, north-east of Hanover: German officials are taken to Allied HQ for interrogation
10 Sgt A Schofield and Trooper O Jeavons in a jeep modified for deep penetration patrols
11 Parachuting jeeps – training exercise
12 Men of D Squadron, 1 SAS, Borneo, 1964
13 Signal centre at SAS operational HQ, Borneo 1964
14 Dyaks of 'Harrison Force' carry a dead enemy soldier, Borneo 1963
15 Training Dyaks for service with the Border Scouts
16 A senior medical NCO leaving a jungle patrol camp
17 An SAS patrol crossing a swift flowing river in northern Borneo
18 Abseiling from a helicopter to Borneo's jungle

Between pages 130 and 131

19   SAS Land Rovers on patrol in the Arabian deserts
20   The barren mountains of Southern Arabia
21   Dropping mail to a patrol from A Squadron in the Oman
22   Signallers of A Squadron HQ on night duty
23   Member of SAS Mountain Troop
24   A 1970s Land Rover equipped for patrols in Europe
25   Display of equipment showing range of Troopers' skills
26   Trooper equipped for free-fall parachuting
27   A climber of Mountain Troop
28   Troopers demonstrating belt equipment
29   A Trooper's belt pouch with contents
30   Troopers firing the 84mm Carl Gustav anti-tank weapon
31   Camouflage, stealth and speed are the hallmarks of SAS
        patrols
32   Fast-moving, shadowy figures: men of the SAS

Picture Credits

The following photographs have been reproduced by kind permission of:
The Imperial War Museum: 1, 2, 3, 4, 5, 6, 7, 8, 9, 10, 11, 12, 13, 14, 16, 18,
19, 20, 21, 22; M. J. Andrews: 15, 17; Photographers International Ltd: 23,
24, 25, 26, 27, 28, 29, 30, 31, 32.

Maps

	page
Theatres of operations North Africa, 1941–43	4–5
Airfields raided by SBS, Crete, 1942–44	48
Dodecanese Islands raided by SBS, 1943 and 1944	57
Location of SAS operations, France and north-west Europe, 1944–45	72–3
Area of operations by D Squadron 1 SAS in Paris-Orlean's 'Gap'	83
Borneo area of operations by 22 SAS, 1962–66	120
Dhofar Province of Oman in which SAS Squadrons operated from 1970–76	154
East Falkland Island on which SAS patrols operated in the summer of 1982	183

Author's Preface

SAS operations have always had their exciting moments. Yet their nature has changed over the years to meet the different types of warfare Britain has been forced to wage in defence of freedom. Their first operation, in November 1941, was a disaster but from such tentative beginnings developed the Special Air Service Regiment, who in the 1980s provide patrols which each have 'intelligence-gathering skills and the capacity to mount highly destructive raids', as the British Secretary of Defence pointed out, in highlighting the unique abilities of these special forces.

This book does not attempt to give a detailed history of the Regiment, but in examining the story of selected operations it shows how men of the Regiment have achieved near miracles in feats of arms, through their skill and courage. Their motto 'Who dares wins' was coined in the days of desert raids and has been their watchword through operations deep in German-occupied Europe in the 1940s, in the jungles of south-east Asia and in the deserts of Arabia during Britain's withdrawal from her Empire, through the tragic uncertainties of Northern Ireland, against terrorists in London and across the bleak uplands of the Falkland Islands. A study of these operations reveals the manner of man who serves in the SAS: an individualist who is hard on his country's enemies, he is also gentle and generous with Allies who are under threats from bullies or the rigours of hostile climates. He is a man who almost inevitably gains your respect for his dedication to his Regiment and the fulfilment of its dangerous roles.

J. D. Ladd
Topsham 1986

In speaking of the achievements of SAS and other voluntary special forces:

> We may feel sure that nothing of which we have any knowledge or record has ever been done by mortal men which surpasses the splendour and daring of their feats of arms.

Sir Winston Churchill,
speech in Westminster Abbey,
21 May 1948

1. Conceived in the Desert

The roar of the bomber's twin engines made conversation impossible among the twelve men sitting on the fuselage floor above the bomb racks. As the engines laboured through dark storm clouds, the vibrations numbed these parachutists' senses as they methodically checked their gear for the last time. The despatcher, an RAF sergeant who would supervise their jump, checked their static lines. These would jerk open the 'chutes as each man fell clear of the Bristol Bombay bomber, and were fixed to so-called strong points in the fuselage. In this obsolete aircraft the fixings looked a mite flimsy, but a man's life could depend on them: in a different aircraft they had already failed twice, and men had plunged to their deaths during training. At that time the lines' clips had twisted free, but now a stout tug by the despatcher on each line satisfied him that the new clips held firm before he moved to the door, nodding to the aircraftsman to open it. Even at a ponderous eighty knots, the rush of cold air sharpened the senses of the jumpers; they saw the sergeant's lips mouth 'Get ready. Watch the light' for they barely heard his words above the roar of wind and engines. Mutely in the rear of the fuselage lay the supply packs of weapons and explosives ready for the airmen to pitch them out after the men; other boxes with their parachutes were clipped to the bomb racks ready for dropping.

One corporal's eyes turned away from this final glance around the plane to study the small lamp mounted by the doorway; his eleven companions did the same. Men eased their shoulders to get more comfortably into their 'chute harnesses, forgetting the cold discomfort of the past 2½ hours of what had been a bumpy switchback of a flight for the latter part of the trip. The dull crack of anti-aircraft shells, felt rather than heard as the plane had banked steeply thirty minutes earlier, had set most of the men's adrenalin racing to key them up for action. Now, as the pilot was having difficulty finding the dropping zone, nerves were steadier, but fear of the unknown was not far away. All wanted to get on with the jump. Then the red light came on. Two minutes to go.

The lieutenant leading the drop was at the door, poised waiting for the green light. It flashed on and he jumped as the despatcher slapped his shoulder. The second man was in position and out of the plane as the corporal blinked to clear the wind tears from his eyes. The jumper's line snaked out before jarring taut for a split second, then trailed slackly from the door, as the corporal moved quickly, ready to go. He did not feel the slap on the shoulder, although all his senses were alert, for at the shouted 'Go!' he was out into the moonless black void, the wind of the slipstream buffeting his face, its noise deafening as he held himself upright, heels together. A sudden jerk and the noise ceased; for brief seconds the gentle stillness gave him a sense of unreality. But where was the ground?

He had dropped from only 150m and should have felt its solid presence in seconds, yet the blackness seemed bottomless as he drifted down. Then, as he gripped his rigging lines, prepared to swing himself clear of unknown difficulties, he was suddenly jarred against a rocky stretch of desert. He came to being dragged across this rough country, his 'chute billowing in the gale-strong wind, at times quite unmanageable even though he followed the drill, rolling onto his stomach as he wrestled to control the rigging lines and collapse the canopy. His efforts were in vain, for no sooner had he got things partly under control than an extra-strong gust snatched them away from him. Nevertheless, he kept his head, despite the bumps and bruising of being dragged along faster than walking pace. So this is how it felt to be tied to a galloping horse, an inconsequential thought he dismissed as with one great effort he turned on his side and hit the release box. There was a merciful unravelling of his harness from his body and he lay semi-conscious for several minutes. A sharp pain in his elbow seemed to be the only indication of serious hurt as he gingerly flexed his ankles before standing up. Then he was almost knocked off his balance by the wind; stinging granules of rock dust, the 'sand' of this desert, stung his face, making breathing difficult and forcing him to turn down wind out into the desert. This gale had blown onshore for several hours and put the jumpers well beyond their intended dropping zone, but the corporal did not know that; he expected to find others from the party who had dropped after him and therefore would be down wind. He never did find them, and this reconstruction was the unfortunate lot of several men who jumped that night of 16/17 November 1941.

The corporal was not the only one lost in this most difficult of jumps. His leader, Captain David Stirling, Scots Guards, was knocked out on landing, taking minutes rather than seconds to free his six feet six inches from his harness. He shouted and shone his torch but his words were lost on the wind, and only with difficulty was he able to bring together ten of his party; the eleventh was missing and not found despite a two-hour search. Like the corporal, he was probably dragged far into the desert, as were most of the ten packages of weapons which had been dropped. Stirling's men found only two of these. One contained Lewes bombs, but there were no fuses and few rations, only enough for one day, and twelve water-bottles (about ten litres) of drinking water. By this time there were only three hours to daylight on Monday.

Their objective was a German airfield near Gazala in Cyrenaica, one of the five which the Detachment were to raid that night in the Gazala-Tmini area. As it should have been only a few hours' march away, Stirling decided to take only Sergeant Tait with him and send the other nine men under Sergeant Yates direct to the planned rendezvous with trucks of the Long Range Desert Group. These, if the parachutists were at the correct dropping zone, should be less than 50km away.

Sergeant Tait was a cheerful professional soldier, and together he and Stirling eventually reached the escarpment, that line of cliffs from which they could see the Mediterranean beyond the coast road. This was the main supply route for German and Italian forces loosely holding a line from the sea at Sollum (on the Egyptian border) 180km to the east of Gazala and well beyond the Allied enclave at Tobruk. The two raiders had marched through the cold dark early on Monday and lain up all Tuesday morning when Stirling realized that they were on a featureless desert plateau and certainly had been dropped well south of their intended landing only fifteen kilometres from the coast. That afternoon a storm threatened, and at 1630 they moved the last six kilometres to the edge of the escarpment, but within the hour the clouds broke in a deluge of rain, filling the normally dry river-bed wadis and blotting out the landscape, to make any reconnaissance of the traffic on the road impossible. The British attack planned for that morning to relieve Tobruk could not therefore get any useful help from Stirling, but he had confirmed his position by radio as east of Gazala. There was no alternative but to head for the rendezvous. This RV lay 65km inland, on an old desert slavers' track, the Trig el Abd, where A Patrol of the Long Range Desert Group would shine a Tilley lamp from a small hill.

They left the escarpment in relentless rain, Stirling's carefully packed cigarettes disintegrating in his sodden kit. They had been over thirty-six hours in the desert by 0700 next morning. When the rain stopped, about dawn, they slumped down in the shade of a hillock and slept for four hours. Their wet clothes had dried on them before they moved off again in the midday haze. Tait was barely able to put his weight on one swollen ankle, twisted no doubt at the time he landed but which had passed virtually unnoticed in the activity of the previous day. Nevertheless, he moved steadily in the direction which Stirling judged would bring them to the RV. By the afternoon they were some twenty kilometres from it when Stirling spotted movement to the south several kilometres away. Through his field-glasses he could make out nine figures heading for the track, and their movement convinced him that this must be Yates and the rest of the party – a deduction reinforced by their route as they turned westward along the track.

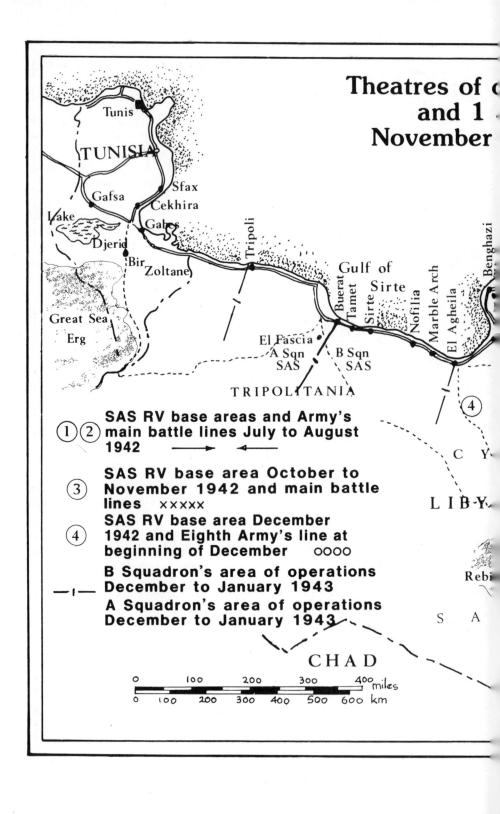

Theatres of ⟨...⟩
and 1⟨...⟩
November ⟨...⟩

SAS RV base areas and Army's main battle lines July to August 1942 ① ②

SAS RV base area October to November 1942 and main battle lines ③ ×××××

SAS RV base area December 1942 and Eighth Army's line at beginning of December ④ ○○○○

B Squadron's area of operations December to January 1943

A Squadron's area of operations December to January 1943

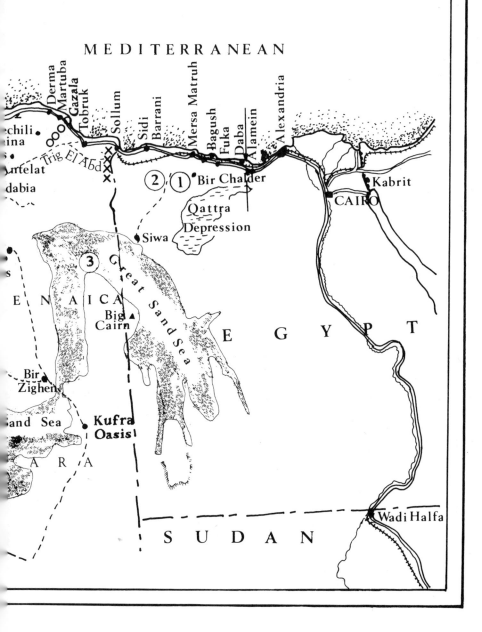

**erations by L Detachment
AS in North Africa
941 to February 1943**

MEDITERRANEAN

Derma
Martuba
Gazala
Tobruk
Sollum
Sidi
Barrani
Mersa Matruh
Bagush
Fuka
Daba
Alamein
Alexandria
chili
ina
rtelat
dabia
Trig El 'Abd
② ① Bir Chalder
Qattra
Depression
Kabrit
CAIRO
Siwa
③
C Y R E N A I C A
Great Sand Sea
Big
Cairn
E G Y P T
Bir
Zighen
and Sea
**Kufra
Oasis**
A R A
Wadi Halfa
S U D A N

Stirling and Tait followed. After the brief tropical dusk, they saw what they thought was a star low in the sky but as they neared it, about 0200 next morning, they saw it was a lamp. Close by in a small ravine were the LRDG trucks under camouflage nets. Here was a welcome with hot tea laced with whisky for the thirsty pair who had existed on a water-bottle apiece during the previous nineteen hours and a handful each of emergency rations. They were cheered to find Lieutenants Fraser and Lewes already at the RV with eight of their ten men. They had also had a disastrous drop and been up to the coast to locate their position before marching to the RV. Paddy Mayne came in soon after first light, having waited nearby to be sure that he had correctly identified the position of the patrol. His experience had been the same as the others, and he had left two badly injured men near the coast.

Sergeant Yates' men had had a torrid three days after leaving the dropping zone early on Monday. Several of the men had been injured as the wind gusted to 150k.m.p.h. at the time they landed, but they marched into the desert. They even came close to reaching the RV before an Axis patrol captured them. Lieutenant Bonnington was thought to have been captured with his men when their plane was talked down by an English voice onto a German airstrip, a deceptively smug tale which the Germans put about at that time. But the raiders' aircraft, hit when its pilot flew low to assess the wind drift by dropping flares, had made a forced landing west of Tobruk. The crew made emergency repairs and took off again but were forced to crash-land for a second time after being attacked by an Me 109, and these raiders were also captured.

This first raid was on 17 November, the date regarded by the Special Air Service Regiment as that of their founding. Even if it was a disaster, the concept was a neat tactic using an economy of manpower for the maximum of destruction.

Lieutenant David Stirling, who put forward these ideas, is a tall, gentle man with a charming smile; modest, he stoops slightly, seemingly in apology for his unusual height, yet he has the ingenuity, inexhaustible energy and gambler's instinct, losing all signs of vague *bonhomie* when there are odds to be counted. He had learned in July 1941 that a fellow officer in 'Layforce', Jock Lewes, had acquired fifty parachutes offloaded in Alexandria, Egypt, for trans-shipment to India. Lewes was encouraged to experiment with these 'chutes, but when he and Stirling made two of the first jumps from a Valencia, an aircraft quite unsuitable for this purpose, the tall Lieutenant snagged his 'chute on the tail of the aircraft, landed heavily and injured his back. In hospital after this, during July, he wrote a set of guide notes, which can be summarized to outline his theory:

a. The Axis forces are vulnerable to attacks on their transports, vehicle parks and aerodromes along the coast.

b. Plans to land the two hundred men of a Commando for such raids against a single target inevitably destroy the element of surprise when their ship must be escorted along the coast, a disproportionately high risk in itself for the Navy.

c. Landing five-man teams with the element of surprise could destroy, say, fifty aircraft on an airfield which a Commando would have to fight to reach.

d. The team might be inserted by parachute or other means such as a submarine or a disguised fishing boat.

He went on to propose that the unit should do its own training and come directly under the Commander-in-Chief Middle East.

The Commander-in-Chief, General Auchinleck, an efficient if cautious Scot, saw the proposals as a safe bet: should they go wrong, the casualties would be few in number; if successful, they could – and eventually did – change the course of major battles. Three days later he briefed Stirling: the Lieutenant would be promoted Captain; he could recruit from 'Layforce' five officers and sixty other ranks to join the unit; and he was to prepare for raids against five airfields the Germans were using as bases for their latest Me 109 F fighters. Teams of four men, not five as originally suggested, were to be the operational basis for raids (interestingly the team strength of British infantry in the 1980s, and used by L Detachment, with only a brief period in the desert when a second-in-command was added to make five-man teams). The Detachment's parent body was a non-existent Special Air Service Brigade, which to Axis agents and others might imply that there were more than sixty-six parachutists in Egypt.

The Australian-born Lewes gave a practical edge to Stirling's theories with such inventions as the Lewes bomb, a blend of plastic explosive (PE) and thermite kneaded together with a lubricant into a bomb the size of a tennis ball. This explosively inflammable mix gave a charge of about 400 grams, which on the boss of a propeller would not only damage the 'prop' but also set alight any petrol or other fuel within range of the blast. Lewes also applied his intellectual talents to methods of training L Detachment.

Another Commando officer recruited at this time was the redoubtable Paddy Mayne, a hefty solicitor who played Rugby football for Ireland. Under a cloud of disfavour for striking his commanding officer, when he agreed to join the Detachment he doubted if the raids would be practical but saw in them a chance to get to grips with the Germans.

Sixty other ranks (enlisted men) were selected from volunteers from 'Layforce' at Geneifa, to begin concentrated training in parachuting and demolitions at Kabrit on the Great Bitter Lake some 150km south of Cairo. Within a few days of their arrival the Detachment had 'won' comfortable furnishings for their tents from the unoccupied huts of a New Zealand camp which they raided one night. Soon their camp was dominated by a 'great framework of swings [standing over ten metres high] with skeletal gauntness against the powder blue sky', on which parachutists did their initial training. It was from Kabrit after only twelve weeks of special training that the five raiding parties moved out to board the Bombay aircraft during the afternoon of Sunday 16 November. Conflicting weather reports of likely ground winds led Stirling to consult his officers before agreeing to carry on with the raid, but all were keen to take off as the last three major raids planned by 'Layforce' had been cancelled earlier in the year. In the event, as we have seen, the landings could hardly have been more hazardous, with only twenty-two of the sixty men who set out returning to Kabrit. Yet the men had shown those resources of personal determination, self-discipline and sheer guts, to achieve near miracles of endurance which would become the hallmark of SAS troopers over the next four decades.

The most successful part of the raiding operations had been the LRDG patrol's recovery of the survivors, as LRDG trucks waited at the RV until the Friday night in case any other teams could be recovered. They then took Stirling and his twenty-one men to Siwa Oasis, nearly 300km to the south-west and across the frontier.

Siwa, with its salt-water lake, innumerable black swarms of flies and old caravan routes, has a dry heat that taxes a man's strength and will to work. To the south, beyond the palm groves, roll the great whale-back dunes running parallel almost north to south in the Great Sand Sea, known to the Arabs as Devil's Country, an area the size of Ireland. It could only be crossed 200km south of Siwa by a route which passed an artesian well at Ain Dalla, the last watering point in over 500km *en route* for Kufra. To the north-west of Siwa lies the Qattara Depression, running further northward to within 50km of the sea near El Alamein, its floor 110m below sea-level and impassable to ordinary vehicles. Kufra was the key settlement to the control of the inner desert, over 1,500km from the coast and stretching for some 2,000km from the Nile westward – an area about the size of the Indian sub-continent. It is haunted by the Ghibili, a hot wind laden with dust, rather than sand, for true sandstorms are rare in these regions, though duststorms occur frequently in the early evening. The great variations of temperature inland – 50°C by noon, to several degrees of frost by 0600 next morning – can lead ill-equipped or at least irresolute men to die from exposure. Yet some SAS troopers crossed these wastes without boots, water or rations, in their determination to survive.

In November 1941 Brigadier D. W. Reid, a massive man with ruddy cheeks and an iron handshake, led his 'Oasis' Force with great skill to take Aujila and then capture the six hundred Italians of the Jalo garrison, despite continual harassment from Axis aircraft. Here, at the former trading centre of the Majabra Arabs, he met Stirling in mid-December, when the Captain returned to the desert for a series of raids in which LRDG Patrols would be used. Their forward base among the sand-blown few huts and Italian buildings, all that remained of this once prosperous settlement, was ideal for L Detachment's purpose: raids which would destroy German aircraft on the airfields at Agedabia and elsewhere on the Gulf of Sirte coast.

Ritchie had been placed in command of the army on 25 November and still had great faith in the enterprise Stirling had shown, while Auchinleck was prepared to let the Captain continue his raids and gave him a free hand to plan the details, helping to overcome the raiders' supply problems since all twenty-two trained men would be needed in the field. Stirling opted for the LRDG as the Detachment's parent organization. He, Major Don Steele, (the officer commanding a patrol of the LRDG) and Brigadier Reid were then able to make their plans at Jalo. Preliminary raids would be made on 14 December, a major raid against Agedabia airfields – the prime objective – on 21 December, to be followed four days later by raids on three successive nights, when an Allied assault on Benghazi was to be near its climax. Ritchie had been reinforced but the Axis forces were short of men and supplies as the Allies controlled the Mediterranean – a situation which they exploited, reaching Derna on 19 December and with forward elements of the 22nd Guards Brigade fifteen kilometres east of Benghazi by 23 December.

At this time the LRDG consisted of: ten patrols, each with specially equipped four-wheel-drive Ford cars and 30-cwt Chevrolet trucks with a range of 1,800km without refuelling; a survey section for making maps; an artillery section with a 4.5-inch (124mm) howitzer, a 25-pounder (88mm) and a light tank, each mounted on a ten-tonner; an air section with two American WACO light aircraft purchased by the War Office; a heavy section of three-ton supply trucks, and a Light Aid Detachment for vehicle maintenance. The first patrol formed by Major (later Colonel) Bagnold had two officers and thirty other ranks with eleven trucks. These each mounted a single machine-gun, supplemented by an early type of Bofors, a 37mm used as an anti-tank gun, and four Boys anti-tank rifles. This and subsequent patrols, including G1 and G2 from the Guards Brigade, had spent the summer of 1941 patrolling from Kufra and Siwa oasis, when their experiences during these 'boring months', to quote the commander of G patrol, led to a number of fundamental developments in their techniques and roles. (One of the latter was to be 'a taxi service for the SAS'.) Their primary job, however, became that of taking traffic censuses on the Axis coast road several thousands of kilometres from the main battle area. They also dropped and picked up agents for the Secret Service, recced terrain which the army might have to cross and occasionally raided enemy transport convoys. This last was only an emergency role by the winter of 1941–2, but, for the LRDG officers working with SAS, emergencies were readily engineered to suit their situations.

The changes in technique related mainly to the size of patrols. By that September they had split the patrols into fifteen- or eighteen-man teams led by an officer, with five vehicles. Their methods of crossing soft sand and navigating thousands of kilometres had improved but were still based on simple ideas pioneered by Bagnold, Britain's leading desert explorer of Africa in the 1930s. He had developed the steel channel strips laid for vehicles to cross soft sand (originally in the Sinai Desert in 1926, where he had used corrugated iron for this purpose). By the early 1940s all vehicles carried such channels in the desert.

Bagnold had also found that a small prismatic compass, difficult to set up in a motor car with varying magnetic interference from tool boxes and other moveable metal loads, took time to use if the navigator had to dismount to get clear of the car's magnetic fields. Even then it could be an inaccurate guide up to 350m out on a day's march of 30km, equivalent to 7km 'adrift' after a 600km drive. His navigators therefore used a sun compass with its horizontal disc marked off in degrees and a central needle casting a shadow not unlike a sundial. The graduated disc was mounted in the car so that it could be rotated as the sun moved across the sky; the needle's shadow then fell to indicate the bearing on which the car was travelling. By reading the milometer distances, the navigator also worked out his position along this bearing. But such dead reckoning could never be infallible, so each night the navigator took star bearings to 'fix' the car's position, using a theodolite and astro-navigation tables from which he read off the longitude and latitude. The first navigators were all old hands in the desert from Bagnold's exploration parties but in 1941 a number of guardsmen and others were trained in astro-navigation for work with patrols, and from 1942 they received an allowance of a shilling per day as 'Land Navigators'.

The 'Old hands' were the men who made the Group successful from the start. Guy Prendergast, a regular soldier commissioned into the Royal Tank Corps in 1925 and who had served with the Sudan Defence Force from 1932 to 1937, is a good example. He took over in the field from Bagnold, who became the army's adviser on long-distance raids. Then there were Bill Kennedy Shaw, a civil servant in Palestine, Pat Clayton of the Egyptian Survey Department (captured in January 1941 when his T Patrol was shot up) and Teddy Mitford, also of the Royal Tank Corps: all had given up leave and spare cash to explore the desert in the 1930s. Often they had joined one of Bagnold's parties, paying their £100-a-head share of expenses in the days when a young officer's pay was about £300 a year.

Radio communication was vital to the success of their road watches and recces, for their information needed to be passed quickly to the army's intelligence sections. Much of it came in a wealth of detail that could not be gleaned by air reconnaissance, although on occasions in the early days they made some specific patrols for information that would have been more easily gained by aerial photographs. Each patrol had its cherished radio truck with a No. 11 set ostensibly with a range of little over 32km and a set to pick up the BBC's time-signals. The radio operators were the best signallers in the army, able to pick up morse from a background 'slush' of atmospherics when working at ranges far beyond the designed operational limits of an 11-set. Their radio links from patrols to the Group's forward base, and from the base to the Cairo citadel compound of Middle East HQ, and to the Eighth Army, were tenuous, for initially these operated on ground aerials at frequencies which meant that sometimes a patrol could not contact base until it was 500km along its route. Later they used aerials suited to the required frequencies.

Their radio procedures followed French civilian routines in order that the base might appear to be a commercial station in Turkey communicating with ships in the Levant. This appears to have deceived the German radio interception services and their direction-finding teams, who had nothing like the comprehensive tracking systems which they used in Europe, because of the distances involved and the limited availability of equipment, most of which was concentrated near the main battle areas. LRDG operators were therefore able to transmit for relatively long periods at night without being D/F-ed and over great distances. G and T patrols even transmitted from Chad to Cairo at one period early in 1941, a link of 2,400km. At base there was a continuous listening watch for emergency calls, and patrols usually came on the air at midday, listening for any fresh orders before moving on that afternoon.

Water was a patrol's most precious possession, as it came to be for SAS desert patrols. Standing order forbade shaving, as this water ration was only a gallon (4.5+ litres) per man per day for all purposes, which included topping up his vehicle's radiator.

The LRDG had suffered a number of losses after Clayton and seven of his patrol were captured: Y Patrol had lost all its officers, and G Patrol lost five trucks. But its soldiers – New Zealanders of R1, R2, T1 and T2 patrols; British Yeomanry and Rhodesians of Y1, Y2, S1 and S2; and the Guards G1 and G2 – had 'learnt to live hard, carrying the minimum amount of food and water . . . [and] how to read the tracks of other men, vehicles and camels so that they could estimate how many and in what direction others had passed before'. Such were the men with whom L Detachment began their raids from Jalo in December 1941.

An emergency situation had arisen in late November when the Eighth Army was embroiled in a battle with Axis Forces between Sollum and Tobruk. Both G1 and G2 Patrols were then ordered to intercept transport on the main and only hard-surfaced road running north from Agedabia 112km to the main Axis base at Benghazi. They were attacked from the air when nearing the coast but Captain Tony Hay led G1 in an attack at dusk on 28 November against a road-house and lorry-park some 50km south of

Benghazi. His eight vehicles, having boldly driven several kilometres down the main highway, turned into the park and fired armour-piercing and incendiary bullets from their machine-guns, while a man on each truck lobbed grenades at some thirty Axis vehicles, before the Patrol escaped into the gathering darkness. They were not followed and, after laying up next day in the desert, returned to the road that dusk to shoot-up a fuel tanker. This was forced off the road, its driver and passenger killed, all other traffic then fleeing back in the directions from which they came before the LRDG trucks drove again into the dark safety of the desert. They spent a further day near the road but were recalled and reached Siwa on 3 December.

The effect of such raids inevitably forced the enemy to withdraw troops from the main battle to protect his lines of communication – a ploy which the SAS have exploited to the full over the years.

Shortly after dawn on Sunday 8 December, a couple of days before they had originally planned to start, Stirling left Jalo to raid the airfield at Sirte. His anxiety to get on with the preliminary raids was spurred by the possibility that the Detachment might at any time be recalled to Cairo. There a number of officers on the GHQ staff, as we have seen, preferred more orthodox methods of warfare to Stirling's ingenious independence. The raids he intended had associations with guerrilla warfare that were regarded in some quarters, even in 1941, as an ungentlemanly way to fight, 'not suited to the forces of the British Empire'. In time the SAS would make a major contribution to altering such naïve military thinking, as we shall see.

Stirling planned to make the maximum use of surprise, and therefore Lewes would attack Agheila airfield on the same night as other patrols of the Detachment hit Sirte. His objective, however, was only half the distance from Jalo that Stirling had to travel, and therefore Lewes did not set out, carried by S2 Patrol, until two days after Stirling. He took with him a Lancia staff car, quite unsuited to desert travel, and (Sergeant Lilley is on record as claiming) it had to be literally carried for a large part of the journey.

S1 Patrol, commanded by Captain Gus Halliman, with Stirling's men 'aboard', followed their usual patrol routine, the stocky, fair-haired Englishman leading his Rhodesians with a practised experience; he was another officer who had served in the Royal Tank Corps before joining the LRDG. He rode in the leading 30-cwt truck with his navigator, Mike Sadler, a Rhodesian; in the second truck were Stirling and Paddy Mayne. Their nine 'troopers'* perched where they could get a footing on the piles

---

* It would be some years before men of the SAS were referred to as troopers, but it seems an appropriate title from the days of these early raids.

of gear. Each of the seven trucks was loaded – indeed almost overloaded, for the LRDG put great faith in the reinforced springs – with petrol, water-cans, blankets and 'cam' (camouflage) nets, not to mention weapons and ammunition, and the seventeen other ranks of the LRDG.

They worked to a well-practised routine ('drill' might sound too formal for these Rhodesians) as Gus Halliman had been with the LRDG for over a year and knew what was required to survive not only against a well-armed enemy but also against the unforgiving hazards of desert travel. As the day warmed up, the men shed their sheepskin jackets; by 1000 hours the sun was well over 20° up in the sky, throwing a sharp shadow from the needle of the sun compass, the pink camouflage of the vehicles blending into the heat haze; by 1100 the blasts of warm air on the ridge tops forced even the aircraft sentries perched atop each truck to discard most of their clothes. By midday, with the sun virtually vertically above them, the shadow on the compass did not reach the graduated dial, so the vehicles were halted. The navigator took a 'fix' on the sun through the smoked glass of his theodolite, the radio operator as usual contacted base for any fresh orders, and the rest lay comparatively comfortably under the shade of a tarpaulin stretched between two trucks. (In case of enemy aircraft flying overhead, the trucks were always camouflaged in the shadow of a steep wadi side or among scrub.) About 0130 they would move on, the day getting cooler in the late afternoon, when the Captain would be looking out for a suitable place to laager before sunset.

The day brought Halliman's Patrol some 150km from Jalo, a day described as 'without incident, no Arabs seen' – no reference to punctures, to trucks bogged in soft sand or to those running repairs required after motoring over grit, sand and rock, which were such everyday events that the LRDG did not refer to them in routine reports. Almost before the trucks had laagered, the cooks had a fire going – it would be mistaken for an Arab camp fire by overflying aircraft – and water on the boil for a brew of tea. Each truck parked across the wind, its folded tarpaulin pinned by two wheels on the lee side with the upper half forming a windbreak and the lower a groundsheet. The drivers checked their day's petrol consumption and made maintenance checks, however, before they could rest.

On 9 and 10 December S1 patrol moved steadily north-westward towards Sirte, having received a signal from Jalo stating that the main battle was static, with Rommel at Gazala and the Eighth Army reorganizing for a further advance.

Just before the midday halt on Wednesday the 11th, 100km south of Sirte, the pilot of an Italian reconnaissance plane, the lightly armed but manœuvrable Gibli (named after the desert wind?), spotted the trucks. They were crossing a rocky stretch of desert and making only some 10k.p.h. with no cover to turn to, so Halliman ordered his black-bearded gunner to open fire. The Gibli had little armour, and if they could shoot it down, the pilot might not be able to radio their position. The other gunners followed suit but failed to hit the plane, its pilot in turn failing to hit them with his two bombs before he flew off. Halliman back-tracked to where he had seen a patch of scrub, not good camouflage as it barely came up to the doors of the trucks but the men flung the 'cam' nets over their vehicles and moved well clear of them. There would be no point in trying to fight off any air attack, as any machine-gun fire would only draw attention to the vehicles now hidden under their netting with its scrim of shreds of coloured hessian. As the men awaited the likely events, three Italian bombers flew over, searching for vehicle tracks. They found them on the edge of the large patch of scrub and turned back in line astern to strafe the scrub, dropping also a number of small bombs. Once the dust had settled and the planes gone, the men picked themselves up to find that no one was hurt and not even a tyre punctured. They therefore had lunch, cans of fruit no doubt, and moved off about 1400 hours, heading for the point where they would drop Stirling and his men. This was intended to be five kilometres from Sirte and a like distance from the coast road, far closer to Axis traffic than they would take vehicles when on reconnaissance.

A second Gibli spotted them just before dark, when they still had 60km to go, but they pressed on, closed up now in convoy no longer spread out as a precaution against air attack. They covered the last 30km without using their headlights, a bumpy, treacherous ride when unseen potholes and soft sand jarred a vehicle and its passengers into unexpectedly harsh stops. This happened to the last vehicle in the convoy, which bogged in soft sand when there was still 1,500m to go, and a change of plan had to be quickly devised. There was also the strong possibility that they might have lost some element of surprise, for the last reconnaissance plane would no doubt alert the Italians to the possibility of raids.

Stirling therefore sent Mayne and eight men to raid Tamet, a new field built in December 1941 45km west of Sirte, while he and Sergeant Brough would move on foot to raid the nearby airfield. Both parties planned to set off their charges at 2300 hours the following night (Thursday 12 December) and then to rendezvous with the radio truck, which was sent back 130km towards Jalo. The other six trucks – three for each party – would pick up the raiders in the early hours of Friday and travel independently to the desert RV.

At this point Halliman realized he was far closer to the coast road than he expected, and maybe they were lucky not to have gone a further 1,500m to the north, for the road bent southward, a kink not shown on the notoriously inaccurate maps. They switched off the truck's engines. They could hear voices and then the sound of a road patrol gathering speed as it moved off – proof that the enemy were on the alert for another raid against the highway traffic. S1 also moved off, making as much noise as possible, while Stirling and his sergeant clung to the side of Halliman's vehicle ready to jump off as soon as they reached firm ground. There were to be no tell-tale footprints suggesting that some of the patrol had not left when the rest moved out with a revving of engines. The trucks carrying Mayne and the rest of the raiding party then moved westward and would lie up next day.

Stirling and Brough soon found that they were much nearer to Sirte airfield than they had expected, and walked onto the dispersal area without let or hindrance, to find a tempting row of bombers. Yet any attack on these that night would only jeopardize Mayne's chance of success, so the two moved on, Stirling stumbling over the sleeping body of a sentry under his blanket. He and his companion let out such shrieks that the garrison was alerted and began firing out to sea as the raiders hurried up rising ground north of the field. They heard a shadow fire fight develop as the garrison tried to prevent an imagined assault from the sea link up with any equally non-existent assault from inland.

Once on the hillside, they crawled into a patch of bushes, had a short sleep and woke to find that they had a good view of their targets, of the beach dunes to the north and of Sirte's white houses to the west. They picked the route by which they would get to the thirty bombers that night, then went back to sleep. (Both slept, apparently, in the typical way of these confident raiders, feeling that no sentry watch was necessary.) When Stirling awoke, he heard women's voices: two Arab girls were gardening on one of the few cultivated patches in that area. The raiders then spent three uncomfortable hours as they lay motionless in their hide without a sneeze or a flexing of cramped muscles.

In the late afternoon, after the gardeners had gone, the bombers began to take off in two and threes. No doubt they were moving forward to fields nearer the front, from where the night attacks would be made against Allied transports. The targets were gone. Even a man of Stirling's resilient spirit must have been a little dejected. He and Brough returned to the road that evening, found no traffic and just before midnight saw the faint glow of fires away in the far distance from below the horizon. Mayne was at work.

There was nothing more to be done at Sirte. Brough cut a small bush and placed it in the middle of the road, the agreed sign for the LRDG trucks, and he and the Captain withdrew a discreet distance to await their arrival. They came spot on time at 0015 hours and, before they left again, Stirling put some mines on the road which blew up later under a tanker. By 0830 they were back at the desert RV. The going had been bad at the start but they had covered 130km in 8¼ hours.

Mayne's party had spent an uneventful Thursday before being dropped within striking distance of the Tamet field. Then Mayne, his great bulk looming through the starglow, led them in single file towards the airfield. Corporal Seekings, a shrewd, thickset countryman with a blond mop of hair, was one of the nine, moving cautiously, as was Corporal Bennett. They could see little in the dark until they came on some buildings with a faint sheet of light escaping from below a hut door. Mayne halted them and moved forward on his own to investigate the hut. He could hear laughter and a babble of talk as if this was a Mess or the aircrew's briefing hut. He flung open the door, conversations froze, then the thud-thud-thud of his Thomson methodically sprayed the room, the last few rounds shooting out the lights. Some of the chatterers recovered from their surprise more quickly than the others, firing from the windows at the shadows outside as Mayne slipped back to join his men. He left four of them as a covering party to keep the survivors occupied while he and the others raced across the field, and in fifteen minutes had placed Lewes bombs, including those which had been carried by the covering party on twenty-three aircraft.

A twenty-fourth aircraft was stalked by Mayne, who could see the glow of instrument lights in its cockpit where he expected to find men working. Their absence and the fact that he had no more bombs no doubt put him in one of those brief black furies to which he was prone, and using his considerable strength he ripped out the instrument panel. He had barely finished when the first bombs went off. The 'half-hour' time-pencil fuses had gone off in twenty minutes.

There was no time to lose, and Mayne set a cracking pace for his teams as he headed for the trucks. The men kept up the pace, nevertheless, as they had little more than their personal weapons and ammunition, for they were travelling light without even water-bottles. The teams joined up where they expected to find the trucks but were momentarily confused by Italian torches being flashed by their pursuers. Then, after using the pre-arranged whistle signals as he followed his compass course, Mayne heard a whistled reply. Seekings, desperate for a drink, was handed one of the large Rhodesian water-bottles as soon as he reached the trucks. He took a great gulp before, unable to catch his breath, he realized he was drinking neat rum. He slept despite the rattle and bumps of the first part of the journey into the desert but was awake when the party arrived at the desert RV to a boisterous welcome: bursts of machine-gun fire (a profligate waste of ammunition but in tune with SAS spirits at the time). Later that Friday morning the seven trucks left for Jalo, where they arrived the following Sunday, the day Fraser left for Agedabia.

Lewes had reached El Agheila without incident the previous Thursday night, but there were no aircraft on the field, which turned out to be only a staging point, for the Axis Air Forces appear to have begun dispersing aircraft to fields which could be guarded, a compromise which gave Allied night bombers meatier targets. Not to be outfoxed by such moves, Lewes had his driver take the Lancia to the road, and as the first sizeable convoy came along he hitched himself to its tail, so to speak, with the LRDG trucks following the Lancia. This convoy was moving towards a road-house Lewes believed was a conference centre for briefing senior officers and which had a vehicle-park nearby. His plan to shoot up the road-house was thwarted when the LRDG truck markings were recognized, but in the resulting gun-battle, as some of Lewes' men kept the Italian sentries busy, others planted bombs in vehicles on the park before Lewes successfully extracted his men and S Patrol's vehicles to return to Jalo. Reports indicate that some thirty vehicles had been destroyed or damaged.

Lieutenant W. ('Bill') Fraser, a neat, clean-looking Gordon Highlander, whose father and grandfather had been senior NCOs in this regiment, was to raid Agedabia airfield on the line of Oasis Force's advance due to start on Tuesday 20 December. Brigadier Reid and his staff had worked out that by Wednesday they would be nearing the area of regular air patrols; therefore anything Fraser could do to hamper these would help the Force. As mentioned earlier, they had already experienced the delays caused by Axis air attacks during their previous advance on Jalo. Fraser with three men left this oasis a few hours before Stirling returned and was dropped by trucks of S Patrol near the airfield on Tuesday night. The raiders found the area stiff with Germans – men of Panzer Grenadier Regiments of 90th Light Division – and the perimeter of the field securely wired, with entanglements that were patrolled by sentries. The team needed four hours to work their way unseen to the wire, at one point having to lie stiff for an hour with Germans and Italians only metres away. Yet they crossed the wire about midnight and were ready to place their bombs.

The parked aircraft, mostly CR42s, an Italian biplane fighter-bomber, were not individually guarded, enabling the raiders in two pairs to 'leapfrog' from one plane to the next for forty-five minutes as they placed their bombs in the thirty-seven aircraft, but they had none left for the last two, for which Fraser later apologized to Stirling. The bombs had begun to explode before they were clear of the field, for the thirty-minute fuses which they used showed some optimism on the time it would take them to get clear. However, had longer fuses been used, there was always the chance that the garrison might have been able to clear those bombs which they found. In the event the confusion as the Lewes bombs went off 'was so great that getting away was no problem'.

As they moved across the desert the next day, they suffered a different hazard, for any patrol which has penetrated deep into enemy territory runs the risk of being mistaken for fair game by their own side. Two RAF Blenheims attacked the trucks, killing two and wounding two of the LRDG before recognition signals were exchanged. Later that day the trucks reached Wadi Faregh, where Brigadier Reid's Force was passing through to their night laager 40km from the airfield. Fraser was back in Jalo a couple of nights later, ready to take part in further raids which Stirling had planned.

Stirling had discussed raiding techniques with his officers, and the lessons of the previous week were considered. In future, whenever possible, a number of guidelines would be followed: no recces would be made with a day's laying up before the raid; raiders would not engage in gun-battles *before* they had planted their bombs; and attempts to use disguised vehicles were to be discontinued – a guideline which Stirling discarded within the next month. The whole success of raids clearly depended on surprise, so they would next strike where the enemy might least expect them: where they had raided before, at Sirte and Tamet, but approaching Sirte by a more westerly route.

Stirling left on Christmas Eve, with Halliman, and made good time before dropping Mayne and five men at Tamet. There they got onto the airfield and destroyed a number of aircraft from a squadron recently flown to Africa. Stirling, however, coming onto the road west of Sirte, found a German armoured column moving up towards the front; it took over four hours to pass, leaving no time for a raid on the airfield. He had to be satisfied with raids along the road against Axis transports, before moving off into the comparative safety of the desert.

Lewes and his men were taken in seven trucks to T2 Patrol of New Zealanders to Nofilia over 200km east of Sirte and *en route* dropped Lieutenant Fraser at Marble Arch, an airfield near Mussolini's monument to his victories over local Arabs in the 1930s. At Nofilia only one plane was destroyed because the few Axis planes on the field were widely dispersed, the bomb on the first plane with a thirty-minute fuse going off before the raiders were clear of the second plane, on which they also planted a bomb. This was probably defused or moved clear of the plane before it exploded as only one plane is known to have been destroyed. Lewes, Sergeant Lilley and their three men successfully reached the LRDG trucks, although the garrison had quickly manned the defences.

The trucks moved off in daylight, heading 75km eastward to an RV with Fraser's team. They had not gone far when they were spotted by an Italian Savoya SM 79 Sparviero, a light bomber with three 12.7 Breda machine-guns and a Lewis, besides more than a ton of bombs. The pilot flew in low, 'all guns firing', and as their vehicles were out in the open, the LRDG machine-gunners replied, but to no great effect. As the plane banked away to turn for another run, the raiders dashed for what little cover they could find in a stretch of desert 'as bare as a billiard table'. On his second run the Savoy's pilot fired at the men. Lewes was hit and died within five minutes. As the Savoya ran out of ammunition, two fighters took up the strafing, and they were followed by other aircraft during the next few hours, until later in the afternoon they abandoned the hunt, no doubt satisfied that they had destroyed their quarry.

The raiders were by no means finished, although ten of the LRDG men had become separated from the rest. The SAS troopers and the rest of T2 found that no one had been seriously hurt after Lewes was killed (by one report, hit while still firing from a truck). The vehicles were all virtual wrecks, but enough parts were salvaged to get one vehicle running, some fifteen men holding each other in their precarious perches on its pile of salvaged tyres, petrol cans and water. They reached the RV south of Marble Arch but could not contact Fraser; after waiting a while, they 'made for Jalo as fast as we could', to quote Sergeant Lilley. It was a journey of great difficulty, with an overloaded vehicle and a continuous need to improvise repairs along the way. Other teams, including Fraser's, had even grimmer journey on foot, covering 300km or more.

The raids of December had accounted for eighty-seven aircraft, according to L Detachment's albeit meagre records in which Stirling avoided an exaggeration by reporting only two-thirds of the numbers claimed by his patrol leaders. Also destroyed were at least forty vehicles including invaluable fuel tankers. Official Italian records give smaller numbers of aircraft – eleven against fifty at Tamet, about fifteen against thirty-seven at Agedabia – a discrepancy perhaps explained by the omission of German losses from the Italian figures. Whatever the precise Axis losses, Auchinleck was satisfied that L Detachment had proved its worth. Stirling was promoted Major and allowed to recruit a further six officers and up to forty other ranks.

A squadron of Free French parachutists of about fifty men commanded by Commander Bergé were put under Stirling's command. These volatile men under their witty commander added a Gallic dimension to the Detachment who would have their successors in French regiments of SAS, of which more later. The first fifty began their training at Kabrit in January under arrangements made by Stirling during his week in Cairo, before returning to Jalo. From there he planned to raid the port of Buerat on the western shore of the Gulf of Sirte, over 300km from Allied positions, investing El Agheila on the Gulf's eastern shore, where Rommel was re-grouping his forces.

The raid on Buerat proved a disappointment as the attack had to be made on the seventh day of their journey from Jalo, without up-to-date intelligence. That morning their radio truck and its signallers had been lost when the raiding party was attacked and scattered by Axis aircraft. Therefore Stirling did not know that there were no supply ships in the port and had to be content with setting fire to warehouses and road transport. Such air attacks had become more frequent, forcing the LRDG to move at night when darkness hid runnels and pot-holes, especially when sabotage raids had for preference to be made on the moonless nights each month.

Stirling and Mayne – who had taken to his bed when left to run the training at Kabrit after Lewes's death – were already legends in the folklore of service bars: both were aggressive in the face of the enemy and official bumbledom, yet gentle in manner with their friends. Stirling's genius might sometimes lead him into apparently impractical ventures from the supply point of view, but with his tireless energy he overcame most of the logistical problems, and many of his men, inspired by their officers' courage, earned promotion which only proven success brought in the Detachment. Some received the coveted, but quite unofficial, honour of being allowed to wear their parachute winged badge on the left breast instead of the right sleeve, as Stirling's reward for distinguished conduct during a raid – an incentive without parallel for new recruits who joined the Detachment. There would be five hundred men on its strength when it became '1 SAS Regiment' in October 1942.

2. 'A Bit Here, A Bit There'

Paddy Mayne, having been relieved of the administrative tedium of organizing training at Kabrit, rejoined Stirling in Cairo as second-in-command. He once described the results of raiding, when asked if there had been 'Good shooting?' with the comment: 'A bit here, a bit there.' This might well describe all the raids of the early months in 1942.

Rommel had received replacement tanks and men by mid-January, enabling him to launch a counter-offensive at 0800 hours on 21 January. He had 173 tanks and 300 serviceable aircraft to support his ground forces, a command renamed *Panzerarmee Afrika*, but the total force of 12,500 Germans and 25,000 Italians was well below its strength on paper – its 'establishment'.

At this time the weather, with duststorms followed by heavy rains, turned the RAF's airfield at Antilla into 'a chocolate blancmange'. Here and elsewhere, therefore, aircraft had to be flown off before they became bogged down, with the result that they were flying from airfields 400km from the Gulf of Sirte, greatly reducing their operational time over the battlefield. By 23 January Rommel's forces were advancing northward up the Gulf coast and on a second axis parallel to it, reaching Benghazi on 28 January. (It was during this time that Stirling was in the desert, pp 19–20, with no radio communications to Jalo or to the LRDG's base, which had pulled back to Siwa.)

Early in February the Eighth Army was consolidating positions on a line running south from Gazala, while Auchinleck rebuilt his force's strength through Tobruk, a slow process, as we have seen. He also partially reorganized the Army into brigade groups, each with infantry in trucks, the so-called 'lorried infantry', tanks and artillery in various combinations to provide closer cohesion between these different units. There had also been, since the first fighting in the desert, the 'Jock' columns. This concept of Brigadier 'Jock' Campbell had its limitations with tip-and-run tactics, as the Brigadier knew, and a tendency to disperse guns in the columns which might better have been deployed in massed artillery.

The Axis Air Forces were less hampered by the weather in the early stages of Rommel's advance because they were flying from relatively drier areas, but once the advance was into the hilly country, the *Jebel* as the

Arabs call mountains, they brought a number of airfields back into operation. Near Benghazi were: Berka 'Main', two kilometres south of the port; its satellite a few kilometres to the east; and Benina, 25km due east of Benghazi, where aircraft were fitted with replacement engines and other major overhauls carried out. Further north among the hills was Barce, with Derna near the coast, and fifteen kilometres to the south-east of Derna was Martuba, each with two forward airstrips; there were also landing strips at Mechili and Tmini, which would be developed as full airfields when the fighting moved eastward, as would the former RAF strips at Antelat and Msus.

During these months in the desert, Stirling had chosen his own targets, and he was soon ready with a plan when GHQ Middle East chose targets for him in June. This was an opportunity for his special force to work in direct concert with the Commander-in-Chief's overall plan, as laid down in 1939 by that master of special forces' warfare Colonel (later Major-General Sir) Colin Gubbins, and which later SAS would exploit to the full. The GHQ Middle East had been asked to take all possible steps, by sea, land and air, to protect two convoys, one sailing from Gibraltar in the west and the other from Alexandria in the east, for Malta. The one from the east would pass within range of the German airfields at Derna and Benghazi on 14 and 15 June. Therefore the torpedo and other bombers on these fields became a vital target to be attacked by all means available.

Plans were accordingly made for four more or less straightforward raids by L Detachment: Stirling would raid Bernina, where he had been twice before, to destroy its workshop hangars; Lieutenant Jacquier, Free French, would raid Barce; Lieutenant Zirnheld, also of the Free French, would raid Berka main, and Mayne would raid its satellite for the second time. A more complex series of raids was also required on Derna West, Derna East and one of Martuba's two fields, areas difficult to approach since Rommel's advance of May; although Mayne had reached Derna in March, by mid-June the Eighth Army was on the retreat for the Egyptian frontier. The Axis reinforcements were concentrated in the Derna area a fortnight earlier, when Stirling and his officers were considering plans for these raids. They knew therefore that some new methods must be evolved for getting onto the airfields.

Stirling discussed the problem with planning staff at GHQ and was put in touch with Captain Buck, an officer in the Indian Army, a fluent German-speaker who had escaped after capture wearing German uniform, getting to the Allied positions comparatively easily. This gave him the idea of forming a sabotage team from anti-Nazi Germans, mostly Jews who lived in Palestine. He was allowed to recruit a German-speaking Guards officer and twelve men, who trained and lived as if in the German army, with identity documents and cover stories that included girlfriends in the Fatherland, from whom the men carried letters; some had pictures of 'German' wives. Buck also recruited two former French Foreign Legionnaires who had later served in the German army as NCOs and were being held as prisoners. These two, the broad-shouldered, jovial Bruckner and the good-natured Esser, were eventually accepted by the others in this Special Interrogation Group – a neat cover for German-speaking saboteurs.

Stirling, Buck and Jordan (whose teams would go to Derna and Martuba) devised a plan for the final stages of their approach to the airfields: Buck's men would drive them in German vehicles through the roadblocks and sentry posts, with the fifteen Frenchmen hidden in the back of the vehicles under tarpaulins and a pile of empty jerry cans. (This was the first but by no means the last time SAS teams would go into action in disguise; on all their earlier raids they had worn British uniforms, even when they whistled their way through Benghazi.) The French had only recently completed their training at Kabrit but were the forerunners of later SAS regiments.

They arrived in Siwa by air early in June and were joined by Buck and his men, driving a military VW (*Knevelwagen*), an Opel, a German equivalent of a three-tonner and a British three-tonner painted in German camouflage colours with the DAK palm-tree insignia and tactical mark-ings. They left Siwa on Saturday 6 June and were escorted for the first six days by a patrol of the LRDG. This first 400km of their journey was negotiated carefully, as the road vehicles were not equipped for the hard going. (By comparison the tall, elegant Lieutenant the Honourable Robin Gurdon, Coldstream Guards, had crossed the 700km from Siwa to the hills south of Benghazi in two days, and come back in the same time, on a recce the previous month.)

They crossed the Trig el Abd before coming into the low hills that run in an east-west line some 65 to 100km from the northern coast. These hills rise to 350m in the north-west and fall to 150m where the coastal escarpment runs south-east of Benghazi – where the coastal plain is 25km wide, northward as the plain narrows. The rolling valleys of this Jebel country are filled with flowers and long grass in places, with stunted trees and scrub on the more exposed hillsides providing plenty of cover. Indeed, as this Benghazi–Derna promontory catches a good deal of Mediterranean rain, it is a pleasant place, or at least was regarded as such by L Detachment, after days in the desert. Derna had a population of thirty thousand, many of whom had evacuated the town, some leaving only at night to avoid the bombing. In the hills nomadic Senussi herded their flocks and were dependable allies, but some robber bands also roamed the hills.

The plan was for Buck's vehicles to slip onto the coast road west of Derna, explaining their journey with documents authorizing them to take the vehicles from Agedabia to the workshops at Derna. What they did not have was the password for June, as army intelligence had been unable to persuade any prisoner to divulge it, although they did have the password for May. They had no trouble from aircraft, friendly or otherwise, as any Allied pilot would have taken the convoy for captured vehicles being escorted by the LRDG, as they passed through barren country from Monday to Thursday. Then the SIG men changed into German uniform and left their British kit with the LRDG. Buck's men were well armed, each man carrying a Luger, a Schmeisser submachine-gun and a primed German 'potato-masher' grenade, and every man's bayonet was sharpened for use as a dagger. The Frenchmen, in khaki overalls and blue fore-and-aft caps, each had a couple of No. 39 fragmentation grenades in their trouser pockets and a .45-inch (12mm) revolver under their overalls. The two 'three-tonners' had loaded heavy machine-guns on special mountings and were hidden by the canopies.

During Friday 12 June, when the convoy was on its way from eastern Mediterranean ports to meet its escorts from Alexandria, Buck and Jordan's convoy was wending its way towards the coast road. They had arranged an RV with Lieutenant Guild's LRDG Patrol for Sunday morning, when his trucks would be hidden near Baltel el Zalegh, 50km south of Derna. The little convoy of 'German' trucks was led by Buck, dressed as a German private with the two German NCOs beside him. An SIG air sentry clung to the back of each vehicle, following the Germans' practice for road convoys. Nothing amiss happened as they drove past Arabs working in the fields and the occasional line of overladen donkeys taking produce to market. Early in the afternoon, while grinding up a particularly steep incline – where the road climbs into the high Jebel, 95km west of Derna – the British three-tonner broke down. There was no option but to take it in tow, and with it hitched behind the German lorry they rounded a bend about 1500 hours to find the first checkpoint on their route. Buck's NCO signalled the sentry to lift the red-and-white barrier; the Italian hesitated and then came to ask for the password. The NCOs flourished their papers, claimed to have been in the desert since May and, after browbeating the duty major, while drinking his wine, were allowed to go on.

Towards evening they came to a road junction where a portly German corporal stepped into the road, holding up his hand to halt them. He, however, only wanted to give them some friendly advice on the dangers of British sabotage raids, advising them to spend the night in the staging area just a kilometre up the road – a suggestion which Buck felt obliged to accept. They pulled into the vehicle-park, the SIG men going off to line up with their mess-tins for an Afrika Korps ration of stew with dumplings and lentils. The Frenchmen, cramped under the tarpaulins in the back of the trucks, could hardly move, for all around the park men were getting out their bedding rolls, settling down for the evening or falling in for some fatigue as orders were shouted.

Although his trucks were some way from the main transport lines, Buck decided that they must move on, if only to give the Frenchmen a chance to stretch their legs, and therefore the little convoy left the park. No one questioned them, and twelve kilometres nearer Derna they pulled off the road for a night's sleep. At some point they apparently repaired the British three-tonner, for they would need the larger vehicles to carry to men onto the airfields.

Discussing how they would recce the airfields, Buck and Jordan decided that they must have the June password. There then followed a 'B'-movie plot that hinged on the fat corporal still being on duty that Saturday morning, the day of the raids. Buck wrote him a note explaining with some dramatic licence why they did not have the password, and two SIG men, Hass and Gottlieb, took it back down the road in the VW. They found the corporal, who took them into a nearby office and gave them details of the challenge 'Siesta' with its reply 'Eldorado'. In the light of future events, it would be interesting to know if he knew who they were, but in all probability he was just being friendly.

Buck then took the convoy, about midday, to a point eight kilometres south of Derna. Here it would not be so easy to explain away their presence as being *en route* for the Derna workshop, although they were within easy reach of the east and west airfields. Jordan and his four corporals were then driven to the perimeter of the airfields, having a chance to see the layout, if only through the narrow gaps in the flaps of the canopy. They noted the positions of Me 110s on the west field and Stukas on the east, but as Martuba was fifteen kilometres further east, Buck decided it was too risky to take a vehicle there, even further from the workshops. After visiting the Derna fields, therefore, they returned to the other trucks parked in an out-of-the-way spot, for no one came near them apparently. However, the Germans may well have been watching the convoy's movements.

At 2100 hours on a starlight night they set off for the airfields, Bruckner, in the uniform of a German private, driving Jordan's and Corporal Bourmont's teams – ten in all – with SIGs Hass and Gottlieb as NCOs sitting by Bruckner. The party under Corporal Tourneret headed for Martuba west airfield, their truck driven by one SIG private with two others dressed as sergeants in German uniform. Buck stayed with the other two vehicles in case the men had to come back on foot to the RV, which at some risk they had used all day.

What should have been a fifteen-minute run took over an hour, because, Bruckner claimed, the engine was over-heating. He finally stopped 200m from the airfield's cinema and went off to look for a key for the toolbox as, he claimed, he had lost his key. A soldier approached the truck, and the SIG men explained to him that the driver had gone for a key. While they were making these explanations, Jordan heard the crunch of many footsteps, setting adrenalin flowing. He pulled back the rear flap, to be grabbed by two soldiers. A circle of them were standing round the truck, their Schmeissers pointing menacingly at the vehicle as an officer called the equivalent of 'All Frenchmen out'. The reply was a grenade thrown by one of Jordan's men, scattering the Germans. This gave him the chance to break free from the men who held him. He ran.

There was a heavy explosion. The French lieutenant glanced back, to see the truck in flames as he raced on. Flares were going up from positions around the perimeter. He sensed the garrison was being turned to, as if to some pre-arranged plan. In the dark and confusion, moving with caution as he made his way towards Buck's vehicles, he took a couple of hours to reach them. He and Buck quickly and rightly assessed the position: Bruckner must have betrayed them. It would not be long – after two hours – before the Germans arrived at the RV. So the two officers and remaining SIG drove off for the LRDG hide-out to the south.

Corporal Bourmont and four others besides Jordan escaped the ring of sub-machine guns; two were picked up next day; another, although wounded, evaded capture for four days. The Corporal and a companion crossed the fifteen kilometres of hill road to an RV which was to be used by the Martuba team. Here they found Corporal Tourneret's team and their SIG escorts, making nine Allies, who then fought off a company of Germans who came to surround them. There are no reports of how they had fared on their airfield, but after a brief fire fight the French were killed or captured, along with three SIG soldiers.

Later Jordan learnt that Hass, probably, was the man who had thrown a grenade into the explosives in the truck. Gottlieb was captured, his identity discovered, and he was shot. Bruckner was flown to Berlin and decorated for his deception, which probably began in the staging area, when he could have slipped away from the others who were queuing for an evening meal. The point at which he became a double agent has not come to light, but fortunately he did not know the exact position of the LRDG patrol, who waited through the following week in case any other Frenchmen turned up. Had Buck deliberately not told his German NCOs of the position of this second RV? Did any of the SIG know it? One suspects that they did. And why did the Germans take more than two hours to reach the forward RV? Or, for that matter, the team raiding Martuba? We can only surmise that Bruckner did not have all the details of the plan; clearly he had expected the Derna party to arrive at the field later than they planned, because he had to delay their approach to fit in with the Germans' intention to surround them.

The four other raids went well, although these targets were 700km from the base at Siwa, and the 'blitz wagon' with another vehicle was damaged by mines on the Trig el Abd track. There was also a possible misunderstanding with the RAF, for they bombed the airfields, although aware of L Detachment's raid. One line of research suggests, however, that bombing the airfields as well as raiding them was a 'belt and braces' affair to ensure the maximum strike against Axis bombers. On Benina, for example, Stirling and his two corporals, Cooper and Seekings, had got onto the airfield without much difficulty as there was no wire, but the RAF bombing began before they reached the workshop hangars. Nevertheless, the raiders destroyed these, eleven aircraft and an anti-aircraft gun, more damage than Stirling felt could have been done by a naval bombardment and at considerably less risk to Allied resources. The Germans would be unable to effect any major repairs to aircraft during the few days the Malta convoy was in range. At Berka main, Zirnheld's Free French team had to fight their way clear of the field but destroyed eleven aircraft, while another Free French team under Jacquier blew up supply dumps at Barce.

Mayne and his three corporals lay in the light of Allied flares, dangerously exposed – an RAF plane crashing within 200m of them – before Lilley got to the first plane. This he found was guarded, and in the ensuing gun-battle the team had to fight their way clear of the field, putting their explosives on a store of petrol before heading for the RV. Once again they lost their way, as they had leaving Derna in March, but this time they were less fortunate, finding themselves in a German bivouac area. Warburton was fired on as he made a run for safety, and was not seen again. Lilley more subtly walked out of the area, but not before he had been scented by an Alsatian, the dog sniffing at the bushes where he was hidden. He punched it on the nose, and its mistress called it to heel. He, Storey and Mayne eventually reached the RV and returned with Stirling's team to G2 Patrol's trucks.

After the teams returned from the airfields near Benghazi, they waited a day in case Warburton had escaped, but when he did not show up, they moved that Monday night to set up another RV-base further north. From there on Tuesday night, with Mayne driving at his usual breakneck speed, Stirling – his wrist in plaster, from a simple road accident – Lilley, Cooper and Seekings went back to Benina to examine the damage. With them was SIG's Karl Kahane, who had served twenty years in the German army before emigrating to Palestine; his swearing when asked for the password at the first road checkpoint, and Mayne's cocked revolver and quick reactions to frighten the man who came to check their truck, got them through in the first of several excitements on what had the elements of a foolhardy venture.

Mayne and Stirling, both in their twenties, vied with each other in the daring each showed when working together, as if to outdare the other. This night they shot up a company of Italians trying to block the Benina–Benghazi road, and put bombs with ten-minute fuses in trucks by the road before turning for the Wadi Qattara, a few kilometres to the south. An Axis truck tried to cut them off from this escape route but, rattling and jolting over rough ground, no one could shoot straight. Mayne took the truck in a headlong but controlled rush down the wadi side, and the Germans did not follow, fearing no doubt that they would be ambushed. Mayne then drove eastward, picking up a track which brought them to the top of the escarpment, after pushing the jeep. They were heading across a plateau, dozing despite the bumpy ride, when a whiff of acid caught Sergeant Lilley's sensitive nostrils. A time-pencil fuse had 'snapped'. In seconds they were all out of the truck before it blew up, leaving them a long walk to a Senussi camp on the way to Gurdon's trucks. At the camp the Arabs fed them before moving off, the raiders being left in an underground *bir* where Gurdon found them the next day with the help of the Senussi. All were back in Siwa on 21 June with the 'blitz wagon' and other vehicles which LRDG fitters had repaired in the desert.

One raid was mounted against German aircraft on Heraklion airfield in Crete, as part of the Detachment's plan to help the safe passage of the Malta convoy. This field had over 60 Ju 88s, the much-feared dive-bombers ready for attacks on Malta dispersed around its perimeter, which – like other fields on the island – would be the target for SAS operations over the years. For Crete at the height of the Desert War had four major aerodromes and a number of landing strips, mainly along the north coast of this mountainous and largely barren island the size of Yorkshire or Puerto Rico. Many of its tough peasant farmers had served in the army in Greece in 1941 and were willing to fight in 1942 when the opportunity offered. That June, Commander Bergé, with Lieutenant the Earl Jellicoe as his second-in-command, landed in Crete in the Detachment's first sea-borne raid, a technique the commandos of the Special Boat Section had used successfully in the Mediterranean since 1941. (George Jellicoe would become the mentor of SAS small boat operations, as we shall see in the next chapter, after the marked success of this first raid.)

Having landed from a submarine, crossed the mountains and got into the airfield, the raiders destroyed twenty-one planes and several fuel stores. But the French paid a heavy price for this achievement, when they were betrayed as they lay up near the southern coast waiting to RV with a submarine. Jellicoe had gone to a nearby village in search for the Cretan agent who would signal in the submarine, when three German patrols closed in on the Frenchmen, who fought in the hope of getting away after dark, but all were killed or captured. This was the second difficult raid the French squadron had undertaken, the first having been at Derna, and they had certainly been allotted the most difficult tasks in this series of raids. Jellicoe successfully came out to the submarine's RV and returned to Egypt.

Despite such valiant endeavours, the raids made little impression on the thousand or so serviceable aircraft the Axis forces had deployed within striking distance of the Malta convoys, not counting planes they had in Libya and on the Italian mainland. The convoy from the east was forced to turn back when a strike force of forty British aircraft could not seriously damage an Italian fleet which was too powerful for the convoy's escorts. Only two of the six ships in the western convoy reached Malta; the others, along with two escorts, were sunk.

Rommel forced the Eighth Army to retreat, Tobruk with its large store depots being overwhelmed on 20 June and Mersa Matruh (in Egypt) a week later. But Rommel's forces finally ran into severe shortages of fuel, ammunition, water and rations, after they had used mainly captured supplies to carry them the 500km from Tobruk to El Alamein. Here Auchinleck set up a defence line across the strip of coastal plain between the sea and the almost impassable Qattara Depression. Rommel's army had expected six weeks in which to reorganize after the capture of Tobruk, but the General forced the pace, for he knew that unless his men could break through quickly into Egypt, their victory would be short lived. In the event, with many units down to thirty per cent of their established strength, Rommel had stuck out his neck a long way.

In these last days of June, Lieutenant-Colonel Prendergast, who commanded the LRDG, withdrew his base from the now isolated Siwa to a wayside railway halt that few if any of his Patrol leaders knew: El Alamein. They continued their road watches at El Agheila, moving patrols there through Kufra far to the south, but in this great emergency for the Army raiding had a high priority in the Commander-in-Chief's plans and he intended that the best use should be made of L Detachment and the LRDG.

Within ten days of Stirling's return to Cairo, he was setting off with thirty-five jeeps and three-ton trucks for the desert. The broad plan was to establish a base in enemy-dominated territory and for three weeks or more to raid the coast road and airfields – a ploy which would become the classic type of SAS operation. For this initial operation he had fifteen American General Purpose (GP) vehicles (jeeps, for short), two of which had a pair of twin K guns, two a pair of single Ks, and his 'wagon's' pair of twin Lewis were also replaced by four of the new Vickers .303-inch (7.7mm) rapid-firing machine-guns. Although these were new to the Detachment, they were obsolete RAF air-cooled guns originally fitted to

Gloster Gladiator biplanes. Their high rate of fire at twelve hundred rounds a minute gave a devastating cone of fire which could cause an aircraft to disintegrate on the ground just as well as in the air. The intention therefore was to use these to defend vehicles caught in an ambush, but they would prove a better weapon of attack than defence, for Stirling was never a man to dwell on defensive tactics.

The convoy set out from Cairo on 2 July, Day 1 of the operation, but by that night the overloaded three-tonners were bogging down so often in the sand that a change of plan was made: six jeeps and six three-tonners, driven by experienced desert veterans and carrying stores for a week to ten days' raiding, made for the desert base. This patch of stony hills and scrub-covered valleys west of Bir Chalda and 130km south of Mersa Matruh on the coast had been recced by the LRDG. Their G Patrols would also be based there, Gurdon having guided the fifty men of Stirling's party to the area in a journey of five days, passing through the southern end of the main battle area, skirting the Depression, getting lost in heavy mists and crossing barren wastes. Should Alexandria fall, the raiders would go south through Kufra, but as a counter-attack was expected by the Eighth Army, such a contingency seemed remote.

The counter-offensive never materialized, for Auchinleck felt that the planned attack by XIII Corps on the rear of the Axis positions might dissipate the Eighth Army's strength. Only a column from 7 Motor Brigade succeeded in evading Axis aircraft, to shell Fuka landing grounds on the evening of Tuesday 7 July. It then withdrew successfully. On the Monday Stirling's teams had left an overnight halt heading north, to lay up that afternoon in their new base area. Early next morning they set out with Stirling's teams of Mayne and nine men who would raid Bagush, with three teams for Fuka and its satellite field, all under the guidance of Gurdon's G2 patrol. Jellicoe, with Timpson's G1 Patrol, headed for El Daba, but as this field was known from last-minute intelligence to be deserted, he and Zirnheld would use their teams to raid the Fuka–Galal road. Two other teams went north-west, to an airfield used for refuelling south of Sidi Barani, with orders to watch the road and report but to destroy aircraft if they found any. This most westerly patrol with men of the LRDG was to stay and make radio reports until withdrawn or their rations ran out.

As Jellico set out, his trucks left a 'little cloud of white dust hanging like a curtain' to screen their departure. Gurdon led out the Fuka-Bagush parties, expecting to be on the escarpment overlooking Fuka in eight hours. This was not to be, for that afternoon they saw what they took to be a 'Jock' column – the column from 7 Motor Brigade with armoured cars and field artillery. This meeting delayed the raiders, who at first believed that these might be captured British vehicles. They crossed the scarred battlefields of earlier actions where derelict vehicles, scorchmarks of petrol fires where men had brewed up, and Bren-carriers without their tracks lay abandoned in retreat. They had to make a detour around an Axis tented camp, with the result that these delays prevented their reaching the escarpment before it was almost dark, at 2000 hours, some four hours later than intended, leaving no chance for a recce in daylight.

The teams now divided: Stirling and Mayne heading west once down the 'scarpe; Fraser and Jordan making for Fuka main; Sharpe for its satellite. At Bagush, 30km westward along the coast, Stirling's plan was to block the road while Mayne's men planted their charges on the nearby airfield. They had the 'blitz wagon' and a jeep each armed with four K-guns, and a three-tonner followed with reserves of explosives, spare tyres and rations. There were no vehicles on the road, an ominous sign that the 'Jock' column had put the Axis forces on their guard, so Stirling drove even faster than usual to be sure that they might have time in hand for trouble, as the rough going down the escarpment had taken over three hours to cross and they were due to have their charges go off at 0100 next morning, giving them only two hours from the time they reached the road. They saw no lights, not even Arab fires, in an eerie emptiness, freshened by the salt wind off the sea. A kilometre short of the field, Stirling drove off the road at a point where Corporals Seekings and Cooper with a trooper were able to get two great boulders into the road.

Mayne and his four men set off for the airfield, leaving two men with the three-tonner. No traffic came past, but the airfield party were an unusually long time. Then a number of bright flashes lit the moonless sky before Mayne returned in a black humour. They had been so long because the airfield sentries were alert and the aircraft parked in widely dispersed groups, but worse: eighteen charges had failed to explode. The fuse normally fired a detonator; this in turn exploded a dry gun-cotton primer the size of a cotton-reel, which exploded the main charge. These detonators had lain so long in the charges on this occasion that the dry gun-cotton had absorbed oil from the 'Lewes' mixture and failed to explode.

Mayne and Stirling were not to be thwarted by such mishaps: they had eight K-guns; why not use them? As they drove to the outer edge of the field farthest from the road, all was quiet, the garrison having damped down the fires from the twenty-two aircraft the 'good' charges had set alight, and no doubt the guards felt that all was over for the night. They got a numbing shock, for the two raiding vehicles, Mayne driving some ten metres behind Stirling, covered three sides of the field in five minutes, firing what might be described as 'broadside bursts' into six groups of aircraft. Some had the burnt-out frames left by the earlier fires showing gauntly in the flickering light of the first plane to catch alight as tracer, armour-piercing and ordinary bullets tore into the aircraft. The gunners had to fire low, in short bursts to conserve ammunition at such rates of fire, but despite the bumpy ride in the jeeps, they hit their targets. The shoot was completed so quickly that the enemy failed to react before the raiders were gone. The three-tonner had already set off for the desert with the men not required for the shoot, as this needed only a driver and two gunners in each jeep.

At the escarpment Jordan was back, having set charges on eight planes before being fired on as he withdrew, a rumpus which alerted guards on Fraser's part of Fuka main and on the satellite field 1,500m away, where Sharpe's team had planted only six charges before they had to leave.

The Medical Officer, Captain J. M. Pleydell and two men had waited on the escarpment, seeing the fireworks below, getting lost once on the edge of a minefield but gathering in the returning teams, who had only one minor casualty. Fraser then led them south about an hour before dawn, due at 0400, giving them time to get clear of the area before Axis patrols reached the high ground. As the raiders were leaving, an RAF Wellington flew over, caught in the airfield searchlights, no doubt aware that all the raiders should have been clear of the area an hour or more before they actually left.

Other teams were making their way south: G2 had done their part in the raiding, after Gurdon had set off eastward down the coast road to shoot up thirty vehicles in a roadside park and their drivers' transit camp. Jellicoe had no luck near El Daba, for not surprisingly there was not the expected jam of Axis vehicles fleeing from the counter-offensive, since this had failed. The French team with him were further down the road, destroying an aircraft low-loader, its tractor and a truck, and taking three prisoners, including two eighteen-year olds who had only recently arrived in Africa. The Sidi Barani recce reached their intended OP but were not due back at the base for some days.

Raiding was, Mayne reportedly remarked, 'a glorious spree', as you 'paid for the fun next morning'. Wednesday 8 July was no exception. The previous evening the trucks may have been seen by a reconnaissance plane, for Fraser's convoy had not gone far when two Me 109s skimmed overhead and the raiders dived from their trucks. Out in the open they had no alternative, but whenever there was the least cover, men stayed stock still, as it is movement on the ground which catches a pilot's eye. In this case Pleydell could clearly see both pilots, but they flew on, probably reporting the trucks' presence by radio, for more planes came to search the area.

At first light the 'blitz wagon', jeep and three-tonner were also crossing flat, open ground, with Stirling looking for somewhere to lay up. He could make out a low grey streak through his field glasses, which in the early morning light he took to be a small ridge of hills, and assessed that they would take an hour to reach. The three vehicles therefore headed for them. Mayne, 800m in the lead, was almost there, Stirling was still in the open and the three-tonner further behind him when two Italian CR 42 fighter-bombers and a Gibli came over, flying low. The pilot of the recce plane dropped his two bombs wide of the 'wagon', while the CR 42s strafed the truck, which blew up after their third pass. During these attacks, Stirling had driven closer to the ridge, but he was forced to dodge behind a small hillock as the fighters now came at him, attacking in turn from different angles as Stirling again dodged the wagon around this 'pimple'. They must inevitably have caught him had he not made a dash for some boulders atop the ridge, crashing the wagon five metres as he dropped to this shelter under the ridge top, where he and his men scrambled into the cover. But the Italians were out of ammunition by this time and flew off. Breakfast of biscuits and Mayne's whisky had to suffice until the midday heat-haze covered the Jeep's move southward, carrying all eleven of the raiders, for no one had been hurt.

Three hours' driving brought the jeep 50km further south, Stirling's team being the first to reach the temporary base. Here cooks, fitters and others from the Detachment and the LRDG patrols who had not been on these raids had improved natural caves in the chalk-like cliff of a small ravine. Birds, lizards, spiky beetles and scorpions lived in the scrub, exploring the bodies of the men as they lay relaxed after a long night of action. Once the vehicles had been checked, nobody moved more than he could help, as all were limited still to one bottle of water a day, kept cool here by burying the bottle in the sand.

The site was none too large, and after one LRDG gunner opened fire on an Axis plane, against orders, others would be back next day. Therefore the raiders moved off at 0300 next morning, to a ridge escarpment that had been recced by the LRDG 40km to the west. Here the long cliff, twenty metres high in places, provided good cover for the next three weeks, with gullies in the cliff hiding trucks under their 'cam' nets over which armfuls of camel thorn and scrub had been liberally spread.

The men, bronzed fit, had the swank of a band of pirates, and on the occasional party night extra rum was issued with 'the lime to follow', in the jesting way men of action make pretence at fine living, although all they have is a mess-tin of 'neaters'. The men would sing on these nights. Almost hesitantly at first, a few voices would take up a song of the time – 'Roll out the Barrel' or 'Kiss me Goodnight, Sergeant Major', then other groups would take up the tune and sing sentimentally of 'My Melancholy Baby' or below the marching songs of their fathers: 'Pack up your Troubles' and 'It's a Long way to Tipperary'. A great roar of sound rose from several dozen pinpoints of cigarettes glowing in the dark, as if to defy the vastness of the desert.

Robin Gurdon guided Mayne and two other parties north to the Fuka escarpment for raids to be put in against the airfields on Sunday night, 12 July, taking the raiders in the late afternoon through a gap in the long sand dune which marked the northern edge of the desert country. His truck was in the open, and the others, after passing through the gap, were moving to an open formation, when three Macchi fighters flew in. Despite Gurdon's friendly wave, they cleared their guns and attacked. At this moment Gurdon's truck refused to start. Ordering his men to take cover, he ran back to the second vehicle but, as it started to move, a long burst of cannon fire set it alight. Gurdon was badly wounded and the driver also hurt. The Captain ordered his men to continue to the escarpment, but for the first time they disobeyed him and turned back for the desert base. He died before they could reach it.

After this series of raids, Stirling went to Cairo, and Mayne took the desert-worn vehicles back to Kabrit, crossing the salt bog of the Qattara Depression in six hours of punishing heat. The fumes from exhausts added to the agony of breathing in any exertion, such as changing a punctured tyre. The heat became so great that petrol vaporized in the fuel pipes leading to a carburettor, necessitating an instant modification to keep the pipe cool.

In Cairo, Stirling organized the replacement jeeps, most of which were armed with K-guns, and was soon heading back for the desert base. He was away only eight days, but long enough for the men who had stayed behind to be on a water ration of half a bottle a day.

A new phase of raiding was to begin from this base, as Axis sentries now guarded each plane at night, while others patrolled the airfield perimeters where barbed wire covered anti-personnel mines. Such defences increasingly absorbed men who might otherwise have been at the main battlefront, as Rommel noted in his diary in August 1942. In later months he found the raiders even more than a nuisance, for they would have destroyed four hundred aircraft when in October his remaining serviceable strength was only 1,025 planes in Africa.

After Stirling's return to the desert base in July 1942, he had plans to trap Axis transports – as his men would later do on other roads – when Rommel was forced to withdraw through the narrow valleys where the coast road crossed the escarpments at Sollum and Halfaya. But the retreat was not to be, or at least not for twelve weeks, by which time the Detachment was chasing different targets. Nor had they been able to mount any successful attacks against night laagers of tanks: these would have required types of charge different to the Lewes bomb, and a jeep – a featherweight against the might of almost any tank – could do no more than drum on its armour with Vickers K-guns. Nevertheless, this was sufficient in a few cases to turn irresolute armoured vehicle crews from their purpose. (In the 1980s there are ways in which modern explosives might make such raids against armour a reasonable bet, but not in the 1940s.)

K-guns against aircraft were, as we have seen, devastatingly destruc-tive, with a technique which Stirling now used for good reasons: the raiders would need little time on the airfield, fully exploiting the element of surprise; such firepower overwhelmed any sentries by individual aircraft; and a rapid withdrawal was possible, getting men and jeeps far from the targets by daylight. However, there were difficulties unless the gunners were well drilled, for in error they might shoot up not only other jeeps but also their own driver as the quarter-ton truck bounced across rough ground. Stirling's gunners soon had the technique mastered: they must fire low enough not to overshoot their targets, which is the usual mistake made in firing at night; they must be able to reload their next belt or magazine as the jeep lurched and bumped across rough ground; and above all they must not fire into their own columns or even swing across their driver's position. He had to keep the jeep on course in its allotted slot in the formation, despite rocks hitting the wheels to wrench the steering from his grasp or an unexpected soft patch lurching the vehicle to a sudden stop. Most important of all: he must not let his jeep wander into other people's line of fire.

During the final rehearsals in the desert, they made several runs, the drivers changing formation from a single line abreast to two columns each of seven trucks some five metres apart with fifteen metres between the columns. Stirling was in the lead flanked by two more jeeps across the head of the columns, giving six guns that fired forward, clearing a path for the rest. Each column fired twenty-eight machine-guns to its flank, 'scything the ground . . . with a vicious spray', the vehicles juddering under the recoil of each burst. At the end of the last practice run, Stirling fired a red Very light and was answered by two arching skywards from the leader of each column; the firing stopped before the vehicles moved up into line abreast. Mayne, leading one column, turned to his front gunner to ask the man if he knew the direction in which they were moving. He glanced at the sky and gave a vague answer. 'You wouldn't get far if you had to walk,' Mayne commented. 'Mind that you are certain of the direction tomorrow night.'

On the next day, Sunday 26 July, the practice was put to good effect, for Stirling's planning and meticulous rehearsals left as little to chance as possible. The jeeps left at about 2100 hours, when it was dark, but the moon was rising. They travelled in an open formation, each jeep follow-ing a little to the left or right of its neighbour's dust cloud. The going was good, with level sand and gravel over which they made 30k.p.h. despite the occasional rock or runnel in a shadow; the gun mountings rattled and the ammunition boxes in the back clumped together when an extra-heavy jar dislodged them. The crews bounced around in the jeep, the driver steadied by his grip on the wheel, the front and rear gunners each hanging on to what hand-holds they could find, as they sped north-east.

Their target, 65km from the forward base, was Sidi Haneish airfield, near Fuka, where the surfaced runways were used by bombers staging to or from the front. Intelligence reports indicated this was a major airfield but, being placed near Axis troop areas, it would have to be approached by the chosen route, or surprise would be lost if eighteen jeeps were to mill around looking for it. Sadler, the raiders' navigator, would have to be spot on, and to check their position as they crossed the Siwa track, Stirling halted the vehicles, while Sadler used his theodolite. The going now became more difficult, with frequent punctures, delaying jeeps by five minutes as a wheel was changed (tyres could be repaired on the move, hopefully before the crew ran out of spare wheels).

About midnight they reached a ridge across their route, and jeeps had to go east and west to find the gully they would climb to the plateau. It proved very steep, a six-metre climb of racing engines after crashing gears to get up speed to charge it. Once on top, the jeeps fanned out before halting for a final check on weapons, to be sure that the ammunition would feed smoothly to each pair of guns. At this point they were fifteen kilometres due south of the target, if Sadler's calculations were right. They set off again, still in open formation except when forced to pass through a rift in some dune in single file, before again opening out the formation. The moon was hidden occasionally by passing clouds, making the drivers' job even more difficult, but they crossed a recent battlefield, and Stirling halted them near a village 1,500m short of the target. They could see no sign of the aerodrome, yet, with every confidence in Sadler, Stirling ordered them forward, a line of dark shadows grinding their way over the rough ground. They had gone hardly 500m when night was turned into day as the airfield lights came on: an unanticipated event. Had they been betrayed? Was surprise lost?

Stirling did not hesitate but put these questions to the direct test. He drove forward onto the runway as he heard the heavy rumble of bombers returning to land. He was 100m from the leading aircraft as it touched down in a hail of machine-gun fire. Sixteen other jeeps opened up along the perimeter before all the lights on the 'flare' path were switched off. A couple of minutes later Stirling fired a green Very light. In its gaudy glare the jeeps formed their two seven-vehicle columns, and two others drew up alongside Stirling, leaving Sadler with his driver and a medic on the perimeter to pick up any casualties.

The noise was deafening; tracer flew in lazy arcs to bounce off the ground beyond the targets. The columns were moving faster now they were on the tarmacadamed roadway leading to the aircraft dispersal areas. They passed through parked lines of Heinkels and Ju 88s: some took time to catch fire; perhaps half a minute would pass before a dull glow in the cockpit turned to a steady blaze. Some fuel tanks went up in a muffled roar of searching flame, yet on other aircraft the undercarriages collapsed as they were chopped down by a swaith of bullets, the fuselage seeming to disintegrate. The roadway took the columns, still in perfect formation, further along the aircraft lines. In places they were a mere 50m from the fires, the men's eyebrows being singed in the heat, while in the light of these fires they could see figures in the distance scurrying around the main building.

The first retaliation was the thud of a mortar bomb dropping just behind the leading jeeps, soon followed by the tattoo of bullets from a Breda machine-gun, its tracer traversing the columns. A front gunner in one of the leading jeeps slumped forward, 'his back curiously straight . . . the head and shoulders resting on the guns'. Though he could not respond to Sandy Scratchley's shout to fire at the Breda, other gunners were soon concentrating on the source of the tracer and silenced it. The mortar bombs had put Stirling's jeep out of action, and fragments split the sump of another jeep; its driver and front gunner, blinded by oil, had a narrow escape as they pulled up without overturning when it veered off the roadway.

The columns had halted. Stirling, collected by one of the jeeps, drove back a little way. He then told the drivers to switch off their engines, and in the silence broken only by the crackle of fires he gave them fresh orders. They were to fire only in short bursts – a number had only one full magazine or less, having used their ammunition with abandon. He would lead them on round the dispersal road, then back out past planes parked on the south side of the field, which they would attack as they left. As they crossed back into the desert, a large figure was seen running from one jeep, moving as if for an imagined try-line. But Mayne was not carrying a rugby ball but an explosive charge which he put on one undamaged plane silhouetted among the fires from the last machine-gun attack.

They were all clear of the airfield before the jeep with the damaged sump seized up. It was destroyed with an explosive charge placed by a machine-gunner. He had to run to catch up with the others, who were moving off, for the raiders intended to put as much distance as possible between them and the airfield before daylight, 2½ hours away. They would move in small groups, Sadler staying two hours to pick up any stragglers, and would hide next day before moving to the ridge 45km south of the airfield, where a dump of petrol and oil would enable them to top up their tanks for the final run to base. Stirling took four jeeps, two of which were damaged and one of which carried the body of the gunner. He had fourteen men in all, the crews of the four jeeps and his own gunners unhurt when the mortar fragment hit their jeep. They drove fast over flat ground, but one of the damaged jeeps had to be destroyed when its engine seemed to seize; there was no time to repair it.

After 50km Stirling realized that he had missed a track at which he had expected to turn on a bearing that would bring him eventually to the refuelling point. By this time it was daylight, but the early morning mist covered their tracks until it cleared. By good fortune they came into the sunshine on the edge of a small ridge with a steep side dropping to a bowl of a valley, where scrub some 1.5m high in gullies around the bowl's edge would provide good hides. In minutes the vehicles were hidden, and they had their first rest after more than twenty-four hours on the move, two of them in the heat of action. All were covered in a yellow-grey dust, their eyes red-rimmed with fatigue. Two men dug a grave for the gunner, buried with the due reverence of two minutes' silence from the men grouped round his grave.

The other parties were as fortunate as Stirling's, except for André Zirnheld's. When the mist lifted, his Frenchmen were on the Matruh-Siwa track, an obvious route south which all had intended to avoid. With no chance in full sunlight to move far away without risk of being seen, they hid the vehicles in the shadow of a small cliff. The hide was not secure enough, for just after midday three Ju 88s flew over very low, turned on seeing them and strafed the jeeps. In nine passes over the vehicles they wounded Zirnheld twice and riddled the jeeps but failed to put two of them out of action. The French were able to move to a better hide once the aircraft had left, but the Lieutenant could barely stand the pain of the bone-shaking short journey.

That night Stirling spent two hours backtracking to find the reference track, from which he set course for the base. One jeep had two punctures which developed into large bursts, making the tyre inner tubes useless, and with only one spare left the crew were forced to run it on its wheel rims. Their speed was therefore down to a few kilometres an hour, and when dawn broke they were in a wilderness of unrecognized desert. Stirling persisted on his compass bearing: his care in backtracking, not for the first time, would justify his confidence, for the next day they reached the base, although they had little petrol left and the surroundings did not seem familiar, until they looked over a rise to see a three-tonner. The French, knowing that their Lieutenant would not survive any distance in the jeep, sent a man the 45km to fetch a doctor, but Zirnheld had died before help arrived. His cross, made from ammunition boxes, bore his name and in French the epitaph 'Died for his country'.

Other parties avoided detection, although Sadler had a close shave after following the others, with only thirty minutes to sunrise. He had watched the Germans with their usual efficiency clear the damaged aircraft to have planes using the runway within a couple of hours of the raid. In the morning mist the navigator with one straggler – a jeep and its three-man crew – were following a desert track when three vehicles loomed out of the mist; the raiders were past the first before they realized a German was leaning up against one truck. His bored expression suggests that he took them for other vehicles from his motorized infantry unit, but the two jeeps were off the track and into the desert before he had time to react to their passing. They lay up several kilometres further south, in scrub on the floor of a valley, and had not been hidden long when a German salvage team came to recover a three-tonner – one reason, no doubt, why three Ju 88s which flew over left them in peace, because the German working party was just twenty metres from the hide.

Mayne, quite unconcerned, had driven, with what might be called 'calculated Irish recklessness', in broad daylight, to arrive at the desert base late on Monday afternoon. 'No planes about' was his laconic answer to any questioning of the wisdom of driving in daylight. No doubt his jeeps, however, had been driven faster and further than others in the last few hours of dark after the raid, and were well south of the Axis main search area, after taking advantage of the morning's fog. Nevertheless, not long after he arrived, six Ju 88s escorted by two Me 109s, weaving across the sky to protect the bombers at a height of 300m, flew over the base but saw no indication of the raiders.

The men and their trucks were well hidden, with, for example, eight jeeps nose-to-tail in one low, long cave. Its entrance was covered by 'cam' nets festooned with pieces of scrub and slung from the wadi side above the cave. The doctor's cave was equally well hidden – he accidentally passed its entrance on several occasions – with mosquito nets inside the camouflage over the entrance. These made it a fly-free haven, its sand floor swept clean of animal droppings and the rock ledges holding medical stores as if in some chemist's shop. The only wounds on the raid were relatively minor for fit men and were treated at the medical cave. There were also facilities for quite substantial overhauls to the vehicles, a recovery truck with a range of spare parts having reached the forward base that July.

The success of the raid for the loss of only two men – the gunner and the French lieutenant – was a remarkable tribute to the tactic of surprise with overwhelming firepower. Yet Stirling was not pleased with the profligate way in which men had used their ammunition in the early part of the raid. He dampened their natural elation that evening with a sharp rebuke: the raid had not been good enough. Gunners had fired at targets beyond the range at which aimed bursts could be sure to destroy planes; some had fired into targets already alight, others had fired too high. The men who ran out of ammunition put their jeeps' crews at risk, for they might well have had a brush with Axis ground forces on the return trip.

In future operations, the gunners would conserve ammunition, for there are strict limits to the amounts which can be carried in jeeps, bearing in mind that sufficient for a two-second burst, from twin machine-guns, weighs about half a kilogram. Firing a ten-second burst, therefore, could take a small but significant amount of the vehicle's total load. On the Sidi

Haneish (spelt Enich on modern maps) raid, the raiders had destroyed probably forty or more planes; sources are vague, but one claims that they destroyed 'every plane on the airfield'. Whatever the exact number, there is no doubt that this was a most economical use of military forces for the cost of two lives and three jeeps.

During the main raid a diversion had been created by the LRDG and a few of the Detachment, who destroyed fifteen planes on Bagush airfield, 25km from the main target, stretching the Axis search-parties over a wider area. The men got off the field without too much difficulty but had to fight off a number of Axis trucks that Monday morning before going to ground. Then, to their surprise, a small Feisler Storch landed nearby, its occupants taking a look at some of the trucks wrecked by the raider's fire. The plane carried a doctor, and both he and the pilot had left the aircraft before it was destroyed by the jeeps' machine-guns. They came back to base as prisoners but would not give their parole and had therefore to be guarded. They were moved with the raiders when Stirling shifted the base another 25km westward, as vehicle tracks were now too obvious an indication of activity. This new base proved safe from air attack, but the raiders were running low on water, and Mayne took a patrol to collect reserves from 'a secret dump near the Matruh-Siwa track'. This was a dangerous area by this time in the high summer of 1942 as Axis forces used it regularly in resupplying Siwa and patrolling against raiding forces.

Although only a few patrols had gone out (rescuing by chance an RASC officer and some men, escaping from Tobruk in a lorry), after the first week at the new base Stirling was recalled with his men to refit for a major series of raids to be mounted in September. They were flown out from an old airstrip 50km from the coast, the Bombays landing along a runway lit by hand-held flares. As only two of three ageing bombers reached the strip, the men were packed together on the fuselage floor.

Mayne brought the vehicles in a convoy during the next few days to reach Kabrit, from where the men were sent on a brief spell of leave. They had left the old base area only a day or two before air reconnaissance showed that Axis armoured cars were searching the area.

In September the Detachment took part in commando-style operations with large numbers of troops, far greater than those for successful deep-penetration raids. Stirling, working to orders from GHQ Middle East, took two hundred men, some with little more than four weeks' training, and over seventy vehicles to raid Benghazi. Not surprisingly, they were seen from the air and ambushed on the ground. The jeeps' firepower enabled them to break out of the encircling Germans and Italians, but there would be no surprise in any attack on Benghazi, and Stirling therefore sensibly withdrew, his convoy being attacked from the air before they reached Jalo. This oasis was to be recaptured by the Sudan Defence Force, as it should have provided a refuelling point on the route back to Kufra oasis. In the event the garrison was still holding out when Stirling arrived, but the Sudan Force provided enough fuel and rations for the surviving jeeps to reach the southern oasis. The casualties had been high, but not as high as Allied losses at Tobruk, after the Germans had been warned of the attack by a double-agent. Men of the Commandos' Special Boat Section were also caught up in this raid, three of them being among the few survivors who broke out of a German ring of infantry and walked 500km to the Allied lines.

These disasters emphasized – in a lesson that MO 4 Staff in the Middle East had yet to learn in 1942 – that small, highly mobile forces can create damage out of all proportion to their size, when more conventional forces almost inevitably fail because their numbers preclude that valuable tactic of surprise. Colonel J. E. Hasledon, a British intelligence officer of great experience in the desert, often working dressed as an Arab in Axis-occupied areas, was killed in the Tobruk raid. He had suggested that a dozen men, some from SIG, might sneak into the Tobruk complex and destroy underground fuel tanks. Stirling had similar proposals for the use of a small force. Yet neither had been able to dissuade the planners from a more ambitious use of large forces, since the Middle East staff believed that such a well-defended target as Tobruk needed the weighty bludgeon of a battle-axe rather than a rapier thrust.

After the bludgeons failed, Stirling's tactics were vindicated, and in October 'L' Detachment became the 1st Special Air Service Regiment with eighty experienced men in 'A' Squadron, some two hundred others being in 'B' Squadron and squads of new volunteers training at Kabrit. The Regiment's operations were co-ordinated with the Eighth Army's plans for an offensive by G Raiding Force, a small staff planning army raids as opposed to those by Secret Service or SOE clandestine forces. It was commanded by Colonel (later General Sir John) 'Shan' Hackett, a man of high intelligence and great charm, who got on well with Stirling. General Montgomery, who had taken command of the Eighth Army from Ritchie on 13 August, did not prove such a friend of SAS that October, although understandably he would not allow experienced volunteers from his battalions to be recruited into the new Regiment. In later months, the General spoke favourably of 'the boy Stirling', but that was after the Regiment's successes of October and November, and influenced probably by Winston Churchill's views. The Prime Minister was always interested in SAS-type operations and once quoted Byron's 'Don Juan' to describe Stirling as 'the mildest mannered man, that ever scuttled ships or cut a throat'.

Mayne's A Squadron went off to cut throats and a lot more besides early in October, concentrating their raids in the area of El Agheila against the railway to Tobruk and the coast road (see Appendix II). They made the approach of over 1,8000km from Cairo through Kufra to establish a forward base at Bir Zalten, 240km – more than a night's drive – from the coast, their raids contributing to the closing of the coast railway on thirteen days in the three weeks before the opening of the Battle of Alamein on 23 October. The Allied advance in the next five weeks had reached El Agheila before Stirling (promoted Lieutenant-Colonel in October) led 'B' Squadron through Kufra to the forward base at Bir Zalten, where he arrived with ninety men, thirty jeeps and twelve three-tonners on 29 November. Stirling planned to raid with the two Squadrons along the 700km of coast road and railway west from Agheila into Tripolitania. With A Squadron continuing to raid the eastern half of these lines of communication, and 'B' in the west, each patrol of two or three jeeps would raid every three days, totalling up to four attacks each night. These would force Rommel's road convoys to travel by day, providing the Allied Air Forces with some juicy targets.

B Squadron had been recruited largely from men just out from the United Kingdom or those who had been serving in Palestine and Iraq. Therefore they had less desert experience than Mayne's Squadron, and when they moved westward early in December, they were an enthusiastic but untried force. On Sunday 13 December, as Montgomery opened his attack from El Agheila, the eight patrols of 'B' Squadron each stood ready to attack a section of coast road, while Oldfield's team covered the gap around Buerat between A and B Squadrons. Each jeep carried two or three men, was armed with at least two K-guns or .5-inch Brownings (with a slower rate of fire at 450rpm but air-cooled like the K-gun) and carried sufficient rations and water (160 litres) for twenty days. Each jeep also carried twelve mines, a Sten, a rifle and sufficient petrol (180 litres) for 650km or further when the going was smooth. Reserves of fuel and rations were cached at a forward base, El Fascia, at the south-east of B Squadron's raiding area and 80km from the coast road. Here also the Squadron's wireless truck was hidden and able to keep touch with the Eighth Army.

The intention was that patrols would return to the forward base only when they ran short of fuel, ammunition or rations, except for those patrols operating near Buerat which could drive back to El Fascia before each dawn. But such activity attracted not only Axis aircraft but also their armoured car patrols, and when Lieutenant Alston went over to the nearby *bir* for a bath in its underground well, his jeep was probably seen, for armoured cars were directed into the wadi where the radio truck may also have been DF-ed. SAS and Axis cars laagered near each other that night but the raiders slipped away and spent Christmas further south. Alston had been joined by Lieutenant Wilfred Thesiger, the well-known explorer, and Lieutenant Martin, of the Free French. They were the only three officers of B Squadron to survive ten days of raids without being killed or captured.

Stirling had left on 13 December for Cairo. The Eighth Army's advance during the next days brought the main battlefield close to Buerat and having made two raids on 13/14 December, Mayne was told to withdraw, for there was no point in destroying roads and installations which the advancing Army would use – a reminder of the need to keep SAS operations far ahead of any advancing Allied forces.

The Allied First Army, of mainly Americans, had landed on 8 November in Algeria and Morocco. With them later would be David Stirling's brother, Lieutenant-Colonel W. ('Bill') S. Stirling, who commanded 2nd SAS which was raised mainly from 62 Commando – hence the phrase 'Stirling and Stirling' for SAS.

The planners working at this time on the invasion of Normandy had foreseen possible roles for the SAS, with Brigadier Antony Head visiting the Middle East to discuss with Hackett how such troops were being used. There were therefore prospects, as Stirling hoped, for an SAS Brigade, as the strength of his forces was growing in January when he had built up a sizeable command: 1 SAS of forty officers and 350 other ranks (a hundred below establishment); the Commandos' Special Boat Section in the Middle East of fifteen and forty; the Free French SAS Squadron of fourteen and eighty, and the Greek Sacred Squadron of fourteen and a hundred (most of whom had served as officers in the King of Greece's armed forces).

Stirling carried in his head the future plans for these forces when in January 1943 he led the patrols sent to reinforce the survivors of B Squadron. (A Squadron were moving to the Lebanon to train in mountain warfare for possible operations in the Caucasus Mountains to aid Turkey and defend Persia should the Germans turn south after their advances between the Black and Caspian Seas.)

That January, Montgomery was also planning to link up with the First Army and invest the remaining Axis forces behind their fortified Mareth line defending Tunis. Stirling left Egypt for El Fascia, an RV 50km from the Mareth Line. The Eighth Army needed to know more about the terrain in this region of Tunisia where Lake Djeria and its marshlands come within 35km of the coast at Gabès. They also wanted some already planned raids carried out quickly, as the advanced elements of the Eighth Army had passed Tripoli and the First Army had reached Gafsa. Therefore, Stirling's patrols, after negotiating the most difficult 'choppy' Grand Sea Erg, hurried north independently to get through the Gabès Gap. With him were twenty-eight men in eight jeeps, and in view of the urgency to disrupt Rommel's supply lines he hurriedly completed a recce of the western positions of Mareth Line, before following other patrols through the Gap. Once north of this, the intention was to raid Sousse, 300km further north. After that he would make contact with the First Army. It was a formidable plan which only a man of Stirling's experience would undertake.

The nine jeeps of the French patrols sent ahead by Stirling were delayed when crossing undulating sands and failed to reach the Gap as planned on Wednesday night (21–2 January); they did get through on the Thursday night, although one jeep was captured by German armoured cars. Later they shot up three large trucks in attempting to break through on the track – off it were impassable dunes – and the hunt for them was up. They lost the wireless car and became separated but nevertheless mined the railway track near Cekhira on the Friday night before the last jeeps were caught on the Saturday. Stirling's three jeeps with fourteen raiders passed through the Gap on the Friday afternoon, twelve hours after the French and in broad daylight. The ground was even more difficult than expected, one jeep taking two hours to free from soft sand. They had probably already been seen by Axis aircraft, but pressed on to lay up 30km north of the Gafsa–Gabès road, in a wadi within 1,500m of a recently built road. Three sergeants, sleeping as ordered after forty-eight hours on the move, were woken quietly by Germans, but they – Sadler, Cooper and the Arab-speaking Frenchman Taxis – later slipped away. Stirling was less fortunate. Trapped in a cave by a German dentist who had been detailed to help the search-parties, the phantom Colonel was taken prisoner. He was a catch the Germans did not realize that they had made, for several days. Several others reached safety, but Stirling's attempts to escape were all thwarted, once by hostile Arabs.

Stirling was not able to take part in the later development of his ideas, but he and his men had proved the value of SAS operations. By setting up concealed bases far into enemy territory, they could operate independently of normal sources of combat stores, and with highly mobile, skilled troops, making the most use of surprise in their tactics, they could create damage out of all proportion to their numbers. Rommel recorded starkly in his diary: 'They caused considerable havoc and seriously disquieted the Italians.'

A fitting commentary from an aggressive leader.

3. The Island Wars and Mainland Raids in the Mediterranean

In the Mediterranean Commando canoeists had been working with the 1st Submarine Flotilla since the summer of 1941 and in several raids during 1942 had blown up railways, attacked ships and made recces. A number of these operations were in support of landings by larger forces including units in the ill-fated attack on Tobruk. Canoe teams had also worked with Stirling because L Detachment did not include any militarily trained canoeists; and the formation of M Detachment for sabotage raids against German transports and aircraft, should they cross the mountains of north Persia, paradoxically involved a possible seaborne raid to Crete. This Detachment began training at Isfahan with 150 men recruited mainly from British troops in Persia and Iraq. Among their instructors was the forthright Cockney Captain Bill Cumper, Royal Engineers, who had served as a sapper in Egypt in the 1930s. The leading expert in the Middle East on sabotage demolitions, he had been recruited by Stirling and not only went on raids but ran many devastating courses to train the SAS.

Teams from M Detachment helped to kidnap the pro-Axis General Zahidi, who commanded local Persian forces in Isfahan, but the raid on Crete was abandoned as German air squadrons had been moved from the target airfield. At this time, in the winter of 1942, other patrols from 1st SAS – of which 'M' Detachment was a part – were still raiding in North Africa, but in the early months of 1943 all the Regiment were withdrawn to Azzib, north of Haifa, for reorganization. A and B Squadrons were brought up to strength to form the Special Raiding Squadron (1st SRS) under Mayne's command. C Squadron was formed for possible operations in north Persia, but Allied victories at Stalingrad and Alamein removed any Axis threat to Persia, and this Squadron apparently became a training cadre. D Squadron was formed for island raids, in part to exploit the idea which Jellicoe had used in Crete the previous summer, the landing of raiders from the sea in small boats. However, Mayne had to use all his considerable persuasive powers to convince GHQ that the SAS should continue in the Middle East.

On 1 April D Squadron with 234 all ranks was officially formed and began to move to Athlit, already familiar to those who had served in M Detachment and who had been in the Commandos' SB Sections, now absorbed into D Squadron with its three Sections: 'M' (not to be confused with M Detachment), 'L' and 'S'. The Section commanders each had a distinguished record of raiding behind them, an obvious but sometimes overlooked reason for the subsequent success of their Sections. Tommy Langton, commanding L, for example, had been with Stirling since the early days. Ian Lapraik ('M') had won an MC and served in the Abyssinian Campaign, where he won the Lion of Judah Medal; he was later captured but escaped near Alamein. He brought with him to join D Squadron several men who had been in the special forces he had trained at one time in Malta, including Lieutenant Dick ('Stud') Stellin, a New Zealander. The OC of S Section, the immaculate David Sutherland, nicknamed 'Dinky', had served in the Commandos' SB Section. In the September he took some of the Commandos' SB Section to Rhodes, from which only he and Marine Duggan, managed with great difficulty to reach the safety of their RV with a submarine.

The Squadron was commanded by Major (later Lieutenant-Colonel) the Earl (George) Jellicoe. A thickset man with curly hair, then aged twenty-five, he had been studying at Cambridge when the war started, but joined Stirling in the late spring of 1942. As the son of a famous admiral, he moved in that circle of friends which gave him confidence in dealing with political as well as military hierarchies, giving his Squadron a more respected position than was the case for most 'private' armies. His diplomatic endeavours in the Dodecanese during the autumn of 1943 were to be frustrated but a year later proved invaluable to the Allied cause in Greece.

The Sections, known as Detachments by September 1943 and later as Squadrons when each had eighty men, enjoyed days of high-spirited training on the Athlit beaches in the spring of that year, when such formalities as the names and titles of D Squadron's patrols were of little consequence. 'No one tried to parade his authority,' John Verney of L Squadron has written, 'nor was there much place for the detestable concept of one-upmanship.' Every man could be seen for what he was, and if this did not match up to the Squadron's needs, then he was sent back to his original unit. Indeed, 'Returned to Unit' (RTU-ed) was the sole, if devastating, punishment for anyone without the self-discipline or will to work in the Squadron. Those who made the grade proved superb soldiers, as their first major operation on Crete in July 1943 proved. They were sent on this raid, as explained below, as part of a larger strategy for the invasion of Sicily.

Although the July 1943 raid on Crete was not the first employment of SAS in a strategic role, it shows how twenty skilled men in the right place at the right time might influence the fortunes of great armies, as it served a double purpose for the planners of the Sicily invasion, who were aware of the ease with which Axis forces could be sent quickly to reinforce that island's defences. The Allies could not land there, however, in overwhelming strength as not only were divisions required for the build-up of forces for Normandy but also there were not enough landing craft to lift more than the assault divisions of the US Seventh and British Eighth Armies. In the air Allied superiority, with 4,328 serviceable aircraft, far outmatched the Axis planes in Sicily, Sardinia and Italy, which totalled only 1,750. Nevertheless, if the Axis defences were concentrated in Sicily, they might inflict a heavy defeat on the seaborne invaders. Therefore two deceptions were planned: the German High Command were led to believe that Sicily was not the intended invasion point but that the Americans would land in Sardinia and/or southern France, while the British would capture Crete as the prelude to an invasion of Greece.

In support of these deceptions SAS patrols landed in Sardinia and, by bold aggression over ten days, helped to give the distinct impression that the Allies were interested in that island. On Crete, an annual venue for the SBS from 1942 to 1944, they could not only create a diversion in this operation 'Albumen' (although why the white of an egg was a suitable code-name for this raid is hard to suggest) but also reduce the possibilities of Axis air squadrons moving to reinforce their Sicilian defences some two to three hours flying time from Crete.

On Crete in the early summer of 1943 were several German squadrons using four main airfields, or so military intelligence led the planners to believe. Sutherland's Section was given the task of attacking three of the airfields; the fourth, at Maleme, was significantly not one of their targets, for this fourth field was the largest and the previous year had been found to be well defended with at least one electrified fence among the several around the perimeter, covered by searchlights and well-positioned machine-gun posts, while dog-patrols moved around the parked aircraft. These defences would be likely to be even more alertly guarded on the planned night for the attacks this year: Thursday/Friday (1/2 July), eight days before the invasion, a timing which allowed for several days of Allied air-attacks on these fields before the Sicily landings. In fact, Maleme never was successfully attacked by raiders but was bombed by Allied aircraft.

Sutherland worked out his detailed plans with Jellicoe on the basis of the Commando SBS and Jellicoe's experience on Crete in 1942. On that raid the Free French patrol had taken over five nights to move south from Heraklion towards the coast before they were betrayed, and Sutherland knew the difficulties in reaching Timbaki, which he had found deserted in July 1942. Therefore ample time was allowed for an approach march from the south coast landing point some 250km by roundabout routes which

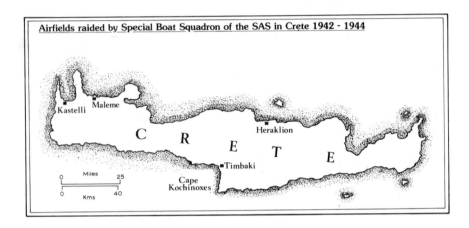

Airfields raided by Special Boat Squadron of the SAS in Crete 1942 - 1944

kept to the mountains and clear of Axis patrols. These routes were so steep in places that men with heavy loads might climb some stretches only by using their hands and feet, a difficulty in mountains which cannot always be foreseen from aerial photographs.

The raiding teams, each of an officer, a sergeant, a corporal and a signaller, would have to carry 'Christmas pudding' bombs of the Lewes type, submachine-guns and emergency rations probably for ten days, which, with grenades and ammunition, made individuals' loads about 30kg. The radio operators carried no explosive charges, but, as their No. 22 sets with their accumulators (wet batteries) weighed 30kg, they could each be carrying over 50kg. Lack of water was also a problem on Crete, and each man must have carried at least one full water-bottle. These loads would have to be hauled from a forward base set up on high ground inland from Cape Kochinoxes, where they would land, to caches within a few hours of each target field.

While intelligence reports suggested that Cape Kochinoxes was clear of enemy patrols, the raiders could expect to find these nearer their targets. They might also have to change targets because of unexpected defences, and no doubt a series of second-choice targets was worked out. To control such changes of plan and keep the teams informed of any new intelligence, Sutherland would set up the forward base where his signallers could also be in touch with the GHQ Middle East's communications centre. His orders were quite specific: Jellicoe told him that he must stay at this base to control the operation. Planning and final preparations were completed on the weekend of 20–21 June, almost three weeks before the invasion of Sicily, and Sutherland, Lamonby and some dozen men boarded an HDML a couple of days later.

The ML came into the small bay near Cape Kochinoxes where the landing was to be made and saw the recognition lights, no doubt, flashed by MO 4's Cretans above a narrow beach between sheer rock walls where the raiders were to land. All being clear, the ML landed the first party from her dory at 0115 that Wednesday night (23 June). Since the water was deep enough for her to get close to the shore, her crew soon ferried the rest of the men and their gear to the beach. Their first job was to establish the forward base, so they cached among rocks the stores needed for the later raids. Their first climb, 40m or so up a nearly vertical small gully behind the landing beach, gave them some inkling of the hard going ahead, as they moved inland to climb several hundred metres into the hills north of the Cape. Their guides lost their way in the dark, and the men with their heavy loads could only move laboriously up into the rocky hills – a slog which took longer than expected, with the result that it was dangerously daylight before they moved up a deep valley to reach a narrower one high in the hills. Small caves along this valley side provided excellent cover, and once Sutherland was satisfied that there were no enemy in the area, they set up camp. By midday he was ready to go back with several of his base party to collect the rations and radio batteries for the raiding parties, a helping hand for those who had far to go that day.

The base was so remote that Sutherland judged it safe for the raiders to leave in the late afternoon, giving them a few hours of daylight in which to make some way towards their first laying-up area, before darkness slowed their progress even more than the hill country did. Lieutenant Anders Lassen was heading for Kastelli airfield, and Lieutenant Kenneth Lamonby for Heraklion; as both their routes lay north-westward, they could keep their patrols together for some days before Lamonby struck north for the coast. These two officers were experienced patrol leaders, although Lassen had been with the SBS for only six weeks.

Lassen had made a number of raids on the French Channel coast and elsewhere while serving in the Small Scale Raiding Force (later 62 Commando) based in the United Kingdom, after joining the British army in 1940. He had been a potential recruit for SOE, although he did not know this, the clandestine services expecting to use him in his native Denmark, but his natural abilities made him such a formidable soldier that he was destined for a short brilliant career with the SBS (he was killed when only twenty-five). During his training he moved so stealthily on one occasion that he got close enough to a stag to kill it with a knife, and the tales of his quick reflexes in action are legion. He had been a cadet in the Danish merchant navy at the time war broke out, but his aristocratic upbringing gave him, like Jellicoe, a disdain for the trivial. This led him to walk out of one meeting of senior officers with a curt 'I go now.' At other times he could charm even the hardest of staff officers and the smelly dogs which he collected on his travels, but his compassion for the underdog – poor Greek peasants or Yugoslav refugees – was in Jellicoe's opinion his outstanding quality.

Lassen's patrol, Sergeant Jack Nicholson, Corporal S. Greaves and later Gunner R. W. Jones, who replaced a signaller, were all to become legends in their own right in the SBS. Nicholson on one occasion landed alone to capture a German officer and had to fight his way clear of German patrols. Greaves died in tragic circumstances only a few months after the Crete raid, and Gunner Jones was killed the following April. The men of Lamonby's patrol were equally effective: Lance-Corporal R. Holmes would later save several of his patrol on Nisiros by a timely burst of Bren fire as he awoke to find Germans around the cave in which he was hidden.

Ken Lamonby had been Jellicoe's instructor in seamanship at Athlit, and now was Sutherland's second-in-command.

The two teams – technically under Lamonby's command at this stage, although such questions of seniority seem unlikely to have arisen – moved mainly at night, lying up during the day in an approach march on which 'very little happened', to quote a contemporary report. After the fifth night the signallers in the teams found the going so hard, with their heavy loads, that it would be impossible for them to beat any hasty retreat with their sets if the teams had to leave their target airfields hurriedly. Therefore the signallers were left at this hide on Sunday morning, and apparently Gunner Jones joined Lassen's team, keeping it at the full strength of four. The signallers by this time were able to keep in touch with Sutherland's base only with difficulty, in part because of the mountains, where reception was notoriously bad, and also because their batteries were losing power. (In the early 1940s these needed recharging after a few hours of transmission, and although various generators were used by SOE and others in the field, Sutherland's patrols did not have one.)

The Cretans had proved most friendly and even helped with the heavier loads at times; others acted as guides through arrangements made by MO 4 officers on the island. One of these guides brought Lassen by Wednesday night to a ridge overlooking Kastelli airfield. Next day local Cretans told him that there were guards a mere ten metres apart, ringing the blastproof shelters, and that each Stuka dive-bomber had its individual guard who was changed every two hours. Lassen thought this an exaggeration but nevertheless revised his plan of attack, for despite his renowned daring he was a prudent man, only taking those risks which

During the last months of World War II, 2 SAS supported Italian
partisans: a heavy machine-gun team from No. 3 Squadron operated
in the hills near Castino, Genoa, aiding partisan harassment of the
German retreat

Lt-Col Blondeel receives the DSO
from Maj-Gen G. Surtees. Blondeel
commanded the Belgian SAS
rescuing 150 Allied airmen near Le
Mans, recceing in the Ardennes and
rescuing British airborne troops near
Arnhem

Major 'Sandy' Scratchly, commanded
a 2 SAS squadron at Termoli

Sgt A. Schofield and Trooper O. Jeavons in a jeep modified for deep penetration patrols in northern France in 1944

SAS teams led the Allies into Holland and Germany: here near Celle, north-east of Hanover, German officials are taken to Allied HQ for interrogation

Parachuting jeeps to advanced bases behind enemy lines was routine
by spring 1945: Shown here is a training exercise

Men of D Squadron 1 SAS in Borneo, 1964

A signals sergeant in the signal centre at SAS operational HQ in Borneo

In the '50s and '60s SAS patrols in Malaya and Borneo worked with locally raised forces: here Dyaks of 'Harrison' Force carry a dead enemy soldier, Borneo, 1963

The SAS trained Dyaks for service with the Border Scouts

A senior medical NCO leaving a jungle patrol camp

Helicopters were often the only means of access to Borneo's jungle areas: men would abseil down to the treetops

An SAS patrol crosses a swift-flowing river in northern Borneo

he had calculated more carefully than he is sometimes given credit for.

During Wednesday the raiders watched the field and found that a sentry guarded each trackway leading from the runways to the blast walls in the aircraft dispersal areas. This further series of sentries meant that movement on these roads would be more difficult than raiders on other fields had experienced once inside the perimeter. However, such precautions absorbing much manpower were a direct result of SAS raids elsewhere, and throughout the Middle East probably absorbed a thousand or more troops. They did not deter Lassen: he decided to create a diversion on the west side of the field, where he and Gunner Jones could distract the garrison's attention while Nicholson and Greaves placed explosive charges on eight Stukas parked at the southern end of the field. The team was briefed and stowed their spare kit for the return march, as they would make the attack in 'light order' carrying little more than six to eight bombs apiece, their Thomas SMGs, ammunition, a few grenades and water-bottles. Silk maps, tiny compasses and other escape kit were hidden in their clothing.

At 2230, having been led by a guide to the point at which he wanted to cross the airfield fence, Lassen began cutting his way through the double apron of Dannert barbed wire. Once through this fence, some ten metres wide, he and Jones walked boldly, if carefully, down the road, their rubber shoes making no noise. Every twenty metres or so they crouched down for a moment to look for the silhouettes of those road sentries, which now would be shown up in the light of a campfire blazing on the raiders' left front. As they neared this fire, where twenty Italians were talking and some singing, Lassen stepped off the road and was challenged by a sentry. Claiming to be a German officer, Lassen bluffed this Italian and a second sentry nearer the Stukas, but a third was not to be fooled – he was possibly a German in the outer ring of guards. But he allowed his attention to be distracted for a fatal moment when Lassen pointed towards the fire, and a moment was all that the Dane needed to draw his automatic and step inside the sentry's levelled rifle. Two shots doubled up the man in an agony of stomach wounds. But the two cracks also aroused other sentries each side of him, and firing broke out. Lassen and Jones each tossed a grenade and behind this tiny barrage moved quickly into an apparently quiet area, leaving the men around the fire shooting at the sentries in the outer ring.

The 'battle' behind them died down but they now came on an anti-aircraft gun battery, and more grenades covered their escape, again into what appeared to be a quiet spot, but there was a sentry there whom Lassen shot. A machine-gun fired about this time, Very lights went up and in the confusion sentries again began firing at each other before Lassen and Jones beat a retreat towards the gap they had made in the wire, but they found time to fuel the battle with more grenades and place charges on a large caterpillar tractor.

Nicholson and Greaves cut their way through the double fence to find they were close to a Ju 88 which had just landed, and when the rumpus of Lassen's first shots distracted the guards, the raiders put a couple of charges on this plane with one probably by the tail and one near a wing route – Mayne's tactic of putting them on the propeller boss had gone out of fashion, probably because the Germans could easily find them there. The raiders could not move further towards the Stukas because three sentries were nearby, exchanging doubts about what the firing meant on the other side of the field. When it died down, the two raiders were able to sneak past the guards and lay charges on a second Ju 88, but there were too many sentries about for them to reach the Stukas – until, that is, ten minutes later, when the burst of automatic fire began the minor battle which developed on the western perimeter; then the sentries no longer watched the planes but were trying to follow the noise of the battle as Lassen and Jones made their exit. Two charges were therefore placed on the nearest Stuka, but one sentry, mindful of his duty, saw the Sergeant and Corporal and fired. They were forced to take cover in a clump of bushes which turned out to be the camouflage and natural cover for a petrol dump. 'This they garlanded with bombs', in the words of one report.

All their fuses having half-hour delays, time was running out, but the sentries by the wings of another Stuka were still intently following the battle, enabling Nicholson to place a charge on its tail. This was almost their last target for a truck came up and more sentries hastily spread around the blast pens, making any more action impossible there. Yet as the raiders retreated towards their hole in the fence, they passed through another clump of bushes where they found a third Stuka. This took the last of their dozen or so charges, and they were through the wire as the first charges blew. Their guide had waited for them despite the fact that searchlights were playing across the hills which they had intended to climb, and he led them by a safe route back to the ridge, where they collected their gear and began to march south, as Lassen and Jones had not arrived by 0200, H-hour that Friday morning, for all the attacks had been at 0115 or thereabouts, which meant that Lassen had allowed himself an hour or so to create his diversion. In practice the charges at Kastelli went off a fraction early and the diversion became a mini-battle.

Nicholson and Greaves followed their orders and reported at the signallers' hide on Saturday night, before making their way back to Sutherland's base in the next week, being passed from village to village. Lassen and Jones had a less easy journey. Their guide may have vanished at the sounds of the nearby shooting, but they reached a position on the ridge by first light. There they could have been caught napping if not in a

near-coma of sleep, but the Dane's remarkable resilience (fed, one suspects, not entirely on Benzedrine) enabled him to stay awake. He therefore saw the search-parties begin to comb the hillside, after his position
had been betrayed. He woke Jones and they crawled clear of danger to
hide in a cave. There, without food but with their two water-bottles, they
lay low for 3½ days. By Monday afternoon the Axis search-parties must
have concluded that they had escaped, and the raiders could move off
and make their way back to the forward base.

Lamonby had been met the previous Tuesday by a Greek colonel who
had been in hiding on the island for two years. His contacts – or possibly
those the teams had met before they decided to leave the signallers a day's
march from the target airfields – told him that Heraklion was no longer
used to park aircraft overnight. This followed German practice in the
Western Desert now that they were aware of the damage SAS patrols
might inflict on ill-guarded planes. Therefore Lamonby and Holmes
headed for Peza village, where a large fuel storage depot was known to be
hidden in a valley.

On the next Wednesday night they were in the hills above the village,
and next day one of the guides went to recce the depot's defences. He
found a way into one wired-off compound by way of a ditch from an
abandoned vineyard; this was to be the starting point of the raid, and
other compounds would be entered by other routes. He also established
the sentries' routine, apparently, for after dark when the raiders reached
the ditch they had to wait twenty minutes. On cue a German officer and
his dog passed the tangle of vines, going on a round of the sentries. With
the German safely past, Lamonby and Holmes scrambled along the ditch
to find fifty or more drums of petrol stacked in the compound. They had
two-hour fuses on their charges and, moving separately around the
drums, set them to explode at 0115 on Friday morning.

Holmes was about to crawl back along the ditch when he heard the
guide move up a bank near the vineyard. A sentry also heard this noise,
and Holmes lay rock-still until he hoped the danger would pass, but the
officer and his dog reappeared. There were several minutes when all
might have come to nothing if Holmes was discovered, not to mention a
long spell of captivity at best for him, but the strong smell of fuel and
Holmes' studied courage in not sweating with fear prevented any scent
reaching the dog before it and the two Germans moved off.

When he had crawled back to the vineyard, there was no sign of the
guide, who knew the layout of the depot, so Lamonby made a solo recce
in the dark, when he found that there were a good number of sentries
about, suggesting that the guard was strengthened at night. The raiders
could not, therefore, lay any more charges without grave risk of being
discovered and seeing the explosives already laid being made safe by the
Germans. Lamonby therefore decided that they should leave the rest of

their charges about the vineyard where they would be hard to find and would certainly cause some distractions when they went off, perhaps deterring any firefighters. He need not have worried about them for, as the raiders watched from high on the hills at about 0115, the drums in the compound went up in a fury of flames that set light to neighbouring compounds. An intense heat split other drums, and soon the surrounding undergrowth was afire, with the whole valley in flames. Later reports suggest that over 200,000 litres of petrol and other fuel went up in the blaze.

Lamonby and Holmes reached the signallers on Saturday night, and a brief message of their success and of Lassen's activities, as reported by Nicholson, was sent to Sutherland. Lamonby apparently waited for Lassen, and they set off for the base on Tuesday or Wednesday. Reports from the guides told of German patrols moving along the coast, and details were briefly radioed to Sutherland, while Lamonby took care to move with particular caution in daylight. This German stratagem of searching the coastline was far more effective than trying to find raiders among the innumerable valleys of the mountains, for any ship or craft coming inshore to collect the raiders was exposed on the open sea.

ML 361 was not due off Cape Kochinoxes until the following Sunday night (11/12 July), by which time the Axis Air Forces would be embroiled in the defence of Sicily and have no time to fly reconnaissance missions looking for the raiders' craft. For good measure, Cairo Radio also proclaimed the safe return of the raiders, without detailing their successes which undoubtedly contributed to the safe passage and landing of the invasion force.

Lieutenant R. ('Ronnie') Rowe, Scots Guards, and his team landed several days after the others, as they had the shortest but still daunting journey to the airfield at Timbaki. This they found – as Sutherland had the previous year – was not in use, they therefore lay up and patrolled the area west of the team's base. Here some thirty Cretans who had helped the raiders were expecting to be taken off with the SBS by Sunday (11 July) all were keyed up in the heat, with water rationed, and only armed threats kept the locals from undisciplined forays to search for more.

That evening two Germans came up the valley but Guardsmen D'Arcy and Conby ambushed them and they surrendered. A second pair, better trained than the first opened fire on the Cretans and then withdrew into the gathering darkness. There was still six hours to wait before the ML was due and Sutherland wanted to avoid any action that might bring the main search-parties to the area. He therefore had the Cretans disarmed, which not only would prevent them precipitating actions against the Germans but ensure that they could be more easily controlled when the ML arrived. Lamonby and his team having rounded up the locals, the Lieutenant stayed in the valley in case the Germans returned.

At 0015 that Monday morning the ML closed into the beach, and in forty-five minutes all the SBS teams, their gear, the two prisoners and apparently some Cretans were aboard. The skipper waited over twenty minutes for Lamonby, but he could not be found, so they sailed without him, reaching Matruh that evening, and were in Cairo the next, 'taking tea at Groppi's fashionable restaurant' – in fact they had coffee and ice-cream, which were shared with the prisoners. The latters' uniforms might well have passed unnoticed among the variety of Allied dress in the room, but they did not, and Rowe was later given an official reprimand for not immediately handing his prisoners to the appropriate security authorities.

Lamonby had been killed, for as he followed the two Germans only one moved while the other covered him. The Lieutenant rose to shoot the one who was moving, and the second shot him, an example of good fieldcraft which makes the bravest stalker cautious of his enemies.

With Sicily conquered, the Allies were about to invade Italy when the Italians sued for peace. Among the forces to surrender would be those on the Dodecanese Islands off the Turkish coast in the southern Aegean, the principal of which was Rhodes. This Greek island was the key to the Allies' quickly gaining control of this area, but they had neither the shipping nor the conventional forces to spare for its occupation. Indeed, the Mediterranean and Middle East commands were so short of landing craft – since the bulk of these were being held for landings in Normandy and the Pacific – that the landings in Italy were consolidated only by juggling the LST convoys from Africa.

The SB Squadron was sent to the Dodecanese, and Lieutenant-Colonel (later Brigadier) D. J. T. Turnbull, as Chief of all Middle East raiding forces, together with Jellicoe, attempted to persuade the Italians to surrender the islands to the Allies. Despite Jellicoe's daring diplomacy when he landed with only a senior interpreter and a signals sergeant to negotiate with the Italian admiral, and despite the defensive battles cleverly fought in an unusual SB role, Germans regained control of these islands and the Squadron withdrew. During the following months, as Appendix II shows, they carried out such a successful campaign of raids on these and other Aegean islands that they made a major contribution to Allied strategy.

The Squadron, being 'soldiers and sailers too' in the Kipling phrase, included some forty Royal Marines and, as L, M and S Squadrons, rotated with one Squadron at a forward base on Kastellorizon where their schooner the *Tewfik* was moored. As the Squadrons changed over about every eighth week, the men were kept battle-sharp, for, to paraphrase one of the senior authorities on such operations: 'The men needed periods of rest, as did bomber crews, if they were not to become careless from sheer strain and fatigue.' Their raids terrorized the German garrisons, but they did more than frighten many of these men into deserting to neutral Turkey: the raiders made the defence of the islands so costly that Hitler had to reinforce the garrisons when he would not concede these islands. He was tricked into this policy as much by Allied clandestine manipulation as by his own intransigence, for British secret services made much of the possibilities of American and British armies joining forces with the Russians in the Balkans. Therefore, as more German forces were drawn into what became for them the vortex of the Aegean, they were trapped by Allied naval and air forces making their subsequent evacuation impossible without heavy losses.

Meanwhile partisan forces in Yugoslavia, Albania and Greece also snared many German divisions, and they were helped to a minor extent by the SBS in the summer of 1944. That May there were more than twenty-six German divisions in these campaigns when they might have been better employed defending the French Channel coast or on the Eastern Front. By June and the time of the Normandy invasion, the garrisons on Leros had been increased by four thousand men and on Kos by two thousand, and the deployment of small garrisons on many islands had been cleverly changed: strong garrisons were placed on selected islands for several weeks and then moved to other islands for another few weeks. SB patrols therefore met no resistance or nearly overwhelming force without that happy – for them – medium of garrisons which they could destroy.

Sutherland summed up the position in a report as being increasingly hazardous for hit-and-run raids, a view expressed more colourfully by Lassen in his fractured English: 'You can do some of it part of the time, for quite a while; but you can't do all of it all the time for very long.' Even he had been forced in late April to abandon an attempt to land thirteen men on Paros, but two of his NCOs individually sneaked ashore, killed a number of Germans and captured an officer.

Part of the SBS's early success in the islands had been due to the German command's suppressing news of the raids, with the result that many garrisons were unprepared when it became their turn for an SBS visit. Such casualness, however, suited the secret services wishing to land agents on the islands, and for a period in the spring of 1944 the SBS had been limited in their choice of targets in order that some garrisons should not be alerted.

When Lapraik's M Squadron came to the forward base to relieve Sutherland's men, he decided on a policy of raiding further north and west into the Sporades and, for example, to Kithira, off the southern tip of Greece. These raids ended in pitched battles or in frustrating non-events, when no Germans could be found. Therefore Colonel Turnbull decided that the tactic of force rather than stealth was required, since a few men,

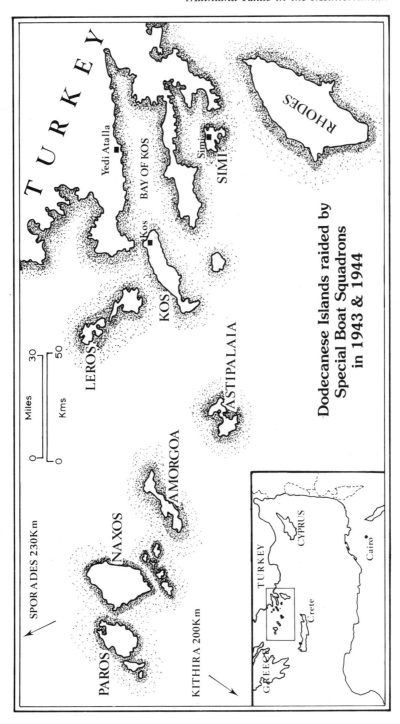

Dodecanese Islands raided by
Special Boat Squadrons
in 1943 & 1944

however skilful, could not break well-organized defences where men were dug in with a good field of fire so that they could not be surprised at close quarters. Such defences can be defeated only by heavier firepower, and the Colonel planned to mount what was in effect a commando-type raid, using Lapraik's M Squadron (81 all ranks) and 139 officers and men of the Greek Sacred Squadron, who, with the small Tactical HQ of the Colonel's Raiding Forces, amounted to a force of 234. Such a number would require a fleet of caiques and ML escorts, but until the threat of two German-controlled Italian destroyers was removed from the area, no sizeable Allied convoy might sail in safety.

The two small but well-armed thousand-ton destroyers were attacked on 17/18 June and badly disabled by three canoe teams from the Royal Marine Boom Patrol Detachment, men of the 'Cockleshell heroes' unit which had sunk several ships in Bordeaux in December 1942. This raid opened the way for Turnbull to mount a raid on Simi, for Allied seapower was too extended to provide more than MLs with their 20-mm cannon for escorts. (A plan to base MTBs in the Aegean came to naught, although SBS teams helped to survey suitable anchorages; but adequate facilities for the maintenance of these powerful coastal craft could not be provided when there were many other priorities for naval engineers.) Simi was chosen for the raid as it was intimidatingly near Rhodes, had a coastline which could not be easily defended and was well known to the SBS. The previous October Lapraik's Squadron had repulsed an initial invasion here by a sizeable German force, before the Squadron was evacuated. The following month, after several recces, they were back in a night raid on the castle headquarters of the garrison and also destroyed several caiques. L Squadron attacked the garrison in February, killing ten or more Germans in their billets, but Lapraik regarded the island very much as his M Squadron's stamping ground.

Simi is more or less a round island with several bays and the harbour town of Simi in the north where the Governor ruled from his old castle-palace. This in 1944 was the German headquarters and looked across the harbour to the west where hills roll towards the sea, making ideal deep-water berths for several shipyards to launch new caiques and schooners. In the centre of the island barren hills rise to nearly a thousand metres; the vineyards and olive groves of the coastal farms are confined to a plain near Simi Harbour and a small area of land twelve kilometres to the south, around St Michael's Monastery. In July 1944 the garrison of a reinforced company or more, was based on the castle, a platoon from this company holding the monastery, and no doubt with a number of OPs and coast-watching station on the high ground. To reach these defences, 'The raiding force had to sail some 120km from their base at Yedi Atalla on the Turkish shore of the Bay of Kos around the long peninsula forming the southern shore of the bay'.

Colonel Turnbull was an experienced organizer of raids and since October 1943 had commanded Raiding Forces Middle East (originally including the 1st Special Raiding Squadron). His Greek Sacred Squadron had trained with the SBS and would prove as valiant warriors as their namesakes of 379 BC, living up to their motto: 'Return victorious or dead' – said to have been the parting words of wives to their warrior husbands off to the wars. Turnbull and Lapraik organized this next raid on Simi with three assault forces, South Force, West Force and the Main Force under Turnbull's direct command, which once ashore would form-up south-east of Simi Harbour and attack the castle-palace.

Final preparations were made during the first week of July, while Captain J. Stewart F. Macbeth made a final recce of the island, returning on Thursday 6 July. The following week the fleet of two schooners with ten MLs infiltrated their way from the anchorage on the Turkish coast, avoiding German coast-watchers, to be off Simi on Thursday night, 13 July. As they approached the island, they joined up in their respective forces, coming into beaches marked by lead lights placed by MO 4's agents. There was no interference on the island from the Germans, for by this stage in the island wars none wandered far from their billets at night. The only casualties in the assault forces were two Greek officers, heavily laden with ammunition: neither could free himself from his equipment when they fell into deep water, and they were drowned. All the rest of the assault forces were in position above their targets by first light, the Greek three-inch mortars opening fire at sunrise on the castle. This proved to be well defended, for the Germans had cleared scrub and other cover for some 500m around the walls, while mortar fire made little impression on them, as the buildings were reinforced with heavy timbers to hold the roofs in place when attacked by aircraft or should they be bombarded from the sea.

Two motorized Ems barges used by the Germans to supply island garrisons had sailed at dawn but met the five MLs which had escorted Main Force and turned back for the shelter of the harbour. There they came under fire from Bren-guns of West Force. Both hoisted white flags before they ran aground, and the crews were captured. Stellin and two of his men cleared Malo Point but were unable to rejoin West Force because, in crossing the sea-wall bridge to the boatyards, they came under accurate fire across the harbour from the castle. They were forced to stay put as the sun rose, for even the slightest movement drew more fire, probably from a sniper on the castle roof. Captain Clynes' West Force, coming from the west, got their explosives into the yards, and under Bill Cumper's expert direction they began destroying caiques (some of twenty tonnes) on the slipways, fuel tanks and the inter-island telephone cable (a favourite target of the SBS in cutting their enemy's communications). About 1000 hours Clynes was told to make even more noise in the yards and to send some of his Bren-gunners to fire on the castle from the west, for the Main Force had reached a stalemate, and only bluff was likely to dislodge the castle's defenders, as after more than three hours' bombardment, the mortars were running short of ammunition. Turnbull had his Force spread across the hills above the castle, trying to create the impression that he had been reinforced, but was still no nearer to cracking the defences than he had been at dawn. Although they had captured several 75-mm coast guns, these could not be repositioned to fire on the castle.

The action by the forty men of South Force had been more successful. To cover an assault on the monastery, Captain Macbeth used his mortars, an unusual weapon for the SBS, as the weight of their ammunition made them an uneconomic way to get explosives to a target when the bombs had to be landed from small ships. The Germans skilfully evacuated the southern defences and held new positions across a small promontory nearby from which they had a clear field of fire and could not be dislodged. They would have to be bluffed into surrender, and to this end Bob Bury, Macbeth's second-in-command, wrote a hasty note in German. The offer of terms was rejected, the German platoon commander claiming that Bury's writing was indecipherable. But a second note, written with the help of a Greek girl who carried it to the German officer, was accepted by him, no doubt because it was expressed in more formal terms, and thirty-three Germans surrendered.

The stalemate in the north would also need some powerful deception if it was to be broken, and Turnbull sent a German petty officer from one of the barges with a note for the German garrison commander, to explain that further resistance would be costly in lives, as the British now held all the island. But the commander shilly-shallied. First the German-speaking RAF liaison officer from Turnbull's HQ, Flight Lieutenant Kenneth Fox, went to parley. He was followed an hour later by the naval liaison officer, also a German-speaker, Lieutenant-Commander Frank Ramseyer. All that happened was the emergence of some Italian *carabinieri* waving a Red Cross flag. For a couple of hours Main Force conserved their ammunition, firing only occasional mortar bombs, one deafening Ramseyer, and bursts of Bren fire to remind the garrison of what was in store should they not surrender. About midday the German commander finally accepted terms. His men had hardly been disarmed when three Messerschmitts flew over, scattering anti-personnel bombs near the SBS positions, and dropped a note into the castle courtyard. This promise of help near at hand came too late although the German commander had radioed for reinforcements as soon as he was attacked five hours earlier.

The garrison had behaved as well-led troops invariably do, with consideration for the local population, and the prisoners joined in some of the afternoon's celebrations with the local people. These were mainly Greek and seemed indifferent to the inevitable consequences when the raiders withdrew as they did that evening with the two Ems barges carrying over 150 prisoners and several pro-Fascist Greeks. Twenty-one Germans had been killed, considerable quantities of military stores destroyed and the Allies' power to strike in the Aegean starkly demonstrated. The raid had also shown that SBS/SAS troopers could be equally proficient in whatever style of operation was required, countering the frequent criticism that such Special Forces could only carry out raids suited to their deep-penetration techniques. In other words, the SBS could attack the targets that the GHQ required and did not have to wait until something especially suited to their talents might come up.

Stellin and a few men stayed on the island and next morning in their slit trenches were comparatively safe as German bombers attacked the harbour, a raid which must have added to the destruction of installations the new garrison would need. The men for this arrived in two motor launches to be met by aimed Bren-gun fire before Stellin withdrew to the hills, from where, that afternoon, he saw the town re-occupied. By nightfall he was waiting for the ML which took his team off the island.

This was the last Aegean action for the SBS, who left the war in these islands to the Sacred Squadron, ably assisted by Ian Lapraik as the Raiding Force HQ's liaison officer and Sergeant Dale of the SBS as a military intelligence expert. Lapraik, a Doctor of Law, was awarded a DSO, an OBE and two MCs, a remarkable record for one who had overcome the effects of two years, from the age of eight, with a tubercular knee in plaster, to become a middle-distance runner, a competent swimmer and a highly respected senior officer, later commanding 21 (Artists) SAS, a territorial unit. His conviction that 'enlightened training was the best that any officer could do for his men' was amply borne out by the few casualties the Squadrons suffered in these operations.

The Squadrons went on to serve in Greece, where their daring won victories more by guile than by force of arms. Later, in the Adriatic, they carried on a less successful island war against well-organized troops of the German XXI Mountain Corps. Their last operations were on Lake Comacchio in northern Italy, where a major attack by commandos, with SBS and other small boat units, convinced the Germans that the main thrust against their Po Valley defences would come in the eastern seaboard, when in fact it came inland at Argenta in April 1945. During these actions Andy Lassen was killed and awarded a VC for his 'magnificent leadership and complete disregard for his personal safety . . . in the fact of overwhelming superiority . . . [he] achieved his objectives', the citation reads.

The SBS had become virtually a separate organization since 1943 from other SAS units operating in the Middle East. The Allies themselves received a sharp lesson that year in the value of surprise raids far from any battlefield. This was brought home to them in North Africa in June, when German parachutists raided an airfield near Bizerta. Although they destroyed only one Boeing Flying Fortress and were captured the day after they landed, their raid caused such a tightening of Allied security that many troop movements were delayed in passing checkpoints.

At this time in North Africa Roy Farran noted that Bill Stirling, 'a mountain of a man . . . radiated an encouraging aura of confidence' to newcomers to his unit, which later became 2 SAS. His boundless energy and drive equalled that of his brother David; he also demanded the same discipline of his men which David had required in 1 SAS, and this entailed a formality which the men of 62 Commando found somewhat tedious, when they were transferred to his unit. They were used to the more relaxed ways of their first commanding officer, Major Gus March-Phillips, who had been killed on a raid. There were also changes in the use of SAS patrols which were landed on the Sicilian beaches, as were Commandos, to spearhead the assault waves. Coming in some minutes before the main landings, 2 SAS and Mayne's SRS each had objectives overlooking a landing area, and cleared these without difficulty. Here and later in Italy they were used in tactical operations closely linked with the immediate development of the main force landings.

As the Allied armies moved north from the toe of Italy, both the SRS and 2 SAS were to link up at Termoli in another tactical landing. The plan for this operation 'Devon' was simple, and since the commandos had been working for some months with the 22nd Landing Craft Flotilla due to put them ashore on 3 October, the orders were written on half a sheet of foolscap. As the landing developed, the Germans counter-attacked about 0815, when they infiltrated towards the town along the coast, but the gap was plugged by 3 Commando, and the SRS made contact with the forward units of 78 Division by a demolished river bridge over the Bifurno, to which they had advanced from the south. These Lancashire Fusiliers were planning to cross this fast-flowing river early that Tuesday afternoon (3 October), but to the north a counter-attack was developing and '40 RM' ambushed one road convoy. A second was approaching from the south up Route 87, and Mayne set an ambush for it about 1100 hours. In the ensuing mêlée one Section (about twenty men) was completely surrounded and the troopers were killed or captured. The Commando Colonel in charge of the landing, John Durnford-Slater, then withdrew all his men into a tighter perimeter about the town before the first armoured cars and tracked carriers of 56 Reconnaissance Regiment were ferried across the Bifurno that Tuesday afternoon, later to be joined by companies of the Lancashire Fusiliers. Also ferried across were Captain (later Major) Roy Farran and two officers with thirteen other ranks with their jeeps of 2 SAS, their numbers reduced by malaria. The Captain had concocted a story which convinced the harassed movement officer that the SAS were urgently required in Termoli.

2 SAS had driven up from the south, the jeeps being attacked for the first time from the air by Me 109s since landing at Taranto three weeks earlier. They found the town quiet, with only sporadic shellfire coming in, but they did not realize it was the quiet before the storm. The Commandos had been relieved from their defensive positions, but next day (Wednesday) 3 Commando and a Troop of the SRS were moved back to hold positions along the two kilometres of the Sinarca River and a railway on the right flank of the British positions. The commandos were in positions on the edge of olive groves looking northward over the small river, and a Troop of the SRS blocked the railway line at a point some 1,200m from the town. The harbour lies on a promontory at the angle where the coast, having run westward, turns south, and the railway followed this line of the coast, making a natural approach to the town from along the Sinarca valley and then southward down the coast railway.

The Colonel stood down the rest of his men – two SRS Troops and 40 RM Commando – as he wanted them to have a proper night's sleep, because they had had only one in the past week, when the weather was stormy on their passage in the LCIs. He wanted them to be 'on top form' next day and therefore left them to rest in the town. Just before dusk a patrol of armoured cars brought in a significant prisoner. He was from 26 Panzer Division, a battle-hardened unit which had been refitting to the north but which, at the time the Commandos were landing, was moving south to join the German Tenth Army. The men of 3 Commando had, however, been reinforced with four six-pounders and a seventeen-pounder anti-tank guns and four Vickers heavy machine-guns of the Kensingtons. There were also Forward Observation Officers with them who could call down artillery fire from across the Bifurno, and that evening, as the sun was setting, four caiques led by a schooner glided into the harbour, bringing in a few more men of 2 SAS.

There were no further signs of the enemy that night, but not long after dawn on Thursday, at 0630, twelve Messerschmitts flew in low. Several bombs fell in the town, including a couple in the street outside 2 SAS's 'rather slummy building' that overlooked the harbour. The SRS Troop on the railway must have seen them and, being stood-to, were ready for whatever might follow. Germans did follow up the air attack, but by infiltrating men through the many open gaps between the defence positions about the town. A patrol from 40 RM shot one man as he threw a grenade, and others were sniping from windows – some may have been civilian Fascists, although the previous day the Colonel had addressed all the male population in the town square 'spreading rumours of a mass execution', as he expressed it, and most of the sniping had stopped.

By midday there was clearly a major attack developing, for the German artillery barrage was growing in intensity, and an SRS truck moving a Section towards the perimeter received a direct hit. This transport was moving the SRS, who, with 40 RM, were stood-to about 1230 to cover the railway goods yard on the north-west edge of the town. Minutes later an 88-mm shell hit the headquarters (lodged in a harbour hotel), killing several men and blowing the Intelligence officer out of the window, where he clung to the sill by instinct before he was hauled to safety by the Colonel, who had been working in the next room with his second-in-command, Major (later Lieutenant-Colonel) Brian M. F. Franks. The artillery fire had obviously been directed at the headquarters because the radio aerials were give-aways to a trained observer. Paddy Mayne and commando patrols searched for this German artillery observer but did not find him.

Out in the olive groves, in rain from low clouds, 3 Commando were watching the enemy overrun a couple of British positions immediately south of them, and saw three Panzer Mark IV tanks edge up to the crossroads nearby. Unfortunately the British anti-tank gunners in this their first action had retired, but the Vickers gunners took a toll of the infantry with the tanks. Meanwhile Major Sandy Scratchley, a veteran of L Detachment, appeared outside Farran's billet. The Major was not pleased to find that 2 SAS, a squadron of which he now commanded, were not engaged in the battle, so he took Farran to the Commando Headquarters, which had been moved to the ground floor of the hotel in 'the room with the strongest walls', where Durnford-Slater and Franks were coolly running their part of the battle.

After taking up positions briefly on the hotel's second-floor balconies, Farran's men were moved out along the railway line to positions near a cemetery. They had not been there long when 3 Commando saw eleven German tanks move towards the town down the Sinarca valley. Six of these turned back as it was growing dark, about 1800, but heavy mortar and machine-gun fire continued, with the occasional armour-piercing shell – intended for Sherman tanks – whistling over the commandos. The Germans were on three sides of the olive groves, and 3 Commando formed a box defence before skilfully withdrawing at 0100 on Friday morning.

The tanks which they had seen moving down the valley the previous afternoon had bumped the SRS, 2 SAS and 40 Commando, holding positions on the railway. The SRS and 2 SAS, albeit in small numbers, were organized by Scratchley into a defence along the line of a ridge across the railway, with the SRS on the left and twenty men of 2 SAS holding the thousand metres from the railway to the sea. The Germans still held the cemetery on the extreme left but continued to be contained there by 40 RM while other Germans attempted to advance down the railway track. Scratchley had two Bofors he employed as anti-tank guns but they probably had little if any armour-piercing rounds, being normally used against aircraft, with the result that at about 1715 the position was getting critical and the Major asked for reinforcement. This came when a City of London Yeomanry Sherman trundled up on the left flank. Its gunner put a round in the dome of the cemetery church to silence one of the most troublesome snipers. Yet others still covered the open tracks of the railway, and crossing them was a difficult, not to say chancy, business.

2 SAS had only one man wounded but Farran was expecting the casualties to be greater, as only a hundred metres down the track was an engine hitched to an ammunition truck; had this been hit by a mortar bomb, the resulting explosion could have been as devastating for friend as for foe. After dark that evening (Thursday), Commando Headquarters managed to get several six-pounder anti-tank guns into positions which covered the beach and the railway. Also a commando patrol found the infiltrating observer in a church tower; a brave man, he refused to surrender and fired his pistol at the patrol but was killed by their answering fire from Bren-guns. The Germans would now be shelling 'blind'. During the cold night the men made do with little rations. 'Our spirits had been low,' Farran wrote, 'until the Sherman arrived.' The Germans resumed shelling the SAS early next morning, and at first light, as the sun rose behind Farran's positions, their infantry came forward again. But 'we could hardly miss' men walking forward, while the SAS Brens and mortars kept up sustained and accurate fire, the attack melting away under this hammering.

At 0655 another strafe by German fighter-bombers heralded an attack from the cemetery which 40 RM repulsed; later that morning they counter-attacked the Germans and gained a foothold in the cemetery but were forced back 50m by intense mortar fire. Their CO, Lieutenant-Colonel J. C. ('Pops') Manners, put in a second attack, and the cemetery was cleared. This secured the left flank of the SAS and SRS positions through which the London Irish put in an attack that afternoon (Friday). The Bren-gunners and mortar men of 2 SAS's detachment 'fired everything they had' as the attack went in and Germans fled along the beach. Only then did Farran realize how many they were and was rewarded for taking care to conserve his detachment's ammunition. The SRS were having equal rewards.

The operation had been a complete success in keeping the Germans on the retreat but was not one for SAS troops. They had neither the organization nor the weaponry for such defensive actions even if they proved capable of sustaining them. After Termoli they were not called on to fight any more battles in Italy 'sandwiched between enemy reinforcements and their front line'.

Bill Stirling had wanted to use the Regiment in a more more suitable role: destroying Axis railways in the area bounded by Bologna, Florence and La Spezia. This triangle lay across the northern Apennine Mountains, its apex at Bologna to the north, with Florence over 75km to the south; the railway which joined them passed through tunnels, one ten kilometres long, and through mountain cuttings. To block this system successfully would require at least two squadrons, say 160 men operating from mountains 2,000m high on the western leg of the triangle. But in the event the Army staff allowed only sixteen officers and men to parachute into the area. They dropped in two groups on the night before the major landings at Salerno, 800km to the south of the groups' DZs. Captain P. H. Pinkney had conceived and led the raid, dropping from an old Albemarle at 2,300m (7,000 ft), with three small teams of the group heading for targets on the main railway lines from Bologna to Florence and to Parto. They came down near a village, and Pinkney – strapped in plaster from a previous back injury – became separated from the seven men in his teams.

This so-called 'southern' group received no answer to their pre-arranged curlew bird-calls and, as the villagers were in some excitement, had to leave the area after ninety minutes without Pinkney. They divided into two teams, as without him they felt there were too few of them to raid in the planned three areas. Crossing hills and forests, they marched for five hours or more each night, laying up by day.

Sergeant Robinson's team reached their target area on the sixth day of the raid, Tuesday 13 September. Next day they successfully derailed a train in an unguarded tunnel. But for several weeks they had to evade the Germans, as the raiders, with the help of Italian soldiers now on the Allied side, made their way to Rimini and then south to the Allied lines. The second team of this Group were captured and shot, as was Captain Pinkney.

The northern Group had also dropped on Tuesday 7 September, but the twenty-three-year old Captain Dudgeon and Trooper Brunt were captured after they used a German truck in an attempt to reach their target tunnels on the Genoa to La Spezia line. Both showed great bravery before the firing squad which later executed them. A second team of two men heading for a different part of this railway line were never seen again after leaving the DZ. But Lieutenant Wedderburn and Sergeant 'Tankey' Challenor on the third or fourth night of the raid derailed an 'up' and a 'down' train in one tunnel, having set charges at both ends of it. They reached the planned RV on the seventh day, but as none of the others arrived, they moved off four days later, having learnt of the Italians' surrender. They could now move by day, provided they kept clear of any German troops, and with the guidance of a friendly farmer found another tunnel, where they derailed a train with the last of their explosive. Then began the long trek south, 500km towards the Allied lines. They spent three weeks of this journey hidden by friendly Italians, while Challenor recovered from a bout of malaria, and by Christmas were still hiding in the mountains, cut off by snowdrifts at times from the valley roads below. On 27 December the Lieutenant was captured and the lady in whose house he was hiding was shot. The Sergeant, hearing firing, escaped to a cave but when out of firewood was caught as he went into the valley for supplies. He later escaped from a prisoner-of-war train, as did the Lieutenant, who was recaptured but escaped a second time.

Such brief descriptions cannot do full justice to the bravery of Pinkney and his teams, for they raided in difficult country and suffered many hardships trying to evade capture. So did other SAS teams in Italy that winter, when in all they derailed fourteen or more trains.

But sixteen men covering an area the size of the Bologna triangle could not be expected seriously to interrupt the flow of German reinforcements to their Italian front. Nor could Pinkney's teams be resupplied, as there was no adequate liaison with clandestine organizations in the area that winter. Later, in part of this very triangle of territory, the operation 'Tombola', in which Roy Farran led No. 3 Squadron of 2 SAS in the early spring of 1945, was remarkably effective in co-ordinating some four hundred partisans of widely differing persuasions. Communists, Republicans and Russian deserters from the German army were supplied with arms by SOE. With their clandestine help, even if on a smaller scale, Bill Stirling's plan might have proved highly successful in 1943.

Whether the SAS were used in their proper roles or flung into infantry battles, they won through with great credit to their Regiment. (Since the days in the Western Desert the Regiments had been raised under a Corps Warrant, as explained in the next chapter.) General M. C. Dempsey, who commanded XIII Corps, wrote of the SAS in Italy: 'I have commanded many units [but] have never met a unit in which I had such confidence.' He attributed their success at Termoli and elsewhere to the serious way they did their training, and to their discipline, fitness, self-confidence and careful planning, qualities which the SAS had in great measure. As was shown in their preparations for the Allied invasion of mainland Europe.

4. Triumph and Tragedy in North-West Europe

David Stirling had conceived the idea of inserting small teams of well-armed and highly trained men deep into enemy territory like the fingers of a hand. These could later come together as a 'fist' to deal a hard blow to those vital enemy installations of railway marshalling yards and main highways on which the enemy depended for the resupply of their front-line troops. Operations by SAS in the Western Desert and later in the Aegean had proved that such raids were possible, even if the 'fingers' tended to prod and probe without necessarily joining to form a mailed fist. Nevertheless, their success had been noted by the staff planning the invasion of Europe in what became 'Overlord' (as we have seen in Brigadier Head's visit to 'Shan' Hackett's headquarters), although in the early stages of this planning for 'Overlord' there was a marked misunderstanding of David Stirling's concept with its strategy of operations against railway centres and other lines of communication far from the battlefield.

Although the precise nature of the roles for the SAS in Europe had yet to be decided, in January 1944 approval was given by the Chiefs of Staff to the formation of an SAS Brigade, as part of 1 Airborne Division which was commanded by General A. F. M. Browning. The Division's organization then included a Headquarters SAS Troop responsible for co-ordinating the SAS operations with the activities and plans of theatre commanders. The Brigade was commanded by Brigadier (later General Sir) Roderick McLeod, who was responsible for its fighting efficiency and availability to meet the demands made on it by various commands, and who was one of the few British regular officers 'to take an informed interest in clandestine warfare'. As the SAS Regiments had not been raised under a Corps Warrant – and would not be so, until after World War II – they technically had no separate existence as regiments in the British order of battle and for administration needed to be a part of some established force. The Airborne Forces HQ was the obvious choice as, apart from 1 Airborne Division, these Forces included glider and parachute units. Neither the Twenty-first Army Group nor the Supreme Headquarters Allied Forces Europe (SHAFE) would take direct command of the Brigade, no doubt because of the complexities of administering it as theatre troops in what was already a complicated series of staffs with many and varied duties. At a later date, however, the Brigade came under the direct command of SHAFE for a period.

There could have been more than administrative difficulties when the SAS were put under command of the Airborne Forces, but the SAS 'had no wish to create any difficulties over the matter', although they resented wearing the red berets of the Airborne, and Mayne for one continued to wear his SAS buff beret. On the operational side, General 'Boy' Browning made those representations which are sometimes necessary to persuade the less imaginative staffs that the Special Forces have a useful role in many campaigns. He thought highly of the SAS, and through his efforts they were incorporated in the battleplan, although not always in the strategic roles to which they were suited and trained.

The first unit to arrive at the Brigade's training area, near Prestwick Aerodrome in Ayrshire, was the Belgian Independent Parachute Squadron (later renamed 5 SAS). They had served in various commands before the spring of 1944, including the 8th Battalion of the (British) Parachute Regiment. Two Free French battalions, 2^e and 3^e RCP, joined the Belgians, as 3 and 4 SAS before 1 and 2 SAS came to Scotland in March from the Mediterranean. F Squadron of the GHQ Reconnaissance Regiment were also drafted to the Brigade. This Phantom unit was one of several squadrons which were the highly mobile 'eyes and ears' of the GHQ, reporting the progress of battles and other up-to-the-minute intelligence by radio, direct to the General Staff. They were all specially trained as signallers, although the majority of the officers came from infantry and cavalry regiments. The commander of F Squadron, Major the Honourable J. J. Astor, was, for example, one of the best radio-operators in the GHQ liaison regiment.

When 1 and 2 SAS reached Ayrshire, they were considerably under strength, for there had been relatively few suitable volunteers in the Middle East and North Africa to expand the SAS after the recruitment of the commando volunteers from 'Layforce' in 1 SAS and men from Lassen's original unit, the Small Scale Raiding Force in 2 SAS. Some expansion and the replacements had come from men serving in holding companies and depots, although some failed to survive the training courses – Major Ian Patterson sent four officers and fifty men back to their units in one clean sweep when he took over training at Athlit. Nor were all the men now serving in the two Regiments experienced parachutists, and the 140 men of 2 SAS included a number who had not been in action. Among those who had were the forty of Sandy Scratchley's Squadron who had been ravaged by malaria. Mayne's 150 men of the SRS had taken again the title of 1 SAS, and the SB Squadrons became independent, although still part of SAS while operating in the Aegean, Adriatic and Italy.

The selection of new volunteers was placed on a more routine basis 'through channels' – one parachute-trained padre, for example, was posted to 1 SAS as there was no vacancy in the Para battalions. An interesting comparison is with the more casual recruitment of men like Roy Farran, whose interview by Bill Stirling in North Africa had been partly conducted while the Colonel was discussing operations with Jellicoe over lunch.

Farran had done his parachute training at Mascarrah in the North African hills, where the weather could be kinder than in Scotland. Despite days when the cloud was too low for jumping, the troopers completed a refresher course, and the new recruits were trained, along with the men of F Squadron who had no parachute experience. They also learnt new techniques, including the use of leg-bags. One of these strapped to a parachutist's leg as he jumped could be lowered from a line fixed to his waist. The bag of kit then hit the ground before he did, a safer way to drop than with an extra heavy load on his back.

Other aspects of the Brigade's training – the use of enemy weapons, maintenance of jeeps, living off the land in survival courses, and long marches with heavy loads when individuals had to make their own way to a distant RV – were all aimed at creating raiders who could operate far from the support of conventional forces. The infantryman who fails to withstand the stress of battle may be sent to the rear, but the SAS trooper has to be of the character and determination which withstand those alarms of finding that the odds have become heavily against his survival or harsh physical difficulties have to be overcome. Otherwise a weak link in a raiding team would endanger his companions, for there was nowhere he could be sent to safety. The selection and training therefore weeded out men unlikely to survive the stress, which might include some who already had distinguished themselves in battle, since courage is not an inexhaustible resource, and a few may have lost their nerve as a result of their previous actions.

The need for good communications was vital to the teams' success, for they would often have priceless intelligence which would become of little value unless it reached the conventional forces quickly. Therefore the Phantom patrols – two with each of the British Regiments – were a key part of the Brigade's operations, and the French and Belgian Regiments' signallers were trained by Phantom. All would work to the Phantom signal centre with its extremely delicate receivers, capable of picking up the weak signals from sets broadcasting in difficult circumstances.

Apart from these conventional radio contacts, the SAS teams were also likely to use the various code messages put out by the BBC for action by the resistance forces. ('Charley will visit his Aunt on Tuesday' could be an indication that a particular German general would be visiting a named headquarters on that day.) They were received by Phantom's signallers or SAS troopers on a miniature receiver, of which there were several designs. One, the MCR 1 or so-called 'Biscuit Receiver', was fitted into a Huntley & Palmers tin and weighed only one kilo, although the tin contained three batteries as well as the set with its five miniature valves. More prosaically, the signallers also used pigeons, for these could fly home with small sketch maps of a target for bombers or similar information not easily put into words, never mind into codes. Codes were of the one-time-pad variety, in which the sender and receiver each used corresponding grids of letters to give an indecipherable random choice of code letters, for only the two sheets matched, and once a transmission had been made, the sender destroyed his 'key' copy.

German direction-finding (D/F) had reached a high point of efficiency by the summer of 1944, and therefore signallers had to change not only location but also frequencies in order to avoid being tracked down. They also had to keep any transmissions as brief as possible, and to help in this a series of six hundred four-letter groups were devised for the commoner messages –*AOAO* indicating 'All containers safely received', and *CGCG* for 'German division advancing towards . . .'. Each four-letter group would be encoded with the rest of the message from a one-time pad, but signallers carried a large silk handkerchief some 50cm square with the four-letter groups of standard message printed on it.

By the summer of 1944 the Brigade had a total strength of 2,500 who were ready to take their part in a variety of operations. Those which had been planned for them before a fitting use for their talents was realized by the Airborne HQ included many with unfortunate parallels to the actions in Italy, with teams dropping between the enemy's front and his tactical reserves. Such tactical rather than strategic operations Bill Stirling knew to be a misuse of his men, and he resigned, as they would have been quickly if not easily destroyed when dropped between the main battle area and the German Panzer reserves, as they were not equipped in those days to destroy tanks, nor could they have easily melted away from search-parties in areas which were strongly held by German forces.

One proposal at that time was to land Squadrons in the Pas de Calais area, where the Germans had been led to believe the invasion forces would land and were ready for them, the SAS providing a final diversion on the eve of Overlord's D-Day, 6 June. In the event a better form of diversion was devised: in the early hours of 6 June, small parties from 1 SAS followed by several dummy parachutists or just the dummies alone, would be dropped to confuse German reports of landings. In 'Titanic 1' an officer and two NCOs were dropped 48km south-west of Dieppe and were followed by two hundred dummy parachutists; their

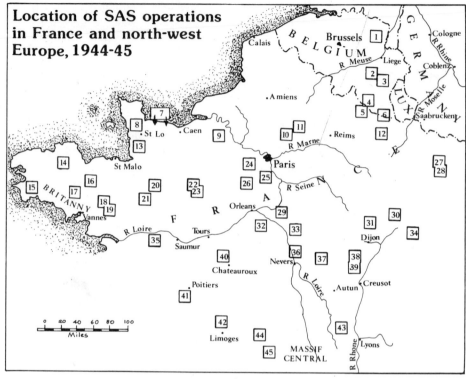

Location of SAS operations in France and north-west Europe, 1944-45

Shown in numbered sequence from north to south in France
and in lettered sequence in Holland and Germany.
See Appendix 2 for summary of each operation.
(*Applies to above, and opposite map*)

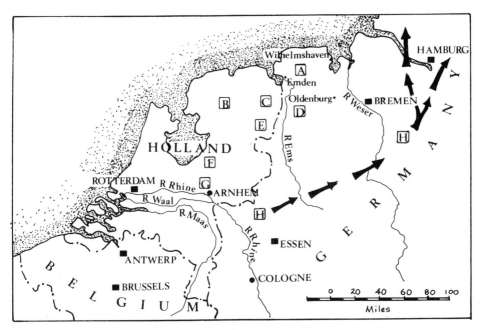

List of Operations

Abel	34	Jockworth	43
Amherst	C		
Archway	H	Keystone	F
		Kipling	29
Barker	39		
Benson	10	Larkspur	E
Bergbank	4	Larkswood	A
Brutus	6	Lost	17
Bulbasket	40	Loyton	28
Bunyan	26		
		Marshall	45
Caliban	1	Moses	41
Chaucer	22		
Cooney	16	Newton	33
		Noah	5
Defoe	13	Normandy Beaches	7
Derry	15		
Dickens	35	Pistol	27
Dingson	18	Portia	B
Dunhill	21		
		Regent	2
Fabian	G	Rupert	12
Franklin	3		
		Samson	42
Gaff	24	Samwest	14
Gain	25	Shakespear	23
Grog	19	Snelgrove	44
		Spenser	36
Haft	20		
Haggard	32	Titanic	8
Harrod	38	Trueform	9
Hardy	31		
Houndsworth	37	Wallace	30
Howard	D	Wolsey	11

only offensive weapons were the recorded noises of small arms fire played over loudspeakers by the SAS teams, who also fired off Very lights. The confusion which they caused led to some delays in the movement of German forces to the main beach-head, south of this diversion. Two of the party reached the main beach-head a fortnight later, despite having had to cross country where German troops were concentrated. Dummies only were dropped in 'Titanic II' (50km north of Dives River) and 'III' (50km south-west of Caen).

In 'Titanic IV' two more teams – Lieutenants Poole and Fowles, each with two Troopers – dropped near Isigny on the south-east corner of the Cherbourg peninsula and 30km north of St Lô, to be followed by two hundred dummies, with the object of diverting German attention from US 101 Airborne Division's landings further west. But in the drop the officers were separated from the men, and the containers with the loudspeakers fell wide of the DZ; indeed, the men discovered that they had been dropped two kilometres from the intended landing point. Nevertheless, they laid out twenty Lewes bombs in an area 450m square and moved north, firing into the air as they went. They lay up 750m from the bombs and heard them go off but saw no German until next day when a cycle patrol passed on the Cartenan road. On the Tuesday evening (6 June) they were approached by Monsieur Le Due of the Resistance, who that night took them to a ruined abbey some five kilometres nearer the coast and where next morning Poole was brought to join them. He had landed with a carrier pigeon strapped to his chest and had sent the bird off home with a message reporting that the party was scattered. For the next three days they made recces of the surrounding country but found no signs of enemy activity. On the Saturday afternoon 'Chick' Fowles was brought to their hide-out, having taken a few shots at Germans and cut telephone lines.

They decided to continue their patrols and did so for the next seventeen days, until a German para regiment moved into the area, when Le Due, having been warned that the Germans knew of the SAS patrols, led them away from the abbey. Some days later they were joined by three American paras who had escaped from a POW camp. They now began a dangerous attempt to get through the German lines and got within sight of the Allied lines on 10 July. But two Germans found their hide and threw in grenades, which wounded Fowles and four others. They then moved into a farmhouse but its owner betrayed them and they were overwhelmed by a platoon of Germans. Fowles slipped away but was wounded a second time and captured. They survived this captivity but Le Due was shot for helping them.

The original deceptions had caused confusion at the German headquarters, which was increased by the wide area over which Allied paratroopers, dropping in strong winds, were scattered north and south of the beach-head – conditions which not only caused the Germans confusion but also gave the Allies some problems.

The major roles for squadrons of the SAS Brigade were finally determined with two main objectives: the establishing of firm bases far into France from where they could stiffen the local resistance forces in raids against vital railway centres, and in mobile columns which in operating across country from their dropping zones would attack German troops on the move – much as L Detachment had attacked Axis forces on the coast roads of Cyrenaica. Both types of operation were intended to slow the German movement of reinforcements heading for Normandy. Allied secret services had already been working to establish organized resistance forces during 1943 and the spring of 1944, training them in military tactics when possible and arming them not only for sabotage raids but also to carry out hit-and-run guerrilla operations for which Bren-guns, Stens, fragmentation grenades and other combat stores were included in the 2,700 tons of items dropped into France alone, during the twelve weeks to the end of June 1944; 2½ times this weight of stores were dropped in the following three months.

To make the best use of these arms the resistance fighters needed two catalysts. One was a military staff which could not always be found from their ranks, while the SOE and other agents, including those of the Free French clandestine bureaux, were too few for such staff work. Secondly, they needed a core of highly trained fighters – the SAS – who could demonstrate what might be achieved.

While these arrangements worked well in the field, there were about a dozen different authorities who had to give their agreement to every SAS operation at that time. Yet because they were organized as a conventional brigade for administrative purposes, once these consents had been received, their supply of combat stores flowed remarkably well to the forward bases. The brigade major, the staff captain and others had deputies to help handle the flood of requests for ammunition, replacement weapons, spares for jeeps and even a pair of size eight medium boots on one occasion. (These last were delivered by air within 4½ hours of the radioed request to the Brigade HQ at Moor Park Golf Course in the north-west London suburbs.) With the true practicality of men who have to get a job done, the staff were not over-cautious in their use of the public telephones, but this does not seem to have led to any breaches of security. Certainly this small staff, far fewer in numbers than those responsible for the general supply of resistance forces (the EMFFI), provided a much better service to the men in the field, in part because they were dropping loads to far fewer destinations and the reception parties were well organized, but also because the Brigade staff had close ties with 38 Group's aircrews.

Much of the responsibility for organizing those dozens of consents fell to Lieutenant-Colonel I. G. Collins, who commanded the small SAS HQ in the Airborne Command. He proved ingenious in arranging those essential approvals from governments in exile, Twenty-first Army Group, SOE and the other authorities involved, and established the routines by which the Brigade requested transport from the RAF. The Lancasters, Halifaxes, Stirlings and Dakotas of 38 Group, sometimes aircraft from 46 Group and the aircraft of the Special Duty Squadron based at Tempsford in Bedfordshire, all flew in support of SAS operations. By early August one Group alone might on a single night fly aircraft from five different fields to drop troopers to over twenty different DZs, as well as seven hundred containers and four jeeps. On the same night, 4/5 August, forty-five men were also landed by glider with eleven jeeps. Indeed, keeping the two thousand men of SAS supplied in the field during that August was a major undertaking as they were also equipping local forces in many cases.

On the night of 5/6 June, when aircraft were at a high premium, advance parties were sent to the four major forward bases which SAS set up, but, perhaps fortunately, the projected 'drops' immediately inland of the invasion beach-head had been cancelled in the planning stage because aircraft were not available for them. This meant that over two thousand of the SAS Brigade were not in action during the first days of the invasion – their turn for action came as the campaign developed. However, of the forty-three operations planned for the initial stages of the Normandy landings (see Appendix II), none could be begun before D-Day, as Twenty-first Army Group was adamant that any pre-empting of the invasion by SAS landings might needlessly jeopardize its secrecy.

The final plan was to land advance parties on the night of 5/6 June in five remote areas of France where SOE already had established contacts with local forces. Each advance party would recce the area for bases suitable for SAS operations and prepare for their Squadron commanders with their Tactical Headquarters to land within a day or two. Once a forward base had been established, more men and later jeeps would be dropped to the Squadrons who would cut German road and rail communications and find targets for the Allied Air Forces and other intelligence. Although the SAS were never a part of de Gaulle's French Forces of the Interior, the military arm of the Resistance Forces, they would work with them when appropriate. But as a number of these *maquis* battalions had been infiltrated by double-agents, SAS patrols tended to keep their bases some kilometres from *maquis* camps, although they often used *maquis* guides and on occasions carried out joint operations.

The five main areas for these operations – 'Houndsworth', 'Bulbasket', 'Dingson', 'Samwest' and 'Gain'–as a glance at the map on page 72–3 will show, put the SAS patrols in strategically placed, if remote, areas. 'Houndsworth', near Dijon in eastern central France, was within striking distance of the main rail and road routes from the Mediterranean coast. From their small camps hidden in the heavily wooded slopes of the Morvan, which rise to over 900m, patrols of Lieutenant-Colonel Bill Fraser's A Squadron, working alongside the *maquis*, made a large area from Dijon to Nevers, half a department of France, uninhabitable to the enemy. The majority of A Squadron were relieved by 'C' in late August, with a total SAS strength of eighteen officers and 126 other ranks in the area at the peak of the operations. These included twenty-two raids cutting the main railway between Paris and Lyons which had carried elements of the German divisions moving north from the Mediterranean coast, and the branch railway from Creusot to Nevers.

This was the largest and the longest-lasting of SAS forward bases in France, not withdrawn until the Americans reached the Morvan on 6 September. During their three months in these mountain forests, they had not only cut the railway links but signalled thirty targets for Allied bombers to attack, killed or wounded over two hundred Germans and taken 132 prisoners. The only serious attempt by the Germans to root out A Squadron was driven off, once Fraser's well-sited six-pounder anti-tank gun had knocked out an armoured car which was supporting a battalion of irresolute infantry.

Near Châteauroux, in the hill country north-west of the Massif Central, the D-Day advance party of 'Bulbasket' landed with the Jedburgh team. Although not SAS, they were one of eighty-six specially trained teams – each with an American, a British and a French officer or NCO – dropped to liaise with *maquis* battalions and provide professional advice to their commanders. They were joined by others of B Squadron of 1 SAS and No. 3 Phantom patrol, making a total of fifty-six all ranks by the end of June, about half of this Squadron commanded by Major John Tonkin. They made twelve attacks on the railway running north to Tours from Poitier and to this rail centre from Limoges to the south-east. Their reports of targets for Allied bombers led twelve Mosquitos to set the large petrol depot ablaze at Châtelhérault in 'the best petrol fire' these pilots had ever seen. But after nearly a month of successful operations, they were betrayed by one of several German agents infiltrated into the *maquis*.

An SS Battalion some five hundred strong encircled the base near Verrières on the night of 2/3 July, searching the woods at first light with mortar and artillery fire. As infantry moved in to follow up this search, the Major told his patrols to make their way to an RV outside the cordon. Each section of patrols at the time had their own camp sites fairly widely dispersed in the woods, but thirty-four men kept together in moving down a forest track, walked into a German ambush and were captured. A wounded officer was clubbed to death with rifle butts before villagers assembled by the Germans to see the fate of 'terrorists', but the other prisoners disappeared. Nothing more was heard of them until the bodies of thirty men were found that autumn in the woods near the base, along with that of an American airman who had evaded capture and reached the Squadron's base. Three men who had been wounded in the ambush were taken to Verrières Hospital, where their capture was reported by the Red Cross. The Germans moved them a few days later, ostensibly to Tours, but they never arrived there.

Those who managed to break out of the woods, including Major Tonkin, eventually made contact with London. An SAS officer, Lieutenant David Surrey-Dane, trained in the selection of airstrip runways, was parachuted in to join Tonkin early in August, and together they found a suitable field on which two Hudson aircraft landed to evacuate the survivors of B Squadron.

As the SS Battalion moved north, the Mosquito Squadron which had benefited from 'Bulbasket's' target information reportedly pursued these Germans at every opportunity until the Battalion was disbanded.

A third forward base, 'Dingson', was established by French teams of 4 SAS, the advance party landing on heathland near Vannes not long after midnight on 5/6 June. The SAS here, under the spirited commander of 4 SAS, the one-armed Commandant P. Bourgoin, soon had over two thousand local supporters in this south-east corner of Brittany. These enthusiastic Bretons gathered in crowds during the first week after D-Day until the base took on the atmosphere of a fairground, with many lights and excited parties of sightseers. However, SAS headquarters met the surprising logistical problem of kitting out these volunteers with British uniforms, boots, small arms, ammunition and food, before they were dispersed to their home areas. To the north, the Commandant had 115 of his Regiment based around St Brieuc on the coast, with thirty picked men of the locality. These, however, had not been picked carefully enough, for they came from two competing factions of the Resistance. Nevertheless, some survived on D+6 when a Russo-German Brigade, mostly men who wished to fight against Moscow rather than the French, put in a set-piece attack on the base, losing 155 casualties, although the Commandant lost only thirty-two. Later thirty of the SAS survivors reorganized the local Resistance into a cohesive force; others were more casual and were caught in local cafés.

The Bretons hid many a trooper in their isolated farms and remote woodlands, enabling their wily Commandant to make the best use of his relatively small forces, which had been joined by six Jedburgh parties. When the Germans attacked 'Dingson' the following week, with another brigade supported this time by armoured cars, the forces in 'Dingson' held them for some hours that Tuesday (18 July). By chance SAS radio signals were picked up by a USAF pilot, and late in the afternoon forty P47 Thunderbolt fighter-bombers joined the battle – a boost not only for the defenders but soon rumoured throughout Brittany, as the Commandant dispersed his forces to those farmhouses and other places of comparative safety. While in hiding these officers and men of 4 SAS trained many Bretons – thirty thousand, or, by one report, as many as eighty thousand of them, embroiled the Germans on rail and road transports to good effect, giving the Americans an almost trouble-free advance to the out-skirts of Brest that August.

They were not the only SAS forces landed in Brittany. Eighteen teams of three to six men in jeeps of 3 SAS were dropped 'blind' near St Malo on the night of D+1/D+2, landing without any reception parties to meet them. (Most of the other landings had been met by SOE and Free French agents, who had organized reception committees.) These jeep patrols of 'Cooney' covered some 75km driving south as they cut railway lines and shot up German troops. This added to the resistance forces' railway sabotage, forcing the German 3 Parachute Division to use scarce petrol supplies in a move by road into Normandy, for they did not dare risk moving by train.

Having blocked the routes from southern France and from Brittany, there remained the Orleans 'gap' which was blocked in part by men of 1 SAS in operation 'Gain'. This most successful series of actions was launched on D+8 (14 June) and, although it ran for only three weeks, achieved near miracles of daring in slowing up a flood of German reinforcements. It was a classical SAS operation.

Summaries in Appendix II, show briefly the fortunes of other SAS patrols, not all of which were sent on strategic missions for which they were so well suited by temperament and training. For example, 'Swan' was an infiltration of German positions by jeeps of 1 SAS moving out of the Normandy beach-head, an operation any competent battalion could perform. But few Allied or Axis troops could carry out operations like 'Gain', 'Wallace' or 'Dingson'.

The American OSS had units which were trained for SAS-type oper-ations and more lavishly equipped than the British. These Operational Groups often included more personnel who were fluent in the local language than was the case in SAS patrols, as many were recruited from first-generation Americans; the OGs in the Adriatic, for example, in-cluded the sons of Yugoslav *émigrés*. Four OG teams, each with thirty-four officers and enlisted men (other ranks) were dropped into southern France from the OSS base in North Africa.

SAS were a law unto themselves in some respects, arming anyone in France who would fight Germans, despite SOE's previous care to make sure that they armed only those likely to fight in the Allied cause and not also feud with other resisters. In action the SAS had no opportunity for such subtle distinctions, and as soldiers, not agents, they were less concerned with the local political niceties. That is not to say that SOE agents involved themselves in politics – they were forbidden to do so – but they had not only to raise underground forces in the difficult years before the Allies landed but also to keep these forces under Allied control as far as was possible. On the other hand the SAS, always operating in uniform, gained local respect by the strength of their firepower and skill at arms. Yet the Squadrons were exposed to betrayal, as we have seen, and an advance party of reinforcements for 'Gain' dropped on 3/4 July to a compromised reception.

'Gain' would be one of the most successful SAS operations, but when Captain Pat Garstin, second-in-command of D Squadron, and his eleven men dropped near La Ferté Alais, south-west of Paris, they were fired on as they landed, even though the correct recognition signals had been given from the DZ. Delays through bad weather, the Germans' capture of a Resistance worker who knew of their intended arrival, and the German counter-intelligence services' efficiency on this occasion led to nine being captured. One died soon afterwards of his wounds, and another was so badly injured that he was taken to the hospital. Three, however, dropping outside the DZ, managed to evade capture and eventually returned home, as did Trooper Jones and Corporal Vaculik of the French SAS. They had been held for five weeks in Paris and although not physically ill-treated were interrogated as the Germans believed they had landed to prepare the way for a major airborne landing.

Then, on the morning of 8 August, they were told that they would be exchanged – presumably on neutral territory – for German agents who were prisoners, requiring them to wear civilian clothes. But when the truck taking them next day to this 'exchange' pulled up by woods 60km north-east of Paris, they half-guessed what was intended. Corporal Vaculik, a German-speaker, asked if they were to be shot and was told that they were. Pat Garstin, hearing this, whispered some last-minute orders and on his shout, once into the woods, they dived off the path. The small German firing party gave chase but when Jones fell, he was thought to be hit and the Germans passed him. Vaculik, forewarned by his conversation with the guards, escaped in a desperate dash for cover, and before the Germans came back, Jones had hidden himself deeper in the wood, despite being handcuffed. These two were later put in touch with each other and with the help of the Resistance reached safety, but the other five were shot. It was a risk all SAS troops ran during these operations, for the Germans treated them as clandestine agents, despite the fact that they wore uniforms.

On the evening of Tuesday 13 June 1944, a small group of French men and women set off for a field in southern Normandy. They had been brought together by Captain R. R. Henquet of SOE's F (French) Section, who had parachuted into France some three weeks earlier to join the Resistance forces. This night they were to receive a second advanced party from 1

SAS's D Squadron, who were to operate in the Orleans gap – Operation 'Gain'. A reconstruction of these operations must in part use some conjecture, since nearly all the participants died in the Allied cause; the following commentary is as close as we are likely to get to the facts of this remarkable operation.

Only the Captain knew of the precise location of the DZ, for the risks of betrayal in this region were high, as we have seen when the first advanced party was captured. But Henquet had been prudent in his choice of contacts when forming the 'Hermit' circuit, as a previous network of agents known as 'Prosper' had been expanded unwisely in this area and destroyed. Therefore Henquet's men in this reception committee had been told only such information as they had to know. Each had his or her cover story as the reason for being out after dark; one, no doubt, posed as a doctor, another as a gamekeeper, and men from nightshift work on the railway could always produce a pass – forged or otherwise – to explain their presence.

The Captain led them to an open field where they set up a line of three brushwood piles some 80m apart, while he stood 30m to the right of this with his signal torch. His radio operator carried the S-phone on his chest, to serve both as a homing beacon for the incoming aircraft and as a radio-telephone link with its radio operator. Cans of petrol were ready by each brushwood pile. The breeze blew gently towards the Captain and his signal torch, so that the incoming plane could cross the base of the 'L' made by the brushwood fires when lit and the recognition signal flashed on the torch, its pilot knowing that he was flying into the wind.

Several of the reception committee were told to stand at intervals along either side of the DZ, parallel to the fires, ready to spot the fall of containers that would be parachuted down on the aircraft's second pass, before the SAS men were dropped. With everyone in position, they waited tensely for the sound of the aircraft's engines. In these moments one remembered the nasty rumours of reception committees being jumped by underworld gangs, as a considerable number of SOE 'drops' and aircraft pick-ups were betrayed to the Gestapo, who arranged to ambush the reception committees or had their hirelings do so.

With perhaps five minutes to go to the expected arrival of the aircraft, a rustle in the hedgerow sets everyone on edge. Hands go to pistols hidden beneath the men's jackets. Henquet's girl courier shivers in the spine-chilling fright that sends your pulse racing when you think that you have been discovered. But the fright turns to heady relief as a horse clumps away from the hedge towards fresh pastures. Soon afterwards Henquet detects the far-off drone of a Dakota and alerts his signaller, who, with a quick flick of his wrist, plugs in the short directional aerial of the S-phone. Its beam vibrates the needle of a direction-indicator on the pilot's consol; keep this needle central and he will fly directly over Henquet's operator.

They even have a brief few seconds of conversation once the plane is nearly overhead. Already the brushwood fires soaked in petrol are alight; they and the flashing of a morse letter have shown the pilots that the DZ is set up. The exchange of passwords on the S-phone confirms that all is clear, as the Dakota makes its first pass. On the second, heading into the wind, several containers are dropped with arms and ammunition, spare parts perhaps for the circuit's generator to recharge radio batteries, cigarettes and some specific items of medical stores which the Captain has requested.

As the men either side of the DZ marked the fall of these large cylinders under their parachutes, they were quickly recovered, while the plane turned for its third pass. Out came six parachutists, to fall neatly within the 'L' of fires and signal torch.

Captain 'Jock' Riding, OC of 2 Troop, and the five NCOs and men as the advance party had been briefed in preparation for their drop. They would establish the first contact with 'Hermit', check the proposed site for their base which the Squadron commander had selected and take in with them the Eureka beacon on which the Stirling bomber that would bring in the Squadron's CO could home. (S-phones had a range of about 1,500km for R/T and their beacon could be detected at 10km by a plane flying at 3,000m, while Rebecca Radar equipment in an aircraft could detect a Eureka beacon at 65km and be guided by the Rebecca dial's moving trace.)

Jock Riding's team parachuted successfully to the DZ and he was bundling his chute in its rigging lines, before men ran from behind the line of fires to help him. The others were down, and all six were led to two waiting black Citroën cars, to be driven along back lanes to a safe house. Once inside, there was the chance for a smoke and to take stock of their helpers. The farmer's wife, with that bustling way of hostesses, welcoming visitors with food and wine, grandfather sitting slightly bemused by the proceedings, while the farmer spoke in low tones to Henquet. The others had slipped away to their own homes as Henquet discouraged their curiosity and SAS parties operated as far as was possible out of contact with civilians.

They were probably visited next morning, however, by Claud de Baissac, SOE's chief of operations in this area. A French-speaker from the British colony of Mauritius, he had proved an outstanding agent, evading in the summer of 1942 the clutches of the compromised 'Carte' circuit, and later was brought out in the aftermath of 'Prosper's' break-up during August 1943. He had returned by a circuitous route to southern Normandy the following February, establishing a vigorous circuit around Chartres, and had helped Henquet establish 'Hermit'. Between them they had supplied much of the military intelligence the Allies received on movements of Germans in the Orleans 'gap' up to this time.

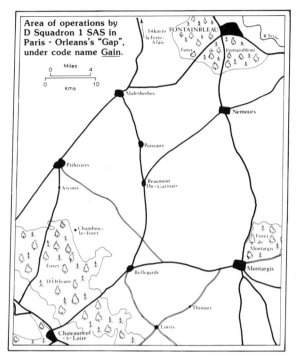

Area of operations by D Squadron 1 SAS in Paris - Orleans's "Gap", under code name Gain.

This 'gap' is a stretch of mostly open country lying between two forests some hundred kilometres apart. To the north is the forest around Fontainebleau, while to the south the Forêt d'Orléans runs in an arc of some forty kilometres around this town on the Loire. In order to force the Germans to use routes through the 'gap', the Seine and Loire bridges had been destroyed by Allied bombing in the week after D-Day, when 12,000lb (6-tonne) 'Tallboy' bombs were used for the first time, to destroy the entrance at Saumur to a tunnel under the Loire. Therefore German reinforcements were using the railway along the north bank of the Loire from Gien to Orleans, then north to Chartres, where it joined a line running south of the Seine, before looping north to Caen behind the beach-head. The line by the Seine brought men and stores from Saarbrücken on the way from Germany – a day's motoring in 1984 but for the Germans in 1944 a much longer time, as any movement by day attracted the attention of Allied fighter-bombers.

The British, on 14 June, had still to capture Caen, and the Americans had not reached the Cherbourg peninsula, while the Germans – unwilling at first to accept that the initial Allied landings were not a feint – had begun only a day or two earlier to move south 1 SS Panzer Division from Bruges in Belgium and 2 Pz Division from Amiens, 60 km north of the Seine; two other armoured Divisions – 9 and 10 Pz – had been refitting in eastern Germany and that week were moved by rail to Saarbrücken. (From the south, moving eventually west of the 'gap', 2 'Das Reich' SS Pz Division had begun an embattled approach march which would take three weeks to complete.) Stores and battle replacements for the casualties in the west also came through the 'gap'. By parking their fuel tankers by day in its woods and using other camouflage, they were able to hide much from even the low-flying photo-reconnaissance sorties of Allied Air Forces. Such pictures could not penetrate below the surface, so to speak, and it was 'eye-ball' recces by SAS patrols which revealed some vital targets. For example, it was an SAS patrol which discovered that the Germans had built bridges below the river surface of the Seine and were bringing convoys at night across these 'fords'. Allied bombers then attacked these 'invisible' bridges.

Good aerial photographs of D Squadron's area had enabled the CO to choose a likely base in the woods west of Pithiviers, in the middle almost of the 'gap'. Jock Riding went on the morning he landed to check these and the proposed DZ to which the Squadron CO, Major Ian Fenwick, and his Tactical HQ would jump on the Friday night. Fenwick was an artist, well known for his cartoons in *Punch*, the humorous weekly, and within the SAS for his dash.

Fenwick's party, seven in all, landed safely from a Stirling bomber, and the Major began almost immediately with a programme of sabotage that would cut the flow of German reinforcements. More of his Squadron were dropped to join him in the course of the following week, yet there were never more than fifty-eight all ranks involved in what became a battle against ten German divisions at different times on the move, a battalion of Tiger tanks, a Flak Corps with sixty 80-mm guns and elements of other units. For the first twelve days D Squadron operated on foot, lugging their explosive charges across rough country at night to set them on the three main lines running through the area. These were defended by renegade Frenchmen of the *Malice*, a Nazi para-military police, who apparently never attacked the raiding parties. On the line which ran due east of their base, from Malesherbes-Puisseaux, they derailed a goods train, causing damage to scarce rolling stock.

What was needed, however, were jeeps to give them mobility, despite the near presence of German forces. Fenwick believed that, by driving with headlights full on, as German vehicles did, his sabotage teams were unlikely to be challenged, for who would expect British saboteurs to drive around so openly?

The vehicles were parachuted packed and chocked in crates with protective skids that could be knocked off the vehicles when it had landed, ready to drive to the field base; its guns were dropped separately, and the jeep's crew – its driver, the commander, who was also front gunner, and the rear gunner – had the job of assembling the weaponry. However, the K-guns, accurate enough at twenty metres, were very erratic at more usual ranges because the mountings vibrated even though a new type of tubular steel fixing had been designed; but one report suggests that these heavier mountings were more apt to break than the flexible improvisations used in Africa. In addition to their twin K-guns, a fifth K-gun was mounted where the driver could fire it while steering with his left hand. (Twin Vickers .303-inch guns were fitted in place of K-guns later in 1944, and some vehicles carried a .5-inch Browning firing to the rear, giving them a heavier punch, even if the weight of this ammunition limited the quantities carried.) The K-guns could clear one of their hundred-round magazines in half a second, as they did in the Desert, shooting a succession of tracer, armour-piercing and incendiary bullets at a target, unless the crew did not want the tell-tale tracer to give their position away, when they used the couple or so of magazines loaded with ball (ordinary) ammunition that most jeeps carried.

Once armed and the fuel pipes connected to the reserve tanks fitted under the driver's seat and over both lockers at the back, a jeep had a range of 1,100km on one filling, always provided there were forty-eight gallons of petrol available. This was dropped in containers packed with jerry cans, but on several occasions SAS patrols had to limit the range of their operations when petrol was short.

Fenwick's patrols, like other SAS Squadrons, were intended to consist of three jeeps, the third carrying a three-inch mortar, but more frequently operated singly or in pairs. All jeeps carried a Bren for dismounted actions, grenades (useful to deter pursuers when, with the pin withdrawn, they were dropped over the back of the fleeing vehicles) and the crew's personal weapons. Various forms of armour plate were added to protect vulnerable parts of the vehicle. The crew had no protection, but relatively few were killed or wounded in their vehicles, considering that about a third of the seventy-five or so jeeps with SAS patrols in north-west Europe were destroyed. More often than not, the crew escaped on foot, D Squadron having more than their fair share of such adventures.

The first parachutage of jeeps was made within a week of the base being set up, apparently when two Halifaxes or Stirlings flew in at 150m, one following the other at an interval of about ten minutes. Each dropped a jeep from its bomb-bay, four white 'chutes billowing out from the black-crated shape in checking its fall from the aircraft, to land it with a thump on the DZ. At other times jeeps survived crash landings after hitting trees, at least one being still drivable although its body had been knocked askew. On the next pass the bombers dropped containers: sheet-metal cylinders 1.75m long, with the Type C hinged along its length which would be filled with carefully packed weapons and clothing. Type H containers of five smaller cylinders, locked together by a pair of retaining rods, carried ammunition, rations and other supplies. As quickly as the reception parties could collect in these containers – carried by four men with a stout stick through each pair of carrying handles – they were loaded onto Resistance trucks or wagons or SAS jeeps. Once back at base, the containers were hidden in ditches, the heavy loads of the H-type being broken up into the more manageable smaller sections, each carried by straps slipped through its two carrying rings. Also dropped were hampers or panniers, wicker baskets that carried radio spares and other light stores. These were carried in the aircraft and tossed through the opening in the floor by one of the crew.

In their final pass over D Squadron's DZ, the aircraft dropped SAS drivers for the jeeps and three or four reinforcements for the patrols. Detailed records of the drops to D Squadron have not been traced, but they had further drops of men and stores before the end of June, when Fenwick moved part of the Squadron to a new base in the forest near Orleans, as this large, tree-covered area was more secure than the smaller woods near Pithiviers. But he left Riding with a couple of patrols at the old base.

On one of the first raids from their new hide-outs, a patrol derailed a train on the line running north from Bellegarde, some ten kilometres to the east of the forest. This, like the cutting of the tracks, caused delays for the Germans, but what could be far more damaging was the destruction of locomotives, for these could not be replaced in a day as a piece of line might be. It seems likely that Henquet's contacts provided information on just such a target in the loco-sheds at Bellegarde. Certainly a recce showed that, although the railway yards here were guarded, they could be entered, as was no doubt explained to men brought to see the lie-of-the-land in daylight. On the night of the raid Fenwick took them back there in three jeeps, guided apparently by men from the Resistance.

The jeeps were hidden, with a couple of men left to guard them, and the raiders got into the yards without any difficulty. There was only one engine in the shed, a disappointment which may have put Fenwick on his guard against possible treachery, but the raid continued and PE charges were placed quickly on the vulnerable parts of the loco: the boiler, wheel couplings and pistons – all of which would then need machine-shop repairs if not complete replacement. The fuses had been set for thirty minutes, leaving time to put charges on other installations, such as the turntable. But as they moved towards these, a shot rang out. Intentionally or not, it was the signal for a company of Germans to move in from positions around the yard. Dodging behind sheds, taking cover behind whatever they could find, the Troopers returned the Germans' fire, keeping them engaged for fifteen minutes or more until the charges on the railway engine went off, checking the Germans, who were momentarily uncertain of what was happening. These few moments gave the SAS, trained to fight at night, the opportunity they needed to move out of the railway yard and back to the jeeps. The fact that they all got away safely says much for the high standard of their training and Fenwick's leadership. Later it was proved that they had been betrayed, but Fenwick must have realized this and no doubt took the precautions which other Squadrons did to move their forest camps without letting the Resistance know their precise location.

Once the railways were put out of action by Allied bombing, Resistance and SAS raids, the Germans had increasingly to use roads. Their vehicles then arrived at the battle area needing maintenance and had used precious petrol which was in short enough supply for vehicles in action. Throughout the first two weeks of July, D Squadron made nightly ravages among these German road convoys. By the end of that month they were ranging further afield, reportedly using over-night camps in the forest of Fontainebleau. They had many successes, with highlights that included the shooting up of a large tank transporter at Ascoux, five kilometres south of Pithiviers, armour-piercing bullets leaving this heavy vehicle beyond repair. On a parallel road another night, incendiary bullets set fire to two trucks, as did the first burst of fire to hit a petrol tanker the following night. But a planned major airborne landing in the 'gap' would be less likely to meet opposition to its initial drops if the Germans were lulled into a false sense of security, so Fenwick was ordered to curb his raiding activity but to continue his intelligence-gathering.

Men of C Squadron dropped to the 'Kipling' area in mid-August had orders not to take offensive action, because of this intended major operation. 'Kipling' was south-east of the 'gap', with bases in the forest of Merryvaux, from which patrols were carrying out recces. Fenwick dispersed his patrols for similar purposes: Jock Riding with Lieutenants Bateman and Parsons took their patrols to the *maquis* centre at Thimory, 60km east of Orleans; Fenwick and Lieutenant Watson 'took off into the blue' but from time to time returned to lay up in the Orleans forest.

While the patrols were moving independently to the *maquis* stronghold, Riding found a good deal of traffic on the main roads and, having passed four Tiger tanks on transporters without incident, since both German and SAS vehicles had their lights off, he planned to move onto back roads. One reason why the Germans paid less attention to SAS jeeps than might have been expected was the similarity when loaded with gear between an open-topped VW and a jeep. Upside down, they looked very similar, which was just as well, for Riding's jeep overturned as his driver swung off the highway. The drill when a vehicle became badly 'ditched' was to unload it, dismantle the guns and haul it upright by muscle power or another jeep. On this occasion Riding's crew had begun to lighten the vehicle when three Frenchmen appeared out of the night and gave a hand. Riding had sent his other jeeps on towards Thimory, probably expecting the righting of his own vehicle to take not more than a few minutes. However, they were still sweating to get the vehicle out of the ditch when the leading car of a German convoy came past. It was followed in the next fifteen minutes by eighty troop-loaded trucks, but none stopped to help what they must have taken for a German VW crew. The British and French had no option but to keep working, for as the convoy passed, any suspicious dash for cover would at best only attract attention and might well have led to the Germans taking an interest in the abandoned vehicle. Finally, after two hours of sweat, when they dared to use their torches only for brief moments, the vehicle was back on the road and they drove to Thimory.

Although keeping a low profile, the patrols made a number of attacks in August. Watson, with his jeeps parked near a level-crossing, ambushed a train in a hail of fire. The technique was not unlike that used against parked aircraft in the desert, and some two dozen such raids were made by the Squadrons that summer.

The Gestapo – or more precisely but without any difference in methods, Himmler's party security and counter-intelligence service, the SD – had an active headquarters in Paris. They had run a most successful wireless 'game' with SOE's F Section, using captured British agents' radios to send back misleading intelligence reports, and during 1942 and '43 had broken up several French and British intelligence circuits. With this record, they were not going to let Allied forces roam unhindered on what the SD regarded as their particular stamping ground!

The second-in-command of their Section based in Paris was the ex-police inspector H. Joseph Kieffer. He arranged for several of his French agents to infiltrate the *maquis* – not difficult in 1944 when the Resistance was expanding faster than SOE or the Free French could possibly vet all recruits to the circuits. One such agent probably found his or her way into 'Hermit' and gave the Germans the location of camps in the woods, but the dispersed SAS patrols were alert. One German officer searching for Watson's men was ambushed and killed by them. The luck which they had so often made for themselves by their boldness would not so much run out as be outsmarted by the Germans. Maybe a particularly successful attack setting fire to sixteen wagons loaded with sugar had given this SAS patrol added confidence, yet all knew that the chances of surviving such actions reduced, partly because of the strain of continually living with danger. That strain was also noticed in the more active Resistance fighters, yet both Allies continued the fight.

One guide, a veteran in his fifties and 'old' to the SAS Troopers, who were mostly in their early twenties, was with Watson on a recce that took them through Fourdan one night, and this Frenchman showed remarkable resilience to the pressures of action.

As they drove through the market square, they passed a parked convoy of trucks with only five sentries watching that no one interfered with whatever was carried behind the trucks' tightly laced canvas covers. The jeep was not stopped and no interest was taken in its passing, therefore a logical deduction was that the convoy's drivers had stopped for a meal break. Such a good target could not be passed up. Watson stopped outside the town, briefed his gunners and prepared to drive back. This time the driver had his foot down, the rear gunner – 'hands clammy with anticipation' – slipped off the safety catches and, taking a firmer grip of the twin handles of his K-guns, steadied himself against the jeep's acceleration. Watson braced himself, while the Frenchman took a firmer hold of the jeep's side – but he seemed more exposed than the others. With luck they should be through the square in ninety seconds, allowing a few quick bursts at their targets before the Germans had time to react – always provided the driver could keep the jeep moving. Watson would hit the sentries with his first burst, while the rear-gunner sent a succession of quick bursts into each truck as they passed it. Watson would also shoot at any troops moving to bring machine-guns into action.

As they swung into the square, Watson's first burst in the direction of the doorway, where the sentries had been talking, found no targets, and as the first truck parked on the roadside burst into flames, there came the angry wasp whispers of bullets flying over the jeep. In a flash Watson grasped the situation: German machine-guns down the street were concentrating their fire on the jeep, ready for its attack. Telling the driver to accelerate, Watson swung his guns to put a short burst towards two trucks, their canvas covers drawn aside to enable machine-gunners to get a clear shot. He expected that they now might find the road blocked. It wasn't. The Germans fired high, and only the Frenchman was hit; he managed to hang on as they raced out of the square. There were more Germans waiting in positions alongside the last stretch of road going out of the village. The jeep was going too fast now for any easy shot at it, the driver swerving to avoid ammunition boxes piled towards the centre of the road. He made the jeep lurch as he flung it back onto the crown of the road, but they were clear of the Germans.

The Frenchman was losing his hold, and as they took the next bend he was half-thrown and half-jumped from his precarious position in the back of the jeep. The rear-gunner saw him struggle towards a garden wall, but there was no chance to stop, for the Germans, alert and fighting, would be following them. When they did, they were not quick enough to catch the jeep, and Watson was safely in the depth of the forest by daylight.

Two days later the Frenchman reached their camp. He had managed to get into the garden and had laid low while the Germans searched the roadside. Then – his wounds dressed by a friend, no doubt – he had walked back to the forest.

The Germans, aware since Rommel's days in the desert of the dangers from SAS raids on road convoys, took steps in the summer of 1944 to protect them. With any sizeable convoy were one or more 'Q' trucks, in all appearances like other transports but carrying machine-gun teams ready for action the moment an SAS ambush was sprung, while infantry in the rear truck of the convoy would dismount and skirmish into the nearby fields in an attempt to encircle the ambush party. On one occasion at dawn a patrol of C Squadron had been shooting up a wagon convoy after the horses had been unhitched for watering, when, to Lieutenant Oates' surprise, the sides of two wagons fell forward. Mounted in these carts were machine-guns and a 20-mm quick-firing cannon, while from two carts at the back of the convoy German infantry advanced towards the jeeps. Oates withdrew without loss. Lieutenant Close on another occasion was less fortunate when his patrol was surprised by a 'Q' truck. He lost one of two jeeps hit by cannon fire, its crew escaping only by leaping onto the second one.

The Germans had also been mounting attacks against *maquis* camps and, as mentioned earlier, had surrounded patrols of B Squadron near Poitiers. In early August they were searching for D Squadron and, after Watson's escape with his crew from Fourdan, made a determined effort to clear the forest of Orleans. There Watson had his patrols in a small camp, with each section given a specific arc to defend in the event of an unexpected attack. Their jeeps were parked and camouflaged so that forest tracks leading to the camp were covered by the K-guns, and although the vehicles used these approaches, they were heavily over-grown with summer foliage. The wheelmarks of the jeeps could have given away a camp, had not the patrols been careful to brush out any signs of these marks, tidy broken branches and in general make sure that there were no obvious signs of their presence. The tall trees not only gave them cover from German spotter aircraft but also dispersed any smoke from their small cooking fires. The routine was relaxed – or as relaxed as it could be deep in enemy-held territory – with the men coming back from a night's patrol to a hot meal and weapon-cleaning before a few hours sleep in a 'bivvy' with its bracken-strewn floor. The jeeps would be serviced, refuelled and re-ammunitioned by their crews during the late afternoon, when patrols were detailed for their night's work.

When *maquis* reports suggested that there might be an attack, a Bren team would be sent several hundred metres down the approach road, so that the enemy would 'bump' into them before reaching the main base, but *maquis* reports had tended to exaggerate both the extent and the strength of German activity. Therefore, whether Watson had any hint of a possible German attack or not, no Bren teams were out on Sunday 6 August. Jock Riding and a signaller, Sergeant Bunfield, were visiting Watson, probably with a new set of one-time code pads, details of call signs and frequencies for use the following week. This was all routine. Then, at about 1500 hours, a shattering burst of high explosive shells sent everyone to firing positions, ready to defend the base or move their camps.

In the first hectic minutes, as more shells burst in the treetops, Watson had the jeeps made ready for a hasty evacuation, but as the German fire was intensified, with mortar bombs falling among the SAS, it was clear that the vehicles would be more of a hindrance than help. The Bren-guns, ammunition and anything useful was therefore taken out of the jeeps, leaving only the K-guns with enough ammunition for a few bursts should infantry come up the tracks towards the base. The bombardment continued for half an hour or so, then grey figures appeared among the trees, moving cautiously to encircle the base.

The Germans had the forest rides and fire-break clearings covered by machine-guns, and while in the thick woodland the SAS had a chance of avoiding capture, if they crossed these open stretches in daylight, they would be picked off by German gunners and marksmen. Skirmishing in woodland is always a battle of individuals' skill at arms, for you can see no more than a few metres in any direction and often are quite unaware of your enemy lying deep in a thicket while he watches you pass. The SAS Troopers, carrying only their weapons and escape haversacks, with maps, chocolate as emergency rations and cigarettes, could move quickly, although each man had as much ammunition as he could stuff in the deep pockets of his jacket.

They managed to keep the cordon at bay, with accurate bursts of fire and telling single shots which made the Germans cautious of any final advance. Nor could the German artillery and mortarmen give any further support, for fear of firing on their own men in the dappled sunlight under the trees. The jeeps had been set alight by the time the Germans reached them, and the crews had moved to new positions, keeping up the accuracy of their occasional bursts of fire throughout the evening. If the SAS could hang on until nightfall, they might make good their escape, as Riding knew while he watched the woods and heard the bursts of fire from time to time. When dusk had turned to a soft velvet dark, about 2200 hours, there were only occasional sounds of fire from a Bren and single carbine shots. The Germans continued to fire sharp bursts into thickets and at imagined movements in the woods, but this ceased about 2300. The German officers had withdrawn their men before they fired on each other in the dark. Riding waited another hour, and then he and his sergeant made their way out of the woods.

Ian Fenwick and his other patrols that Sunday had been in their base near the *maquis* battalion at Thimory, preparing for a visit from Paddy Mayne, who had signalled that he wanted to parachute in to a DZ on the Monday night. On the Monday, however, Fenwick heard of the attack on the forest base, albeit a somewhat exaggerated version (no doubt based on the boasts of the German infantry on their return to Orleans); that all the jeeps had been destroyed and their crews killed or captured. He immediately deferred the arrangements for Mayne's drop and set out to look for any survivors of Watson's patrols, taking one jeep driven by his regular driver, Corporal Duffy, Sergeant Dunkley and two Frenchmen, Lance-Corporal Menginou, who, like a number of others in 4 SAS Regiment, was attached to the British patrol as a translator, and a sergeant in the French Forces of the Interior who would act as a guide.

They made good time in daylight along secondary roads, crossed several main highways and were driving along the road that skirted the Orleans forest when a Frenchwoman stepped into the road, waving them to stop. The Germans, she said breathlessly, were awaiting for them in Chambon-le-Forêt, a sizeable village a few kilometres down the road. Fenwick might have skirted round the village but took the bolder course, no doubt expecting the Germans to be parked in a convoy on the roadside and not exactly 'waiting for him'. Nevertheless, as they entered Chambon, the K-guns were cleared for action and the jeep was travelling at speed.

As they neared the village centre, they were met not only by machine-gun fire but also by shots from 20-mm quick-firing guns. Nevertheless, they were past the first ambush position before a 20-mm shell killed the Major. A burst of fire from a second series of ambush positions caused Duffy to lose control of the jeep as he was wounded. Both Frenchmen were killed. Before Duffy lost consciousness after the jeep crashed, he saw the sergeant with blood on his face being led away in handcuffs. Duffy later came to in a hospital in Orleans before being moved to a German hospital in Fontainebleau.

A series of radio messages confirmed Colonel Mayne's intention to come over 'to see for himself the situation' and giving Riding command of the Squadron. A few days later Colonel 'Paddy' with Mike Sadler, the desert navigator who was now Mayne's aide in the field, parachuted to a DZ in the 'Houndsworth' area. At Fraser's A Squadron base here in the Morvan, Paddy was clearly glad to be back with his men, who held him in as great esteem as had his Squadron in the Middle East. Even in 1944 he was a legendary figure not only in the SAS.

Mayne noted the gaunt look of many of A Squadron after eight weeks of action, their thin faces and tired eyes showing that they had been under tension too long. He noted other details, such as Fraser's request for a dress kilt to be dropped to him. Such formality no doubt met with Mayne's approval only because it made the men more likely to feel that things were pretty normal if their officers dressed for conferences with maquis leaders. Much the same consideration prompted the Colonel's dislike of men wearing their berets at a jaunty angle – this smacked of bravado when he wanted professional soldiers.

He decided that 'A' should be relieved by C Squadron before the strains of their operations made them careless, when raiders needed to be at their sharpest on patrols in the 'Houndsworth' area, as the Germans were in strength not fifteen kilometres from the base at Mazignen.

Having made arrangements from this change-over, the Colonel and Sadler motored through enemy-patrolled areas for some 150km north-west to visit 'Gain'. There he arranged for Lieutenant Bateman to act as liaison officer with 'Agrippa', a *maquis* leader in whose battalion area 'D' had regrouped after Fenwick was killed. Parsons was sent with his men back to the Orleans forest, where they would continue to watch German movements, sending reports that would be vitally important to the planners of the major airborne operation in the 'gap'. Parsons would also be able to give some warning to 'Agrippa' should the Germans appear to be moving troops from Orleans against this *maquis*. Paddy then returned to Britain, but only for a brief spell.

On Thursday 10 August the expected attack was made on Agrippa's battalion. That Parsons had been able to give any warning seems unlikely, because the Germans had surrounded the *maquis* with infantry supported by eighteen armoured cars, impervious to the bazooka shots with which the Frenchmen tried to defend their camps. They therefore wisely decided to abandon the base, around which the woods were already alight after the Germans had used flame-throwers. Three *maquis* trucks broke through these fires, followed in a 'clapped-out' civilian car by Bateman and his team with an American airman who had joined the SAS patrols after his plane had been shot down. They reached the main road, but on the open ground here an armoured car overtook the SAS party, machine-gunning their car as it passed.

The Troopers dived for cover but Wilson, who was wounded, could not get out of the rear seat. He saw the American, also wounded, struggling to get back to the car for cover before he was killed by the armoured car's machine-gunner. Four Germans then approached the SAS's unreliable vehicle, unaware that Wilson was still inside it, and paid the price for their casualness: he shot three with his Colt at fifteen metres, and the fourth ran off. The armoured car's gunner then sprayed the crashed vehicle again, wounding Wilson for a second time. He regained consciousness to find that he was tied to a tree. A German officer, watching, his eyes flicker open, immediately began asking how many SAS were with the *maquis*, slapping Wilson's face despite his broken jaw to force an answer, but since he got no reply, Wilson was taken to Orleans with one of the *maquis*. This Frenchman was shot in the Trooper's hearing, just to prove 'what happened to terrorists'. Wilson still refused to give away any useful information and was therefore bundled off to another interrogation centre, of which he remembers nothing. When he finally came to his senses, he was in Orleans Hospital, where the

Americans found him when they arrived two days later, on 16 August.

The advance of Patton's army had been spectacular, and in the following week they covered the 150km to reach the Seine. The planned airborne landing was therefore unnecessary and was cancelled about 20 August, for the Resistance forces, aided by D Squadron, had dominated the Orleans 'gap', not only making possible Patton's rapid advance but also preventing the German First Army from the south-east of France effecting a link with the armies caught in the Falaise 'pocket'. Other Squadrons made their contribution but Ian Fenwick's D Squadron had plugged the 'gap' with exemplary ingenuity and courage.

Three days after the Americans reached Orleans, Mayne had a Troop and twenty jeeps of C Squadron lashed in Dakotas and flown to the city. A few days later they motored to 'Kipling', where – since the major airborne landings had been cancelled – Captain D. Ian Harrison's patrols had begun attacking German convoys. In one of these, two jeeps had shot up in daylight an SS Battalion's transports parked in Les Ormes, a fierce gun-battle developing at close quarters. Harrison was wounded more than once, his driver, 'Curly' Hall, killed and their jeep knocked out. Harrison escaped capture only by his courage in fighting off Germans who got within a few metres of him, as he stood exposed in the street, his guns jamming before the second jeep was turned round to escape down the dusty round. This was the last they saw of the Germans for some time, although SAS patrols ranged up to 80km from the 'Kipling' base between 25 and 29 August. The rest of the Squadron drove to join them from Orleans that week.

At the end of the month 'C's' twenty-four jeeps in four groups motored the 110km from 'Kipling' to 'Houndsworth'. A few days later, on 5 September, A Squadron left there bound for Britain, their convoy of surviving jeeps, requisitioned cars and two nearly new German troop-transports forming a column nearly a kilometre long. They drove off along what were now well-worn tracks from the camps – they had not seen a German reconnaissance plane for weeks, apparently. ('C's' operations during the rest of the month are summarized in Appendix II.) They took to flying Union Jacks on the jeeps for better identification by the *maquis* and several times were nearly attacked by Allied fighter aircraft; one jeep's crew managed to let off their identification yellow smoke signals only in the nick of time on one occasion. At this time, bad weather for flying made movement safer but reduced the number of drops to resupply bases, and for days at a time the patrols were limited to short distances because they were short of petrol. That September any Allied bombers unable to find a DZ had a series of dropping points at which their loads might be 'left' in France for use by local forces, rather than taking the containers back to the UK. This was not much help to SAS but is indicative of the Allied organization in support of the French Forces of the Interior. By mid-September, however, C Squadron had received their first drop to re-supply them in daylight.

Elements of the German First Army's rearguard now seemed trapped, or about to be, and German stragglers were found by 'C'. Lieutenant Mycock found more than the normal small bunch of these towards the end of the month. His patrol had been in contact with the French army coming up from the Mediterranean landings six weeks earlier, and he led their tanks into Autun, a town just south of the Morvan bases. The French had barely liberated this town when a column of three thousand Germans was seen to be approaching it. Mycock set out to contact its commander and succeeded in persuading him to surrender after a brief exchange of shots in which a Trooper was wounded in the thigh. But the main German forces had quit the area, and 'C' were moved to Cosne on the east bank of the Loire, where they lived in requisitioned hotels and used a large garage to give the jeeps the major overhauls that they urgently needed.

The SAS operations in France had continued despite betrayals and the activities of Kieffer and his SD. The extent of this was not realized until the full story of B Squadron's losses unfolded. When the thirty bodies of those captured at Poitiers were found, they were not at first identified as being SAS men. Only when Tonkin was shown a newspaper report and made further investigations did the full horror of the events become clearer. Having captured these uniformed soldiers in battle, the German army had passed them over to the SD, who held them in prison in Paris for a month. Then Kieffer had them dressed in civilian clothes and taken back to the Poitiers area, where they were shot with Sten-guns, a British weapon used extensively by the *maquis*. The records were fudged and their deaths shown as being in action near their base, which might have suggested that they had died in some misunderstanding between Allies. As they were being taken into the wood, one Trooper realized that the execution party were armed only with Stens, an inaccurate weapon at ranges over 50m, and he took the chance to make a run for it. Escaping through the woods, he was found by the Resistance and hidden; he survived to give evidence at the Nuremberg trials in 1947 which led to Kieffer's execution.

Duffy also survived after being moved to Fontainebleau, for French wardmaids smuggled a German doctor's white coat into the ward and he walked out of the hospital, despite the shoes the girls gave him being two sizes too small. He was saluted by the gate sentry and, once clear of the hospital, took off his shoes, before walking fifteen kilometres with badly blistered feet, having only a brief rest in a woodman's hut and a short lift on a carthorse, a ride that nearly led to his recapture: but the two German motorcyclists who stopped him only wanted to know the way.

He was hidden by the Resistance until the Americans reached Milly.

The success of these deep-penetration raids and bases far behind the enemy battlefront was due to the forceful, independent characters like Duffy, who, in his own words, had been 'parked in a ward full of bloody Gerries'. There was a bit of a fracas there, before he was moved to the ward from which he escaped. A host of similar incidents, when SAS men on their own continued the fight, underline this attitude of mind which, with their high standard of training, had made the SAS so formidable a force.

Trooper Jamieson, for example, was the hidden Bren-gunner covering a team from A Squadron cutting the railway near Digoin when a German platoon took up ambush positions within metres of his hide. As the SAS team moved off the railway, having laid their charges, Jamieson let fly a burst which knocked out a Spandau crew, and in the next ninety minutes, using his Colt when no Bren ammunition was left, he enabled the team to escape before diving into a river and swimming clear of the ambush.

Sergeant Foster of 2 SAS, his jeep separated from the 'Wallace' columns, crashed into a German staff car in which he killed four senior officers before motoring the rest of the 50km to the base in Châtillon Forest. Sergeant F. ('Chalky') White DCM, MM – awards won in Africa – had three fingers shot off one hand after Captain Roy Bradford and Craftsman Jim Devine had been killed, yet White kept firing, enabling the survivors of this jeep's crew including himself to escape.

Lieutenant 'Monty' Goddard of C Squadron, shooting a Vickers from the hip at ten metres range, killed the crew of a German mobile anti-aircraft gun and dropped a grenade into the truck towing the gun but was killed as he attacked a second gun in this battery. Lieutenant David Leigh, an experienced SAS officer leading seven jeeps in one of the 'Wallace' columns, was killed trying to extricate the crews from an unexpected encounter with a strong German roadblock alerted by a previous column. Many of Leigh's men were wounded, but those who escaped made their way to the Allied lines, and later some were parachuted to rejoin the 'Wallace' columns.

These few examples of the many actions in France follow the tradition established by SAS in the African deserts and brought to France by the leavening of experienced men in the SAS patrols.

Lieutenant Bill Fraser, who won his first Military Cross with L Detachment 'in a successful raid on the aerodrome east of Agedabia' on the night of 21/22 December 1941, won a bar to his MC in 1944 when, as the Major commanding A Squadron, 'his untiring leadership and spirit kept his men alert and their morale high', to quote again from the citations. His courage and resource reinforced his men's respect for him. His personal leadership included an attack on 29 August in which he led his six-man jeep crew against two large German convoys in succession; with his

Bren-gunner, he engaged a third, setting up such confusion that the Germans could be heard shooting at each other over an hour after the Major had withdrawn.

Sergeant-Major Bob Lilley – whom we left in the deserts of North Africa – was the Sergeant-Major of 'C' and given command of some of its more difficult patrols. Reg Seekings, one-time corporal in David Stirling's vehicle crew, was Squadron Sergeant-Major of 'A'. Wounded in the German attack on 'Houndsworth', he was 'as smart as he was tough and goodhearted'; he retained his touch of genius with things mechanical and left 'Houndsworth' driving a Ford V8 coupé, a German bullet still lodged in his neck.

The highlights of these operations had been the daring of SAS raids, but more important in military terms was 'the large amount of invaluable information about enemy movements' sent back each day from the Squadrons in France. It was particularly valuable because the jeep crews were trained observers and knew what was significant to report, including the absence of Axis forces from some areas, while *maquis* reports tended to include unreliable exaggerations – understandably, as they were made by civilians with little training. SAS reports had often to be based on 'eye-ball' inspections of a target – there were none of the electronic surveillance aids used in the 1980s – which meant that John Tonkin had to crawl into a wood to tap each of eleven railway tankers to be sure that they were loaded. They were. A signal flashed to London in clear brought RAF Typhoons at first light to set the tankers on fire with rockets, one of twenty-nine major targets which 1 SAS alone pinpointed for aerial attack between June and September.

Apart from the six-pounder anti-tank gun dropped to A Squadron, the Squadrons in France had no heavier weapon than three-inch (76mm) mortars, but Major Roy Farran's 3 Squadron of 2 SAS were to prove that heavier weapons' destructive power could be devastating beyond their conventional use in bombardments. 3 Squadron had served briefly in France but had been in an area quickly reached by the advancing Americans. The Squadron's CO, Major Michael Rooney, had trained them to a high pitch of efficiency to which Farran attributed much of their success when in March 1945 they were operating behind the German front in north-west Italy, Farran having taken command after Rooney broke his back in a parachute accident. They carried out several operations (see Appendix II) before a troop took part in 'Tombola'.

In this operation an advance party dropped on 4 March, including Farran, although he had been told to stay in Bari with the Squadron HQ for co-ordination of operations with SOE. Under Farran's leadership, before the Germans' final withdrawal six weeks later, fifty of the Squadron had raised a battalion of guerrillas to form a most effective fighting force, although they were an unlikely combination of Allies: Russians who had escaped from German prison camps, Italian Communists and youths escaping from forced labour in Florence, to the south-east of the snow-covered hills where Farran based his men. After as little as three weeks' training this *Battalione Alleata* made a two-day march and attacked the villas of a German Corps headquarters. The three 'companies', twenty-four British, twenty Italians and thirty Russians, then made a fighting withdrawal in which only six of the Russians forming the covering party were captured and three British killed, although several others who were wounded were evacuated only with great difficulty.

They made other fighting patrols, moved their main location eastwards and had devastating success in harassing the German retreat down the Pavullo-Modena road, where Route 12 runs through a high valley. Working to orders from General Mark Clark's Fifteenth Army, the Squadron attacked the retreating 232 and 114 German Divisions which had been facing the US IV Corps. In these attacks they used with deadly effect a 75-mm howitzer that had been parachuted to them. They positioned this gun, and an American 4½-inch (120mm) mortar and a captured 36-mm quick-firing gun, at various places where they dominated Route 12. The '75' once overlooked several hamlets from its mountain position; at another site it covered the ford across the Secchia River; once it even fired into the town square of Reggio with 'five rounds rapid' when this town was 80km north of the main battle area, causing such uncertainties about the strength and depth of the Allied advance as to force the Germans to retreat further before forming a new defensive line.

Such actions always cause confusion which completely demoralizes a retreating force, and, as had been realized by a few senior officers long before SAS came into existence, this type of operation could have disrupted the *Blitzkrieg* through France in 1940. More importantly, if an SAS force had existed, it would have kept the Allied headquarters informed of German movements, which in the event were running far less smoothly than reports suggested. No one knew at the Allied headquarters that over half the Germans' tanks were stuck on the roadsides with mechanical breakdowns.

Operations in Italy and France had the advantage in 1944 of help from local people, and while patrols avoided too much involvement with civilians for fear of betrayals, they received considerable help from ordinary men and women, often at the cost of the lives of their helpers. SAS's battles in Germany, however, enjoyed no such support. But before crossing the German borders, there were other operations which had limited success.

C Squadron, after re-fitting in central France, moved, as did other Squadrons, to Holland in October 1944. There each patrol of 'C' worked with a Field Security Section (the military equivalent of counterespionage forces) of the Second Army. As jeep patrols could move more swiftly than even light-armoured forces, they were to raid ahead of the army, seizing important Nazis and German documents from administrative offices before either might vanish in the general retreat. But by November the Second Army were holding static positions along the line of the River Maas, and there was little for the SAS patrols to do. In February they were concentrated in Antwerp, where a German parachute landing was expected but never materialized, and the Squadrons returned home to the UK for leave in March and training for the Far East.

In March 1945, however, Germany had still to be defeated, and the Allies' final thrust was expected to meet not only fierce opposition but also a fanatical civilian resistance after the military forces had surrendered. Although Special Forces of SAS or Commando units in 1945 were not trained or equipped for anti-terrorist roles, there was probably the notion in some quarters that they could be used for this purpose. Be that as it may, the Allies undoubtedly wanted a quick and complete victory and therefore brought back to mainland Europe not only SAS Squadrons but also Commando Brigades which had been training in Britain for the war in Japan.

✚ Brigadier J. M. Calvert had taken command of the SAS Brigade on McLeod's appointment to the General Headquarters in India. The 'new' Brigadier is known as 'Mad Mike', but he was – and is – neither 'mad' nor as devil-may-care as he is sometimes portrayed but a deep thinking and brave commander. A Cambridge University 'double blue' who had once resigned his commission to join a ski-battalion training in 1940 to fight in Finland, by 1944 he held thirteen decorations for gallantry, a number of these won during raids behind Japanese lines in Burma. He had the unenviable task of sending his men into actions for which they were not equipped and which did not suit their methods.

In the last airborne operation by SAS in World War II, Operation 'Amherst', fifty parties, half of them British and half French, dropped 'blind' to nineteen DZs in north-east Holland about ten kilometres ahead of the advancing first Canadian Army. Each party of some fourteen, including two officers, was dropped with great accuracy from forty-seven Stirlings of 38 Group RAF using radar-assisted navigation. The sky was completely overcast that night, 6/7 April 1945, and therefore jeeps were not sent in as had been planned, but the teams carried out their various jobs: preventing the Germans demolishing the Steenwijk airfield installations; capturing eighteen bridges on the line of the Canadians' advance, and radioing back intelligence reports on German dispositions – all actions which they were to complete in seventy-two hours with the help of the Dutch Resistance, to the satisfaction of the Canadians and the confusion of the Germans, at relatively little cost, although taking twelve per cent casualties including twenty-nine killed, when considering the hazards of such drops close to German defences.

In a parallel operation ahead of II Canadian Corps, forty jeeps of the Belgian SAS made recces in north Holland and later further east but had over a third of the crews killed or injured, many being casualties when the jeeps ran into mines laid in roads and others in roadblocks covered by Germans in prepared machine-gun positions. This operation 'Larkswood' had shown again the difficulties of operating close to the main battle area, as did 'Howard', when two squadrons of 1 SAS tried to recce the countryside into which 4 Canadian Armoured Division were advancing.

1 SAS, now with C Squadron, reached the unit in Germany on 9 April, the day the Canadians took the bridge over the Ems River at Meppen, from where they planned to advance north-eastward to Oldenburg, 75km inside the German border. 1 SAS were to infiltrate through the German lines, with two columns moving parallel to the Canadians' left (west) flank and intending to converge at several RVs along their route. In the misty dawn next day, the crews of Canadian Sherman tanks 'blinked incredulously as the tiny vehicles' roared across the bridge. But 'mechanized mess-tins' were not the vehicles with which to tackle prepared defences when machine-gun bullets were easily absorbed by earth and concrete strongpoints. At the first canal 'C' reached, the bridge was down, and well-sited defences on the far bank prevented any attempt to cross, as others did further east on this Kusten Canal. Eventually 'C' crossed where 'B' had found a route, and during the morning the jeeps, with their customary dash, burst their way through roadblocks, bypassed others by taking to the dusty lanes and in places quickly improvised bridges.

As the leading jeep came over the hill into the open valley where Borgerwald lies, there was no reason to suspect that the town was any more dangerous than half a dozen others they had passed through. But here the Germans had an organized defence in some depth, and when the leading jeep was knocked out, the CO of 'B', Major Tony Bond, and a Trooper were killed. The other jeep crews tried to work their way around the strongpoints but were pinned down by heavy fire. Then down the road came Colonel Paddy, driving his jeep at a breakneck pace, its .5-inch thumping as he swept past the key strongpoint, to turn in a flurry of dust as he picked up two wounded men. Then he was back up the valley track, despite the enemy's machine-gun fire. He made two more trips, rescuing the survivors of the leading jeeps and to bring out the two bodies. The columns moved on, skirting Borgerwald to find less determined resistance at the next village, where sixty Germans surrendered.

When they stopped for lunch in the woods near Esterwegen, Germans took shots at them. One, spotted by Lieutenant Peter Davis, came out when challenged but not with his hands up – he shot the lieutenant in the shoulder and made good his escape. The column moved on and by evening were laagered about twenty kilometres into Germany. Black smoke hung in the spring air above burning farms, and white sheets of surrender had been hung from many a house and even some trees. As they drew up, the jeeps in a defensive circle, the Colonel's '.5' was thumping again, for he had seen movement in a ditch. A cycle patrol with *Panzerfausts*, the German one-shot anti-tank rockets, were killed or captured, except for two who escaped in the gathering darkness. Away to the right the Canadian artillery rumbled and the SAS sentries were alert.

They were not disturbed, however, and next morning continued to battle their way through villages, taking more prisoners than there were men in the jeep crews. B Squadron were pinned down in a village about midday, a troop of 'C' moving 300m to the flank of the village to give 'B' some covering fire. But their twelve jeeps on an exposed track were a sitting target, unable to distinguish friend from foe. Then, while Ian Harrison and his CO were deciding the next step, German mortars opened up, and only two crews of the leading vehicles managed to scoot out of sight round a bend in the road. The rest took to the roadside ditch, which was full of stinking water but safer than the track being plastered with mortar bombs. Crawling through culverts and along this metre-deep stagnant strip of water was all the more difficult as their jackets filled with water. Nevertheless, they crawled clear of the jeeps. Harrison had gone ahead several hundred metres, once having to dodge bullets as he climbed across a blocked culvert, before he saw Davis's Troop coming down the road. He might well have been shot by them had he not waved his beret on the end of his carbine.

Davis' Troop opened up on the village with their .5s, and in the blast of this concentrated fire the mortar-crews took cover. These Germans ceased firing long enough for several jeeps to pick up C Troop from the ditch before machine-guns opened up. The Troop had lost two jeeps taken away by the Germans and seven damaged by mortar fire, but those that might be repaired were later towed out along a track that could not be seen from the village. That night both B and C Squadrons laagered in a wood and lay low, 50km from their crossing of the Meppen Bridge thirty hours earlier and with half as far to go again to reach Oldenburg. They were brewing up before preparing an evening meal when two jeeps came in, flying white flags. They had taken a badly injured officer to a German hospital and believed that they had been followed to the RV. Mayne immediately moved his Squadrons deeper into the woods, from where they later heard German mortar and shell fire, as the Germans probed the forest.

At dawn a patrol left to contact the Canadians, who were apparently out of radio contact. (That was not unusual; even in France signallers at times had to send messages via London to neighbouring units not far away in the French mountains.) The Germans were on the sentry almost before he could shout a warning, and their machine-guns poured a steady stream of fire into the clearing around which the jeeps were parked, with the German prisoners lying in the open. Giving their parole, they were allowed to move into 'dead' ground, a shallow dip which would give them some cover. Five SAS Bren-gunners moved forward, without any orders to do so, firing into trees as they searched for the machine-gun, while Peter Davis's jeeps kept up a steady stream of fire at the unseen enemy who seemed to be attacking from his side of the laager. The Bren-gunners were forced to give ground as the Germans stalked them in turn through the wood, where the Colonel was also looking for shots, with his camera.

The battle was hanging on a thread of decision, for the Germans had all the advantages of cover and knowing the ground, no doubt. Then a Canadian flame-throwing tank with some light carriers came crashing through the trees. For C and B Squadrons there was one more spell of refit and reorganization when patrols were regrouped after their casualties, during a forty-eight hours in Lorup before they were on the move again. This time they were on the right (east) flank of the Canadians, but there was no opportunity for headlong dashes up country lanes as they advanced from Vrees.

German youths and old men and women, armed as local home defence units with *Panzerfausts*, thickened the defences of many towns, while on the Canadians' front German paratroops fought doggedly to defend each roadblock and river crossing. The jeep patrols worked with the screen of armoured reconnaissance moving ahead of 4 Canadian Division, in the conventional way of armour, bumping the stronger centres of resistance, which were left for heavier armour to attack, clearing minor strongpoints and mopping up infantry positions left behind the Canadian advance.

After ten days they were nearing Garrle, from Vrees, when an independent armoured brigade was tasked with breaking through the last few kilometres to Oldenburg. The Squadrons were put under its command and had covered only part of this distance by 4 May, when the Germans in the area ceased fighting four days before their country capitulated. For B and C Squadrons the way was virtually over.

Lieutenant-Colonel Brian Franks was at this time heading for Kiel. His 430 men in seventy-five jeeps from 1 and 2 SAS, with a few 15-cwt and three-ton trucks for re-supply, had come from west of the Rhine, across the Weser and the Elbe, working with the armoured reconnaissance forces under a series of commands as different divisions took the lead in the drive to the Baltic. Franks' patrols were the first Allied troops to reach Kiel that May. They had been in nine major actions, killed an estimated two hundred Germans and captured 233.

The final figures for SAS operations in north-west Europe show that two thousand SAS personnel – British, French and Belgian Regiments with a number of other nationalities serving in their ranks – had suffered 16½ per cent casualties in putting six times their number (12,517) of Germans out of action when they were either killed or captured. The SAS record of seven trains destroyed, 122 railway lines cut and about seven hundred motor vehicles destroyed or captured is equivalent to only a small proportion of those destroyed by Allied Air Forces, but more than their numbers they were of significant consequence in one aspect: the dynamic effect they had in boosting the morale of Resistance forces.

The operations in March and April 1945 provided no roles for the SAS, but any commander in 1945 was pleased to have them under his charge, for their reputation was formidable, and such first-rate troops will always achieve some success in whatever role they are given. David Stirling came back from the Colditz prison with some pertinent ideas on roles for the Regiments in the Far East, and in the second week of May 1 and 2 SAS returned to the UK to prepare for them. Stirling's scheme for operations included the use of SAS regiments to stiffen a guerrilla army in northern China, making attacks on Manchurian railways carrying not only military forces but also vital raw materials for the Japanese as they prepared for a war of attrition. This would have been the largest and possibly the longest SAS operation had not the atom bombs put a quick end to the war, saving the estimated million Allied casualties had the Japanese homeland had to be invaded.

In 1945 the British General Staff could see no proper role for the SAS, although the Americans began training their Ranger Battalions, the equivalent of British Commandos, to operate against the Russian lines of communication should they attack western Europe. Therefore when 1 and 2 SAS returned from Norway, where they had been disarming without difficulty some 300,000 Germans, they were disbanded. They and the Brigade HQ finally closed down on 8 October, after the Belgian Regiment had transferred to the Belgian Army's command the previous month and the French had formally transferred to their national army on 1 October. For the men the change to peacetime can be summed up in the words of the Reverend J. F. McLuskey MC, their padre in 'Houndsworth', who had climbed a hill ridge to say his prayers at the foot of a large pinetree, high in the Morvan: 'in years of greater security, it was often to prove a much harder climb.'

5. New Regiments, New Roles

In 1946 the War Office, prompted by *Calvert, Franks and other senior officers who had served in SAS, set up an enquiry by the Tactical Investigation Committee which examined possible roles for the SAS in the future. From the Committee's analysis of SAS operations in World War II they concluded – to paraphrase the report – that, in the fluid fighting to be expected in any future war, there would be roles like those of 'Wallace' if not of 'Houndsworth', when well-trained small military forces could achieve results out of all proportion to the numbers of men committed behind an enemy's main battle areas. Significantly the report also pointed out that, 'The SAS does not necessarily drain the infantry of its best men' – the main objection by infantry colonels to the formation of special forces – 'but will often take . . . a man of great individuality [who] may not fit into an orthodox unit as well as he does in a specialist force.' This individuality of the SAS Trooper came to distinguish him from other soldiers, who tend to work in teams. Although working in the 1980s in the standard British Army four-man module, two pairs of 'buddies', with the three modules to an SAS Troop, Troopers can work as a team when appropriate.

In 1947, however, the formation of a new regular regiment was politically impossible when the British were seeking to reduce their military forces. Therefore a Territorial Unit of reservists was formed, amalgamating the SAS with the Artists' Rifles, whose origins as a volunteer regiment went back to 1860 – its commanding officer had always been, until the turn of the century, a professional artist, a sculptor or a painter. In the World Wars the Regiment's staffs had been the nucleus of officer-training units before it was re-formed in 1947 as 21 SAS (Artists) Regiment TA. '21' came from the 1 and 2 of earlier SAS regiments, reversing the numbers because there was already a 12 Airborne TA battalion. Their first CO was Lieutenant-Colonel B. M. F. Franks DSO, MC, TD, with Major L. E. O. T. Hart OBE as his second-in-command. Hart had been the Brigade Major in 1944–5, heading its administration.

Recruiting began in September 1947, and some 180 former SAS officers and men joined as reservists, a number of former officers joining in the ranks, as did all the men who later gained commissions in this regiment, which by the Artists' tradition had always been officered by men who had first served in the ranks. Briefly '21' was under the command of the Rifle Brigade, but details of the Regiment's special needs in equipment and weapons for its deep penetration patrols were understood only by its officers, and while the War Office appreciated these intended roles, there was no one to question its specific needs. For this reason and for what would later become reasons of security, with the Brigadier responsible to the Army Staff in some situations of political delicacy, '21' became the senior regiment of the SAS Corps, ranking after the infantry in seniority and with power to raise other regiments as and when the War Office (later the Ministry of Defence) required them. In any future war there would not then be the hotch-potch of private 'armies' that there had been among the special forces of World War II. But the Corps is far smaller than the generally accepted size of such a formation, its numbers being in hundreds rather than ten thousand or more.

The selection and training of recruits to '21' maintained the high if not an even higher standard than that which Stirling had set for his recruits to L Detachment in 1941. And the Regiment's commanding officers who succeeded Colonel Franks, were – like him – able to draw on first-hand operational experience and also had those traits of leadership which command respect and are essential to the success of any part-time unit, when the enthusiasm of volunteers needs constantly motivating if they are to maintain their efficiency.

21 (Artists) SAS were preparing to send M Troop to Korea (at the American General MacArthur's request) when in 1951 it was diverted to Malaya. When the Chinese entered the Korean War, SAS-type patrols, with their inherent risks of political involvement for those local people who might work with them, apparently deterred the British government from allowing '21' to operate there. As we have seen, SAS were not the unit for battlefield reconnaissance.

In Malaya they began what became a key job for SAS, operating against terrorists, or 'bandits' as they were called in Malaya when twelve hundred pro-Communist Chinese took to the jungles in 1948. Many of these men and women had fought the Japanese and been armed by the wartime Allies; they supported Mao Tse-tung and saw his defeat of the Nationalists as an example of what Communists might achieve. In June 1948 they began murdering planters, Chinese foremen on estates and many local political leaders. These raids were made from permanent bandit camps, some with huts for lectures and other training facilities for two hundred men and women. One such camp was found by 'Ferret' force, a paramilitary unit drawn from army volunteers, from former members of SOE's Force 136 and other civilians. The 'Ferret' scouts led fighting patrols from regular infantry battalions, making the first offensive sweeps into the jungle, aided by forty-seven Dyak trackers, the first of many such Iban tribesmen from Borneo who served with the British forces in Malaya during the next decade. 'Ferret' force proved that the British did not have to remain always on the defensive, but the Force had to be disbanded when many of its 'leading lights' had to return to their civilian or more conventional military posts.

The Communist terrorists continued to attack civilian fieldworkers, in an attempt to frighten them into deserting the rubber plantations and tin mines, and by 1950 had killed twelve hundred people, including policemen and soldiers, although half as many again of the bandits had been killed or captured.

The Commander-in-Chief of Far East Land Forces at this time was General Sir John Harding, who told Mike Calvert to study the situation, as Calvert's experiences in Burma in 1942 and his analytical turn of mind seemed likely to produce solutions. He then spent six months in a personal tour of Malaya and – as befitted the former SAS Brigadier who had reverted to his substantive rank of major – spent time with infantry patrols and made long journeys through terrorists areas but was 'only[!] ambushed twice'. His clear insight into what was needed is reflected in his subsequent report which led to two innovations: 410 squatters' villages were moved from the jungle fringes to wire-fenced enclosures which could be defended against terrorist raids; and Calvert was ordered to form the special force which he had suggested, to harass the Communists in their jungle hide-outs. Calvert's suggested name was also given to this force: the Malayan Scouts (SAS). But, as so often happens, this special force – or at least its commander – was given far too many tasks when politicians were looking for quick results once a decision had been made to form the unit. Calvert found that he was organizing its new headquarters, masterminding its recruits' eight-week training programme in Johore and preparing for their first operation 400km to the north, near Ipoh.

The first recruits included volunteers who – like Major C. E. ('Dare') Newell, OBE – had served with SOE in Malaya in 1945; Newell as well as some other recruits had been in 'Ferret' Force, and some volunteers had wartime experience with SAS. Ten volunteers were deserters from the French Foreign Legion but others were less qualified by experience, being merely bored with peacetime routines in infantry regiments. Under the pressures to start operations Calvert could not be as particular as he would have liked over the standard of recruits. He made time to widen his search for suitable men, visiting Rhodesia where a thousand volunteers offered to join, and his staff were able to select some 120 to form C Squadron.

As there was this opportunity to be selective, 'C' would prove one of the most professional of the SAS Squadrons, serving in Malaya for over three years despite the men being prone to jungle illnesses. Two of the Squadron were killed in action before it returned to Rhodesia (modern Zimbabwe). There it was later to become the nucleus of the Rhodesian SAS Regiment, although it continued to be known as C Squadron for many years (see Appendix II).

Calvert also brought together in Johore an intelligence section of men experienced in jungle operations from the time seven years earlier when they had worked with him in Burma, including Hong Kong Chinese to act as interpreters. The head of this 'Int' Section was Major (later Lieutenant-Colonel) John M. Woodhouse, Dorset Regiment. He had joined the army as a private in 1941. A linguist, he had served for two years as an interpreter with the Russians. He had a mature sense of military priorities, putting battle discipline before the buttons-and-bows of uniform, and during his service with the Malayan Scouts came to realize that they would have to develop their own training and tactical techniques which differed in some respects from the veterans' experiences fighting the Japanese.

The Scouts were joined in January 1951 by M Squadron of 21 SAS – redesignated 'B' of the Scouts – while their A Squadron, a hundred strong, was completing its training course. This included throwing grenades and diving for cover in the deep monsoon drains running through their camp area, one of several lessons with live ammunition that disregarded the normal safety rules for field firing ranges. Since there was neither the time nor facilities for such routines, all training – much in the way Calvert had known it in 1940 – had to take place on football pitches and other clear spaces around the camp. This and A Squadron's hard drinking were criticized at the time by the more prosaic officers of B and C Squadrons and would be a lingering criticism of SAS standards for the next ten years. What was not realized by these officers, who were aware of the problems of maintaining the very existence of their Regiment against pressures at home for their disbandment, was Calvert's quite different concept of the Scouts as an *ad hoc* unit. He thought that it might be the forerunner of others, formed in particular regions for operations during the British withdrawal from their Empire, when such units – Calvert argued – could be formed and disbanded more readily than squadrons drawn entirely from a British regiment.

His tactical plan for the Scouts in Malaya was to use patrols based for long periods deep in the jungle, where they could make contact with the aborigines, the Sakai, who were being coerced by the terrorists into providing them with food. The Scouts would also harass the terrorists in their bases, but since Malaya is a hilly country about the size of England but three-quarters of it covered by jungle or swamps in the coastal plains, finding these bases would need the patience for a long campaign. This had barely begun for the Scouts before in November Calvert was invalided home 'a very sick man' with a distressing collection of tropical diseases picked up during twelve years' service, much of the time in the Far East.

But a start had been made: one of the Scouts' patrols spent 103 days in the jungle when seven days was considered a long time for British soldiers to live in these forests. This patrol and others also began the first of what would become a less-featured but important aspect of SAS activities: their help for local communities. In 1951 their medics took penicillin and simpler medicines into the jungle, holding sick-parades for aborigines with skin- and other diseases. But the patrols' main task was to send out three- or four-man patrols from their jungle base to ambush the tracks used by terrorists returning to a jungle hide-out. The patrols had some success, and only two SAS Troopers were killed in these penetrations before the jungle bases were withdrawn.

An infantry officer with no Special Forces experience, Lieutenant-Colonel John Sloane, Argyll and Sutherland Highlanders, took over from Calvert. He then reorganized the Scouts which now had a fourth – D Squadron – recruited from miscellaneous volunteers. 'Dare' Newell among several other officers was persuaded to stay with the unit, when they had intended to transfer to more regular formations. Meanwhile, the patrols were kept to the jungle fringes and defended jungle forts, helping the Malay Police Field Force. They would be back in the jungle in February, the month John Woodhouse returned to the United Kingdom. Woodhouse's contribution to the future roles of the SAS would be fundamental, as explained later, while the operations in Malaya led to tactical rather than broader developments, as is shown by a comparison of the first parachute operation in February 1952 and the achievements of D Squadron, who spent over three weeks in the swamps of Telok Anson, six years later.

The jungle-clad hills of Malaya have great trees 70m tall, their interlocking top branches forming a canopy high above the shadowy and damp ground. Like all the rain-forests of south-east Asia, they flourish in a regular rainfall on most days, for, while some months are wetter than others in various regions, only the extreme north-west of Malaya has a marked dry season. In such wet, dank, primary jungle, with its steamy morning mists under the high canopy's continuous shade, a man never gets sun-tanned, while the jungle floor has only a meagre covering of leaves, since these are shed year round, and so a footmark can show clearly. Most people are familiar with jungle noises, if only from watching TV: the screech and jabber of monkeys, the bird calls and the snort of disturbed wild pigs; what is not so often realized is how still the jungle can be, sheltered under its canopy from all but the strongest winds. Apart from the jungle vines, the *rotan*, with its strong but string-like trailing creepers with their backward pointing thorns, the primary jungle is relatively clear of undergrowth often offering less cover from the view of your enemies than might be imagined.

The heavy, near-impassable growth of bamboo thickets, thorns and sharp-edged *lalang* (grass clumps as much as twice the height of a man) forms what is called secondary jungle, growing where the tall trees have been felled. It is in this that you might unexpectedly come across a wild pig or a poisonous snake, although even these animals and reptiles keep clear of man, as do tigers unless they are old and unable to catch less dangerous eating. (One officer in later years made a hobby of catching snakes, which in Borneo made the Iban trackers, and no doubt others, wary of picking up his rucksack when he called for it.)

Each jungle tends to have its own characteristics and animal life, however. In Malaya the water buffalo could circle a man before charging him without any provocation. In Borneo wild pig were possibly the most dangerous in that they would charge a man quite fearlessly if they felt cornered, giving his position away to the enemy. The troopers were therefore given a pig-repellant of a highly poisonous paste that could be smeared near a hide to discourage these pigs.

The jungles in Malaya rise and fall on the hill contours, making for slippery, steep climbs and ankle-snagging descents among tree routes off the paths. SAS – the Malayan Scouts officially became 22 SAS in 1952 – never normally patrolled along what few jungle paths there were, for these were obvious routes to be mined or ambushed; instead they moved over untrodden ground, finding their way more often by compass and such information as aerial photographs revealed than from maps.

Chasing terrorists in such terrain, when a patrol was doing well to cover a kilometre in an hour, was made the more difficult by the terrorists' knowledge of troop movements. Information was passed back to their jungle camps by a network of spies, many of whom moved from their homes to tin-mines along the only clear tracks beside waterpipes from jungle reservoirs. Others worked in the field around defended villages. Therefore, if the British were going to catch the jungle terrorists in their bases, they would need more than foot patrols.

Yet the British infantry, Gurkha and Police Patrols matching those of 22 SAS had cut off much of the food supplies going into the jungle; they had booby-trapped caches of rice found ready for the terrorists to collect, and, with the removal of squatters from the jungle fringes, the terrorists were forced to grow much of their own food in this *ulu* by making clearings in which farming was not difficult because vegetables grow in weeks rather than months in this climate. The snag from the terrorists' point of view was that these clearings could be seen from the air, although they were far into the jungle. To reach them, however, would take foot patrols days, if not weeks.

John Cooper, one-time member of David Stirling's desert patrol, now a Captain, and Alastair MacGregor, who had served in Jellicoe's Squadron, had both joined the Malaya Scouts. They saw the possibilities, albeit hazardous ones, for the use of parachutes to land on the jungle canopy. This was a technique which relied on luck more than they would have wished, because a successful landing depended on the chance of falling into a tree with branches that held the chute. If it did, the Trooper had still to rope himself down 30m or more to the ground. Their experimental jumps carrying 30m of rope into treetops were followed up by the Scouts' Second-in-Command, Major Hugh Mercer, and by February 1952 fifty-four men had been trained in this technique, ready for the first operational jump onto the jungle canopy. They were to form the 'stop' or blocking party in the remote Belum Valley where aerial reconnaissance had shown that the terrorists were growing food.

This long mountain valley near the Thai border was to be searched by Gurkha, Commando, Police and SAS patrols. The two SAS Squadrons which made this march included a patrol led by Major Woodhouse, soon to leave for the UK. His men were on the move ten hours a day with only occasional and brief halts. The harsh sun in the open river beds which they followed at times baked their bodies and feet, after hours in the continuous damp of the jungle. They also crossed a couple of rivers on bamboo rafts quickly built with the help of the Sakai, before reaching the heart of the valley.

The blocking party had an easier approach in a Valetta aircraft, although, having jumped from only 225m, there was less than half a minute to spot and steer for a 'solid' tree. The descent by the first man out, the 'drifter' in this operation, as in other 'blind' daylight drops, showed the strength and direction of the wind near the DZ; then those following stood a better chance of landing in this case in a small, natural clearing. Sergeant Ken Kidd, the 'drifter' in this jump, smashed into branches firm enough to hold his 'chute 45m above the ground and he roped down. The others were dropped in 'sticks' of three, all landing without serious mishaps.

The foot patrols reached the terrorists' farm after five days of tough going, but the enemy had decamped, warned of the patrols' approach by the Communist agents in the few villages along the route. Nor did the men in the 'block' see any terrorists, who must have spotted the Valetta circling over the DZ. A great deal of effort had gone into the operation for the relatively small gain from the destruction of this farm.

In February 1958, when the Security Forces had nearly a decade of experience in anti-terrorist techniques, these had been improved, particularly through the close co-operation of integrated military and police headquarters down to battalion level. Informers' tips and the results of routine police observation could, therefore, quickly bring a patrol to follow up the sighting of a terrorist or for cordons to be thrown around their temporary hide-outs, when they ventured outside the jungle. These techniques had killed, captured or forced the surrender of over nine thousand Communists leaving only a hard core of two thousand activists. Nor did they have the hold they had once enjoyed over village communities, in part because these understandably now supported the authorities as clearly the winning side, but also because many must have been out of sympathy with the Communists' ruthless ways. As for the Communists, now there was no longer the chance to dominate and rule even one region, they were scattered in savage bands bent on sheer terrorism without any immediate political aim. Typical of these were two groups in the Telok Anson swamps, whose leader, Ah Hoi, had slashed with his knife the pregnant wife of a man he believed was an informer. She died, held down by his accomplices before a crowd of terrified villagers.

These terrorists, little over a day's march through rubber plantations from the Federation's capital, Kuala Lumpur, had murdered a number of estate workers, their threat causing large numbers of the Security Forces to be tied down on guard duties around the plantations, before 22 SAS put D Squadron into the swamp. Their CO, the tall, red-haired Major Harry Thompson, Royal Highland Fusiliers, planned to search this watery area, the size of central London (30km by 15), using two Troops of his 37 men to flush out Ah Hoi, while the other two Troops and his small HQ were held ready to pounce once the terrorists were found. The searchers would be secretly dropped from a Beverly to the jungle canopy five kilometres from the coastal (west) edge of the swamp, from where they would patrol eastward towards the heart of the terrorists' maze of rust-brown water, stunted mangroves and glutinous, stinking mud. (The brown stain of this water was caused by iron, to which the men attributed the fact that 'swamp life was comparatively healthy', for in their previous experience of long spells in the swamps – continuously in water all day and sleeping at night in a hammock or on an improvised raft – there had been less sickness than among jungle patrols.)

The two troops dropped as planned with food for two weeks, but Trooper Mulcahy's parachute failed to catch in the branches of the big tree he landed on; this collapsed his canopy and he crashed to the ground, breaking his back. Both patrols had then to clear a DZ for a helicopter to 'cassevac' Mulcahy, after the pilot had hovered 'one wheel on a log' over soft ground as the stretcher was loaded.

Captain (later Brigadier) Peter de la Billière then led his Troop along the line of the Tengi River on the first of ten frustratingly difficult days, when much of the Captain's inexhaustible determination would be needed. They saw signs of the enemy, but only minute signs, such as a dislodged piece of bark or a twisted leaf. A few men in the SAS, such as Sergeant Bob

Turnbull, could read these as clearly as any Iban tracker and better than many of them. (He could also fire his pump-shot gun with accuracy at a speed which made an almost continuous bang of the first few shots. A quiet Yorkshireman, he spoke fluent Malay.) The SAS patrols had themselves to travel without leaving any tell-tale signs of their passing, as they moved out in four-man teams to search for signs of their enemy.

Each day, from the steamy mists of dawn, men forced their way through stinking mud and rotting vegetation, wading sometimes neck-deep in the marsh channels, swimming open water at other times. Before nightfall they looked for somewhere to lay up, where two strong young trees were close enough to sling a hammock, or they might make a raft to sleep on if they were to use the same spot for a couple of days. During the secret stages of their search, they could not be re-supplied by helicopters, which would have revealed that some of the Security Forces were in the swamp. Within a couple of days each man smelt of bog, his rotting clothes adding to the stench, although – since he lived in it – he did not notice it, nor did his companions.

The terrorists moved upriver, and while patrols from de la Billière's Troops saw none of them, Sergeant Sandilands' men caught a glimpse of two on the eighth day. The Sergeant and a corporal then swam silently, drifting a log across open water, and were able to get a shot at these two, wounding one. Following the wounded man with caution in case he ambushed them, they found a camp six kilometres into the swamp, the radioed report of which led Thompson to put his two remaining Troops into the swamp from the east. A military and police cordon was then put around the whole area, but ten days of patient movement were needed to close this trap, and after three weeks in this mire the Troopers moving from the west were feeling the effects of being almost continuously in water. Their once close-cropped hair was now matted; legs ripped by thorns were infected and ulcerated; leeches – dropping from branches – had drained men of some blood, before a lit cigarette put an end to the painless bite, though the head left under the skin might turn sceptic.

Then the tiny figure of a sickly girl, Ah Niet, appeared at one of the checkpoints in the cordon. Swimming out of the swamp, she had brought Ah Hoi's offer of terms for his surrender: £3,500 for each of his gang and freedom for those already in prison. The reply was firm: the 'Baby-Killer', as villagers called Ah Hoi, had twenty-four hours to surrender or he would be killed in the swamp. At dusk he emerged with some of his men, carrying torches and an insolent conviction that his 'cause' would triumph in the end. Thompson was there with a Troop he had flown to this checkpoint. They went back into the swamp, following Ah Niet as she swam 300m so quietly that for months she had come and gone undetected. She was to lead them to another group ready to surrender, but her '4 foot 6 inches starved of vitamins', and no doubt with other ills beside this beri-beri, was too weak to go on. The Major therefore held his Troop at the swamp edge until, as he had no doubt expected, these terrorists also surrendered a day or two later. The Squadron had been instrumental in the capture of some ten hardcore terrorists. Ah Hoi was sent by the authorities to China, reflecting political considerations.

22 SAS would become as familiar with the politics of emerging nations as with jungle techniques, and in the six years between the unsuccessful operations in the Belum Valley and their successes in the swamp of Telok Anson many things had changed. The most significant in the field was the re-imposition of discipline, or, more correctly, self-discipline.

The Regiment, about 560 strong, had by 1956 five Squadrons, including one drawn from the Parachute Regiment, but that year the Rhodesian C Squadron had been replaced by New Zealanders. The operations of the original C Squadron had been less successful than their keenness might have achieved, had not some been prejudiced against 'natives'. The New Zealanders, like the Rhodesians, were more prone to jungle ailments than the British, which at the time was put down to their higher living standards, with daily showers at home and years of more hygienic conditions robbing them of some natural immunity to sickness.

The SAS's ability to win the support of aborigines, once the neighbourhood bullies had been eliminated, made a lasting impression on all who came to know of the Regiment's work. Their gentle strength in dealing with backward peoples' misfortunes enabled them to make friends among isolated peoples, as much one suspects, through the mutual sharing of hardships as for the invaluable intelligence gained through such friendships. Whatever the reasons, the Regiment gained recognition, with a number of senior officers of the British Army, as having an invaluable role to play in low-intensity operations. It was a far cry from the roles for which the SAS had been re-formed in 1947, although 22 SAS's highly successful operation in the Oman in 1958–9 (see Chapter 7) was a portent of the Regiment's political value, as a highly trained semi-clandestine force. Theirs was a role which could not be carried out by one of the more orthodox regiments, bound as they must be by more public arrangements for their deployments.

Two influences in the late 1950s were also shaping the Regiment's future: it was making its continuation more assured through Woodhouse's principles for selection and training; and terrorism was becoming more sophisticated and in some respects co-ordinated as it spread worldwide.

However, some years would pass before 22 SAS and its TA counterpart 21 SAS were finally established as a permanent entity, not only in the British order of battle but also in the eyes of their political masters. Meanwhile, as in other units, the Regiment's strength was reduced in the

defence cuts of the late 1950s (as shown in Appendix II). The Sabre
Squadrons of 22 SAS came to Britain for the first time in 1959 and, having
no regimental depot, were briefly based in Malvern, Worcestershire.
Before this time their training and selection had been carried out since the
early 1950s at the Airborne Forces HQ and Parachute Regiment's Depot in
Aldershot, Surrey. There, in 1952, Woodhouse ran the first selection
courses that chose men who were something more than 'average',
whatever had been the intentions of the Tactical Investigation Committee
six years earlier. The Regiment's one-time adjutant, Major Dare Newell,
Secretary of the SAS Regimental Association, in 1955 described the type of
man they were looking to recruit from serving soldiers, as 'the individualist with a sense of self-discipline . . . [he] will always fit well into a team
when team-work is required'. Selection now also involved 'psychological
tests', a term – never mind a method – hardly heard of in 1944.

Most SAS recruits in the 1980s still come from the serving British Army,
and the only ones who may join from civilian life are those who have
served in 21 SAS as Territorial Reservists. The potential recruit is, therefore, likely to be a mature man in his mid or late twenties, who knows
something of the world as well as of soldiering. They are often senior
NCOs who accept a cut in pay, as Troopers receive only the same pay as
corporals in other regiments; however, during his first year the 'senior'
will continue to enjoy his original rate of pay. All those other ranks who
are finally accepted are with the Regiment for a three-year tour, which will
be renewed until they reach retirement age, normally in their mid-forties,
unless, because of some disability, they return to their original regiment
at the end of perhaps a second or third tour with SAS.

In the changing nature of British society during the last decade, a
better-informed and wider-educated type of man was not impressed by
the insincerity of earlier methods to confuse recruits with a seductive
'Hop into the lorry, mate', when any man who took the instructor's offer
of an easy way prematurely to end a long march might be returned to his
unit for lack of determination. There is also a tendency in these days of
mobile warfare, when infantry travel in personnel carriers as often as they
march to battle, for soldiers to be less accustomed to the physical
demands of marching made on SAS patrols. Therefore the emphasis in
selection courses, not only for the SAS, was changed, and by the late
1970s the first ten days of selection courses were directed at giving
potential recruits an opportunity to improve their physical fitness and to
weed out those whose motives for volunteering stem more from mis-
placed expectations of daring-do than hard soldiering.

At this early stage they begin to discover the meticulous approach of
SAS to security: six-figure map references are remembered, never written
down; you do not fold your map conventionally, to have your target area
on top and therefore of use to an enemy who captures you, but keep it in

its original folds; nor do you move anywhere on an exercise without your rifle. If a man forgets such fundamental rules, he is ordered to do, say, twenty press-ups; an acceptable punishment that can be instantly applied and then forgotten – at least, forgotten by the NCO who gave it, but remembered by the recruit, who is unlikely to make the same punishable mistake a second time.

Officers are selected by an even more stringent screening, as befits those whose rank depends on merit not regulations and who are likely to serve terms with SAS at different times during their military career. But with only a total strength of some 750 all ranks, the prospects for senior command in the SAS are meagre. Since 1979 SAS officers do not necessarily have to pass the entrance examination before attending Staff College; this recognizes that an officer serving in some far-flung jungle does not have the opportunities for study which an officer based in Germany may have. That is not to say that SAS officers do not study – they have to – but their specialized courses are not those taught at any Staff College.

The SAS officers of World War II tended to come from what then was the relatively small educated class of university graduates and young men who had moved in the world of the professions. Today's officers are selected from a wider background. For the young SAS lieutenant, there may be a marginally extra reward, since he will be paid as a captain when commanding an SAS Troop, but he must keep himself fitter, with perhaps more exercise runs in lunch breaks, than if he had remained an infantry officer. Certainly he is likely to spend more time in undisclosed distant countries than had he continued to serve in the NATO forces. SAS officers also usually read more widely than officers in line regiments or the gunners (Royal Artillery), the Royal Corps of Transport and other Corps of the British Army from which SAS officers volunteer. So do the Troopers, with their individualistic traits of 'playing a good game of chess as he drank a bottle of scotch' or 'arrived with a book of poetry', to quote some comments from those who met them in the Falkland Islands. The reader of poetry also carried four different personal weapons, but that is another story.

Those officers and men who fail the selection course have been told that to do so is no disgrace; for SAS are at pains not to break men, as perhaps ninety per cent of all volunteers, officers and men, give up or fail the selection course. No figures are published for this failure rate, but when B Squadron was being raised in 1964, eighty of the 120 volunteers on one course dropped out at their own request. Only the best complete the testing course, which includes fourteen weeks of intensified training with firearms, including sophisticated weapons not issued to infantry soldiers. Those who pass the course are 'badged', being formally given their SAS beret and its winged-dagger badge, and will go on to more specialized courses. But for some officers and men in the Regiment, including Woodhouse, a recruit's final acceptance does not come until he has completed his first three years in SAS or distinguished himself in an operation.

The specialist courses will, for example, equip the medic, as we have seen, to perform surgery and cure tropical diseases, and yet he is a fighting soldier carrying arms like the rest of the patrol. The signaller is also much more highly skilled than his counterpart in other units. He is an expert in high-speed Morse transmissions, broadcast and received more easily than voice in the difficult areas for radio communications where mountains, distance and atmospherics make radioed speech unintelligible. Languages have always been an important study of SAS since the days in Malaya, when the NCO conversing with villagers in their own language gave them reassurance, while he could accurately interpret any information which they provided. Therefore occasionally SAS men have been withdrawn by helicopter from jungle patrols to attend a specific language course, aimed at providing linguists for the next region in which the Regiment expect that they may be required.

More general but nevertheless specialist courses prepare men for free-fall parachuting, the 'High Altitude, Low Opening' (HALO) technique for inserting patrols in a way which is difficult to detect on an enemy's radar screen; others are trained for mountain and cold-weather warfare, a third group for operations from canoes and other small boats, while a fourth group are trained in astro-navigation and techniques which parallel those of the deep-penetration raids of 1944 by jeep, or at least in one of its successors, the Land Rover.

Standard Operating Procedures (SOPs) have been laid down for the more usual situations those Troops and their patrols might meet. Yet SOPs were not immutable dictates, for by the evolution of such procedures the SAS have kept ahead of the changing nature of warfare, as it moved out of the jungles and mountains into the suburbs and towns. The procedures are wide ranging as the Regiment expect to deploy anywhere in the world, and to be operational without need to acclimatize to the extremes of weather in a particular region. The senior officers hedge their bets by keeping world affairs under constant review.

The Regiment has been based in Hereford since 1960. HQ facilities include an intelligence unit co-ordinating no doubt political as well as military intelligence, saucily called 'the Kremlin' by those in the know. There is also a signals centre which can keep in touch with units worldwide, as reports from the Falklands have shown. While one HQ group evaluates and develops new equipment, another prepares contingency plans for possible future operations, and the Training Wing runs the basic courses described earlier. There also a man's training may include safe-breaking, the use of foreign armies' weapons and more covert anti-terrorist techniques which cannot be described without needlessly putting men's lives at risk.

Senior officers commanding an operation may find that the Squadron Major attached to his forces on occasions takes orders only from the general in overall command of a campaign. This arises because a Sabre Squadron or other elements of the Regiment are usually attached to a general's headquarters in order to ensure the best use of SAS units in a particular theatre. This is a chain of command which has its critics in military circles, for there is undoubtedly a feeling that SAS 'work to Hereford' and not even to the theatre Commander. This is a misunderstanding brought about by the Sabre Squadron's direct radio links with the Hereford HQ and perhaps by SAS's enthusiasm to get into action, for – being the supreme professionals they are – they understandably enjoy exercising their talents. Yet in the days when they were less well known, the Commanding Officer of 22 SAS had to sell the idea of employing them in Borneo, because the War Office staff had not included any Squadrons of the Regiment in the force being sent there in December 1962. Yet only a few months earlier, the Director-General of Military Training had visited '22' during their advanced training in America. Impressed, he saw their potential and within eight weeks they were being re-equipped.

6. Refinements in Low-Key Tactics: Borneo 1962–6

The Regiment's new equipment in 1962 included long-distance radios. These would enable a patrol's report of significance to reach British diplomats via Hereford, in time often for political decisions to be made before British forces might be drawn inadvertently into a major battle. Such swift and direct communication could also, incidentally, give the staff at Hereford news of operations more quickly than it might by more conventional means reach the general in charge of them. In a nuclear war, the SAS's special communications would be vital in transmitting intelligence from patrols in Europe. A key role, which was seen by some officers in 1962 as having a higher priority for the Regiment than their part in low intensity brush-fire wars. Woodhouse, however, as the Commanding Officer of 22 SAS at that time opted for some Squadrons at least to be sent to Borneo, where there would be the opportunity for action after the British had met their treaty obligations when the Sultanate of Brunei, its neighbouring state of Sarawak to the west and surrounding the Sultanate, and Sabah to the east, were threatened. All three states lie along the northern coast of Borneo and had opted to join the embryo federation of mainland states, Malaysia.

There had been a revolt in the former British protectorate of Brunei and after this was quelled in December, the northern Borneo states were threatened by Indonesia. This island republic of 87 million people is the most populous state in south-east Asia stretching from Sumatra, through Java and southern Borneo (Kalimantan) across many small islands to the western half of Timor. Much of this territory had formed the Dutch East Indies until 1949. The flamboyant Indonesian President Sukarno intended to bring not only northern Borneo but also mainland Malaysia into his republic. The Brunei rising was quickly put down in December 1962 but Indonesian propaganda against the mainland Malayan States which in September 1963 became Malaysia continued to the extent that British security forces in Borneo were prudently strengthened during the early months of 1963.

Sukarno was not a Communist but made an ally of the Chinese

Communists in Borneo and used a number of his own saboteurs to infiltrate the Borneo territories. These had been trained for clandestine operations against the last Dutch territory in the islands, but in August 1962 this area of western New Guinea passed into Indonesian sovereignty, and Indonesian agents were no longer needed there. Sukarno also allowed the Communists to train potential guerrillas in Kalimantan; small groups of this clandestine Communist organization, the CCO, then infiltrated across the border into Sarawak and Sabah on their way to help the TNKU, which had organized the unsuccessful Brunei rising, as the self-styled North Kalimantan National Army. Indonesia also had at this time an efficient Marine Corps, able to infiltrate patrols across the border but hindered more than helped by the TNKU's ill-disciplined forces.

Woodhouse visited the War Office that December, offering not only his Regiment's jungle expertise but also their new long-distance communications. His arguments were persuasive: in the last days of December he was called to Borneo, to discuss with Major-General Walter Walker, the Director of Operations, ways in which SAS might help the security forces. The General's first thoughts were not what the Colonel had in mind but he offered to undertake them, knowing that things could more easily be changed when he had men in the likely battle areas. Three days after Colonel Woodhouse's arrival in Borneo, A Squadron was being flown to the Far East, where they were held at Singapore and told to acclimatize, although prepared to move straight into the jungle. Many of the Squadron were old hands at jungle warfare from the Malayan campaign, but as yet military staffs had not accepted the SAS's readiness to deploy without the usual fourteen days to get used to tropical heat – or to Arctic cold, for that matter. (This was a policy that by the early 1970s would be reflected in the screening of recruits at Hereford, through questionnaires which indicated to professional psychologists on the staff which volunteers had the ability to acclimatize quickly.)

When the Squadron reached Borneo, General Walker at first intended to use them as a mobile reserve, to be parachuted onto the jungle canopy to recapture any of the larger villages' few helicopter landing pads, should the Indonesians capture one of these. Such a role was, as Woodhouse pointed out, a waste of the talents of his men, a waste which, no doubt in the light of the Malayan experience, would have caused them unacceptably high casualties in such jumps. A much more effective role was then agreed by the General: SAS patrols could provide early warning of any incursion across the border by TNKU parties or Indonesian military forces.

This border ran for over 1,500km across the jungles and mountain ranges which in places were over 1,000m high, with much of this terrain being poorly mapped and in places not mapped at all. For A Squadron this jungle frontier would offer opportunities to achieve even greater

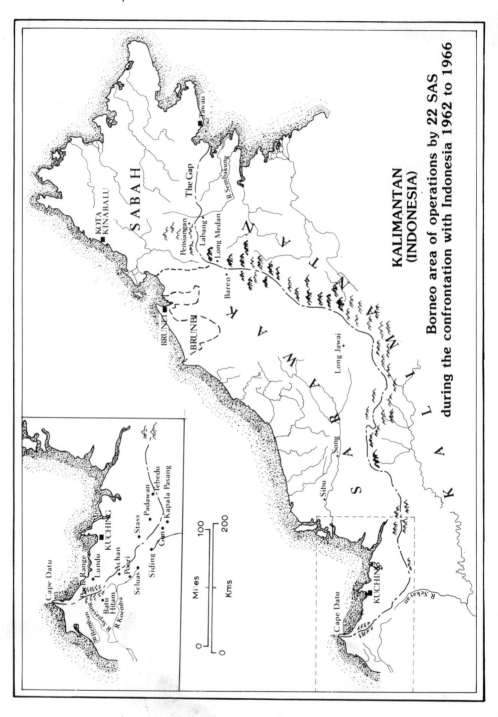

Borneo area of operations by 22 SAS during the confrontation with Indonesia 1962 to 1966

success in gathering intelligence than had been possible in Malaya, although the principles were much the same. Small SAS patrols lived in the jungle for months at a time, made friends with isolated villagers and through these close ties obtained vastly more intelligence than might be expected from four or fewer men alone covering long stretches of the border.

The four years of the campaign began with this 'battle' for hearts and minds between January 1963 and the first attack led by regular Indonesian forces who crossed the border in a small raid that April, which has come to be regarded as the beginning of the confrontation with Indonesia. Thereafter the security forces countered such aggression by cutting the intruders' line of retreat to the border, until in June 1964 the British began a series of cross-border raids in which Indonesians were harassed in their forward camps, hindering their build-up of forces before they could mount attacks. An army coup in March 1966, however, reduced President Sukarno to little more than a political figurehead, and in the uncertainties of Indonesia's intentions major cross-border operations ceased, although a few Communist and Indonesian raids continued, probably without the knowledge of the ruling generals in the Indonesian capital of Jakarta, 1,200 kilometres away in Java. The generals accepted peace terms on 11 August that year, and the Malaysian Federation remained an independent state which includes the northern Borneo Territories.

The SAS's part in this 'confrontation' is summarized in Appendix II, but three examples illustrate the nature of their different operations: hearts-and-minds, reconnaissance and a cross-border raid, although the distinctions are often blurred by the very nature of SAS patrols which have intelligence-gathering skills while possessing firepower far beyond the capabilities of ordinary soldiers. In the early days of Borneo, the Troopers' compassionate understanding of the local tribesman was their greatest strength.

Many parts of Borneo were far wilder than Malaya. Its swamps were if anything more impenetrable—those of the Koemba River were so broad and deep that at least three patrols were unable to cross them, while those of its Sentimo tributary although shallower were even longer, covering some thirty square kilometres. The early mornings, especially in these areas of swamp and near the coast, were invariably misty, the strong sun not breaking through until mid-morning, and by most afternoons heavy thunder clouds deluged the forests, their electric storms making radio communication difficult if not always impossible. A Squadron soon settled into such weather patterns and found the confusion of trackless jungle a challenge, its inhabitants living in longhouses by the rivers which flowed swiftly from the watershed ridges along the border and might rise ten metres in flood during a single night. The ubiquitous wild pigs, scorpions and snakes infested this jungle as they did in Malaya.

Major Edwards positioned his four small troops at an interval of not less than 150km along the Sabah and Sarawak border. The Squadron was below even its small established strength but, by using only two or three men in some patrols, could field a total of twenty-one such teams from the four troops. They each also covered such far-ranging areas that some did not meet others in their troop until the Squadron was withdrawn after four months.

Since 'A' was below strength in officers and men, Squadron Sergeant-Major Lawrence Smith doubled as Edwards's second-in-command. Among other duties he made the area recces a 2i/c would normally carry out, when the Squadron might be moved to a new location. In one case, looking at the prospects in Sarawak's First Division, the most westerly of the five 'counties' of that state, Smith contrived to sail with a local merchant millionaire along part of the coast of Kalimantan, finding no Indonesian activity. In 1965 he was awarded an MC, gaining this award for commissioned officers although himself a Warrant Officer, because he had performed the job of operations officer, mounting SAS patrols and liaising with army battalions, with great skill in covering a front of 500km. Several times he also personally led patrols for exacting reconnaissances or fighting raids. Smith was not the only SAS man whose responsibilities exceeded those normally undertaken for his rank: a Trooper would lead a patrol of several men if no NCOs were available. But then these Troopers were remarkable men.

Two or sometimes three men would remain in the jungle, 30km – thirty hours of jungle marching – from patrols east and west of them. Their contacts, perhaps after a brief introduction by the Troop Commander to a longhouse headman, would be established by their patience and under-standing of these primitive peoples. Land Dyaks, Muruts and Punans each had their tribal customs and way of life along the border. The Land Dyaks whom A Squadron met in February 1963 were more superstitious than most. Should the shrieking flight of a hornbill be in an unpropitious direction across a track, there would be no more hunting that day, and the hunters would return to their longhouse. This village-within-a-village might house fifteen families in such unhygienic conditions that part of the slatted floor served as a communal lavatory; its floor and the bare wooden walls on ancient timber stilts may have creaked alarmingly but bad spirits were kept at bay by the shrunken heads festooned on the doorposts that topped the entrance stairways.

These Land Dyaks have for generations kept themselves to themselves, siting their longhouses on readily defended hilltops, although more usually Borneo people live on a river bank. But those on the hills overlooking the valley leading north to Pensiangan covered one possible route for the Indonesians to reach oil-rich Brunei, here only 40km from the border.

Captain Ray England's patrols worked on this part of the border, covering these valleys and a couple of other possible entry routes across the mountains further west. Although that early spring no Indonesian invasion developed, Communist agents slipped across the border, and more than one Communist cell had malevolent influences on the few Chinese settlements in the area. The patrols therefore always moved ready for action with five metres or more between each man, closing up only in secondary jungle to keep the man ahead just in view. At this time, when Indonesian regular units had not crossed the border, the patrols used the jungle tracks: two-metre-wide trade routes with river bridges, or less frequently used paths that crossed streams on single logs.

In the early days the Troopers did not usually sleep in Dyak villages, since the Dyaks' love of gossip might unintentionally betray a patrol's presence. Therefore they visited villages but slipped away before nightfall to a jungle hide, where a typical patrol had its *bashas* with more often a waterproofed sheet than a leaf-roofed covering. Here a man cooked for himself, or they might cook in pairs, supplementing their tins of sardines or dehydrated rations with fresh meat or fish caught for the pot. Snake and monitor lizard meats were curried; monkey came to be preferred by some to wild boar. Either of these might be stunned before being killed, with its meat untainted by the virulent nerve poison shot 50m on the 10cm slim bamboo dart from a Dyak blowpipe.

As the patrols became more secure in the villagers' trust of them, and their presence was seen as protection from possible Indonesian attacks, the Troopers came to live on the edge of a village or even sometimes in the longhouses. Women would make them gifts of vegetables, and there was also rice and tapioca from the clearings nearby that were cultivated until the land was exhausted and a new jungle clearing had to be made, with the jungle reclaiming the old fields to create that thick secondary growth.

The trust in a patrol came mainly from the medic's work: his quarter of an aspirin dissolved in milk could be all that was needed to bring down a baby's fever, or a simple pill might cure a headman's raging toothache. These were far better gifts than the traditional trinkets bartered with primitive peoples for their friendship, and a good deal more sincere help. Yet a charming legacy of earlier times was the gift of beads from Punan tribesmen of the River Rejong in exchange for portable radios and other SAS favours. These encompassed Fortnum & Mason food hampers flown out at one Troop Commander's personal expense and Sergeant 'Gipsy' Smith's water-powered generator improvised with a wooden paddle-wheel in a mountain stream to power six-volt lighting in one longhouse.

All the time that patrols were making friends, they were watching and noting events. News came in village gossip as people lined up for medical treatment and later by more specific reports. The patrol also recced the country around the twenty-five or so longhouse settlements in its area, noting routes an intruding force might follow, ambush positions, potential DZs, occasionally clearing a small area for helicopter landings or secretly caching food. They learnt and noted which Dyaks might be influential in steadying the villagers if trouble came, and a few who might 'stir it'. They knew which settlements were short of salt, an important item of diet for good health in the Tropics, and encouraged the Dyaks to continue their cross-border trade in this and other products, such as wild rubber, rice and pepper.

The traders brought back news from Kalimantan. In mid-April one had seen seventy Indonesian soldiers in jungle green patrolling the headwaters of the Sekayan. Another told of twenty 'Indo' soldiers in the Kalimantan village of Kapala Pasang. A hundred were seen on the track across the border moving to Gun, where the villagers had been ordered to build two camps each for a hundred men and to improve the state of the main trading track. One difficulty was to persuade the Dyaks not to exaggerate numbers in making these reports, so the length of the queue for a morning's medical checks had at times to serve also as a guide to how many 'Indos' a trader or porter had seen.

Urgent reports were fed back to the Troop signaller, who would at times be the only man at the Troop HQ. He received messages not only from patrols but sometimes from a headman's runner, sifting what was urgent from what was routine, which could go back to the Squadron HQ with the next chopper flight. The Troop Commander was more often out with his patrols than in, say, Padawan, where Captain England based his signaller. A Squadron's CO was also away from his base for a time in March 1963 when he walked along most of the border alone, 'becoming like an animal . . . very, very alert', as he explains. He slept in 'hideyholes' which were less conspicuous than *bashas*, linking up with SAS patrols along this 1,500km route. Some villagers spoke Malay, which most headmen understood, and he relied on the generosity of villagers for much of his food. His only protection was his Armalite, although a man alone cannot continuously guard himself against attack, which is why the SAS patrolled usually with at least two men.

One patrol, led by Corporal George Stainforth, on loan to 'A' from D Squadron, was in the Long Jawai area that March and had already made reliable friends among the longhouses in the valleys hereabouts, which provided a possible route across the mountains from Kalimantan into Sarawak. His Dyak friends told him of two strangers moving through the area, enabling the Corporal to track down these intruders, whom he arrested. They later turned out to be senior organizers of the terrorists based in Indonesia. When 'A' was replaced by 'D' that May, Stainforth remained on Long Jawai and did not leave with his Squadron until August. He had been six months in the jungle and become so much a part of the villagers' lives that he was told all they knew of Indonesian activities across the hills, including the build-up of uniformed forces opposite Long Jawai valley.

The raid by thirty men led by Indonesian regulars in April had quickly penetrated three kilometres from the border on the western coastal plain of Sarawak to attack Tebedu. Therefore General Walker was expecting more infiltration by regular forces, although the few incursions that spring were made by CCO or bands of terrorists from bases in Indonesia. The movement of the largest of these, along the Indonesian side of the border, was monitored through Dyak reports to SAS patrols, and when it did cross the frontier, it was quickly captured. Many of these seventy would-be guerrillas were young Chinese enthusiasts, but there were several older Communists, including the former headmaster of a school in Brunei. This was the enemy's first major defeat since the Brunei revolt was put down, after which the security forces had seen little action, apart from isolated incidents with CCO infiltrators.

The first SAS casualties came sadly in May when a helicopter flying in bad weather to visit SAS patrols crashed, killing all nine people aboard. Such accidents emphasize that the risks in such jungle campaigns are not confined to ground patrols, for nearly as many British casualties were caused in flying accidents as by the Indonesians. But in this accident the SAS lost key personnel: the second-in-command of 22 SAS, Major R. H. D. Norman MBE, MC, an experienced Special Forces officer who had served behind the Japanese lines in 1945; Major Harry Thompson MC, who had masterminded the successful search of his Telok Anson swamps in Malaya and was due to take command of the Regiment the following year; and his signaller, Corporal 'Spud' Murphy.

General Walker had described 1963 as the year which began with the end of a revolution and ended with the beginning of a war. However, this war did not become a series of pitched battles, because Walker adopted a bold policy. He sent many of his Commonwealth military and police forces into the jungles to dominate the routes which intruders might take in crossing the border. Although the SAS Squadrons formed only a small part of this force, their intelligence gathered in 1963 made a significant contribution to final victory.

In subsequent years SAS's fighting patrols were perhaps 'pretty small beer', in the words of Colonel (later Major-General) Farrar-Hockley, one of Walker's senior staff officers, yet their knowledge of the peoples and terrain of the border was passed on to a far wider number of the Security Forces than many people realized. SAS NCOs guided Gurkha and British infantry patrols, trained Dyaks to be intelligence Scouts and filled in many blanks on the maps of Borneo which were used by other Regiments in the campaigns. Yet by the very nature of their high standards their numbers were always bound to be limited.

At Walker's prompting they were, however, to re-form B Squadron in

January 1964, and two years later formed 'G', drawn from Guardsmen who had been carrying out SAS-type patrols with the Guards' Independent Parachute Company on the central Sarawak border. 'G' was distinguishable from other SAS Squadrons only by the height of its Troopers and perhaps by the difficulties they had in picking up local dialects.

A half-squadron of the New Zealand SAS and a squadron from Australia also served in the campaign (see Appendix II), but 22 SAS pioneered the techniques and demonstrated the way in which local people could be encouraged to help the Security Forces, although this was through the Dyaks' loyalties to individuals rather than any to the Malaysian cause. But the friends passed on this information to good effect, as Walker's 'eyes and ears with a sting', as he called them, worked closely with the regular battalions in their areas. SAS patrols were also meticulous in obeying orders not to cross the border, since there was a uninformed element in the Army's headquarters which regarded SAS as likely to sting the enemy and provoke him, just for the fun of it.

Stainforth's patrol at Long Jawai, lying 50km from the border, had been left only six weeks when the village was attacked. The SAS patrol had been replaced here by a large patrol of twenty-one Border Scouts, three policemen and six men of 1/2nd Gurkha Rifles, who put up a fierce resistance when attacked by four times their number of well-equipped Indonesian troops. All but three of this security patrol were killed or captured in this dawn attack, launched after several Indonesians had infiltrated into the village two days earlier. The Dyaks had not mentioned their presence, although there seems no doubt that they would have warned Stainforth. The absence of any radio contact with 1/2nd's headquarters was put down to atmospherics, without their realizing that the two Gurkha signallers had been killed.

When the three survivors reached the headquarters four days later, the Battalion's reaction was professionally swift and effective. Gurkhas were flown to cut-off points on the Indonesian company's line of retreat to the border, where most of the intruders were killed in ambushes. But the loss of the Security Patrol highlighted the limitations of using Border Scouts in defensive rolls, although they had been trained by the Gurkhas to use their weapons in elementary infantry tactics guarding settlements. Walker decided that most of these Dyaks would be better employed gathering intelligence, and responsibility for their training was then given to SAS and the Gurkha Independent Parachute Company, who also recruited some old friends from ten years earlier in Malaya, one suspects more by knowing where they might be found than by sheer luck. Three Iban trackers, for example, old friends of D Squadron's quartermaster, Sergeant-Major Frank Williams, formed the nucleus of one Scout section, while so many other Dyaks volunteered that D Squadron had to devote most of their time to training them but continued to send a few patrols to the border. The training of these descendants of head-hunting warriors taxed even the most patient of instructors, for the Dyaks had a casual approach to loaded shotguns which they thoughtlessly might point in the direction of friend as well as foe.

The Squadrons had up to September 1963 had only makeshift head-quarters, but that month SAS took over a house lent by the Sultan of Brunei. It had a conveniently frightening ghost from the days when it was a Japanese interrogation centre, which discouraged local interest in the 'ops' room, 'COMMCEN' (communications centre) and sleeping quarters, with their added luxury of showers. The Scouts were now trained to look for signs of intruders along the border and no longer wore uniforms, making them less obviously members of the Security Forces should they meet any Indonesians. In time they would work in twos and threes with SAS patrols along the border, or themselves patrol between longhouse settlements. As the number of these Scouts increased, SAS set up several training centres elsewhere in northern Borneo, and in western Sarawak during the late summer of 1964 a selected forty Iban Dyaks were trained for cross-border operations. We shall meet them again across the border under their commander, Major John Edwards, who had commanded A Squadron.

Before this hunting began, the SAS had to search for their quarry in increasingly hostile conditions by the winter of 1963/4, as Indonesian forces were making more frequent intrusions into Sarawak and Sabah. They had also built up their forces in border camps such as those the Dyaks had reported the previous April, and their influence among these border people was growing. Gossipers might now tell the 'Indos' as much about an SAS patrol as they told its Troopers about their enemies. Therefore the patrols went back to living entirely in the jungle, often relying on their two Border Scouts for local information or visiting a longhouse for only a brief stay. At times, in the interest of good manners and better relationships, a stay might be prolonged by offers of hospitality. Then the Troopers might sit chewing the stinking *jarit* from a split bamboo filled with raw pork, salt and rice, that had been buried for a month to putrefy rather than cook by normal means. As the Trooper tried not to throw up these revolting mouthfuls, he could but wonder if an Indonesian bullet might put an end to his nausea before he had to be sick. The patrols continued, however, to use Dyaks from time to time as porters or to fell trees for a helicopter landing zones, but four of these woodcutters were killed by Indonesians, one of several incidents which made the Dyaks less co-operative than they had been.

The Security Forces had closely watched the more likely crossing points: the comparatively flat plains along stretches of Sarawak's western borders; the valley tracks leading through Stass, some 50km to the

Sarawak capital of Kuching on the coast; at Long Jawai in the 3rd Division, as we have seen; in the valleys south of Pensiangan; and on the waterways of the mangrove-lined estuaries in eastern Sabah around Kalabakan, where a company of a hundred men once infiltrated across the border without much difficulty. All these were points noted, with a military man's eye for country, by Major Edwards when he first made his long walk near the frontier. He and others also saw the possibility for small, well-trained Indonesian patrols to intrude into Sarawak and Sabah by less obvious routes. One of these he had not crossed because it lay through jungle which was uninhabited as there were few rivers. Virtually unexplored, this stretch of jungle, known as the Gap, lay east of the Pensiamgan valleys of Sabah.

In June 1943 Captain Andrew Dennison with the 'old Malay hand' Sergeant Eddie Lillico took a patrol into this jungle. His three Troopers, with three local Muruts and five constables from the Police Field Force, found only signs that some Muruts had been hunting there. These stocky, hardworking people had taken to the SAS Troopers, who could hold their own with the hard-drinking tribesmen in three-day festive sessions on *tapoi*, the rough cider of these jungles made from rice, even if they found *jarit* not to their liking.

A year later another patrol found signs of an Indo patrol in the Gap, but they came across in force further west, near Kabu in the Pensiangan valleys. Forty strong, they were probably intending to make a fighting recce since they asked one Murut where the SAS patrols might be found. He duly reported this to Sergeant Alf Gerry who then 'whistled up' a Gurkha company. Such step-up tactics, by which helicopter-borne reinforcements answered a border patrol's radio call, not only took their toll of intruders but impressed the locals with the Security Forces' ability to meet force with force, although – as mentioned earlier – it did not impress them so much that they did not continue to pass information to the Indonesians.

In the winter of 1964/5 – marked only by the calendar and not by much change in the tropical weather of Borneo – SAS patrols of B Squadron were concentrated (if that does not make them sound too thick on the ground) in western Sarawak. There, south of the border, were the headwaters of the Koemba River flowing into Indonesian territory and the Sekayan, which would be the backdrop to aggressive patrols described later. Ninety kilometres to the west lies the Pueh Range, high hills with a peak of 1,500m and a favourite route in 1964 for CCO agents infiltrating through the jungle to reach Lundu, where the police Special Branch knew a number of Communist cells were active.

Corporal Bigglestone with three men was sent over this range in 1964 to find a CCO forward base used by terrorists being infiltrated from Kalimantan and called – the Special Branch understood – Batu Hitam (Black

Rock). On striking west from the border which ran north-south along the mountain ridge, the patrol left the infantry platoon which had provided an escort as far as the border, and moved into Indonesian jungle where they could as easily be ambushed as ambush an Indo patrol. Since they had to avoid villages and any contact with local people, they carried in their Bergens all that they might need for at least two weeks in the jungle, but they were not allowed to carry more than 22kg since an excessively heavy Bergen rucksack in tropical heat could overtax the strength of even an SAS Trooper. He wore a long-sleeved bush shirt and slacks tucked into his gaiters above army boots, which had moulded composition soles, cunningly re-cut to leave the pattern of an Indonesian, not a British, footprint on the jungle floor. The rest of his rig was clearly British; only in the early months of the campaign had there been any attempts to dress Troopers as civilians, which proves an impractical disguise if you are carrying an Armalite, never mind the strange appearance of men in jeans tailored for the smaller figures of a shop's local customers. Most men wore a soft, long, peaked, close-fitting cap or the 'floppy' hat that was standard army issue; only a yellow band sewn in the lining would be a recognition sign to friendly forces, when the hat was put on inside out. Their rations would provide only 3,500 calories a day, or as little as two thousand for those who chose to make the standard fourteen-day pack last for twenty-one days, to save weight in their Bergen. Yet to stay fully fit on such active patrolling a man needs five thousand calories a day.

They lay up each night, their *bashas* hidden in the jungle, and turned to long before dawn, packing away the parachute-silk sleeping-bags, which gave little warmth on the high mountain range which could be surprisingly cold at night. All signs of their overnight bivvy were carefully removed; even tree branches that had been disturbed were pushed back into natural positions. They would march for an hour before breakfast; that the corporal allowed them to brew tea for this meal seems unlikely: they would get by with a biscuit and half a tin of sardines washed down with a drink of water. This would be purified by dissolving a couple of tablets in water from a pool or by drawing it from a fast-flowing mountain stream, for, despite the abundance of water, all manner of debilitating 'bugs' infested any slow-moving stream. For lunch a man might have a few more biscuits and a tin of cheese, keeping the meatier items in his ration pack for supper just before nightfall. There would be no cooking on this patrol: you were safer, if cold and hungry, not attracting the attention of a Dyak hunter, if not an Indonesian patrol, to the smells of cooking.

When they halted for a break on the march, the men sat on their Bergens, cradling their rifles as alert as ever. If they talked, it was only to exchange brief sentences in a whisper, while the corporal rechecked his route, although he had marched most of the time with his compass in his hand. The lead scout, who always has the most exacting job, calling for continuous concentration on any patrol, might pass over the repeater shotgun to the Trooper who would take the lead on the next leg. As they moved further west, he needed to be alert to a chance meeting with a Dyak, for they came out of the wilder forests towards the settlements along the Sempayang River where there were many paddyfields, for growing rice hereabouts in traditional watery beds. These crops of seedlings, which would not be harvested until April, gave no cover, and the patrol kept mainly to a jungle-covered spur from which there was a view of the river.

The one Dyak they met, from whom the corporal got no worthwhile information, was obviously terrified. He was so insistent that Batu Hitam should be avoided that there was clearly some mystery about it, but all that the patrol found was a longhouse at the location they had been given, with no sign of an enemy camp. Other patrols from B Squadron continued the search, one spending ten days on the jungle-covered spur from which they could watch the river and a trading track beyond it. This ran northwards to the village of Bemban and was seen to be the supply route to an Indo camp, but apart from indications that these troops had been in the forests they saw only a couple of soldiers.

Edwards' Cross Border Scouts also searched in these jungles for the terrorist camp. He would take thirty men across the border and set up a forward base, from which Lance-Corporal Jim Penny and Trooper Dave Abbott led some patrols. The Ibans did not know this country and were as apt as the Troopers to find themselves in difficult swamp near the river, but in February they found many footprints, confirming that one part of the jungle had been used by the Indonesians or the CCO for training. Later that year two SAS patrols mapped part of the area but saw no one fifteen kilometres north of Bigglestone's longhouse at Batu Hitam. Other patrols from A Squadron failed to find the CCO in the late spring, even though a defector tried to point out the route from the border. But that May an Army unit successfully sprang two ambushes in which thirty-two Indos from Bemban were killed.

The Indonesian base near Bemban continued to be watched discreetly by Edwards' Scouts, who had some success, in part because his Scouts provided good intelligence, information that confirmed there was a CCO staging camp on the route to Batu Hitam. He had personally led patrols but – to get ahead of the chronology of our story – was later forbidden to do so because of his detailed knowledge of British intelligence. He had moved his base in the summer of 1965 to a longhouse built on a lonely part of the coast, easier to re-supply secretly from the sea than to risk overland portage. From this 'island', as it was known, his Scout patrols were at times led by SAS Troopers, although at times they were not strictly supposed to cross the border when diplomatic initiatives limited British offensives.

SAS Land Rovers patrolled the Arabian deserts in the 1960s

The barren mountains of Southern Arabia where the SAS perfected
their survival and ambush techniques

Dropping mail to a patrol from
A Squadron in the Oman

Signallers of A Squadron HQ on night duty ready to receive radio
reports from patrols in the Oman desert

Members of SAS Mountain Troops fought in the Antarctic regions bordering the South Atlantic in 1982

A 1970s Land Rover equipped for patrols in Europe with single General Purpose Machine-Guns (GPMGs) firing forward and to the rear

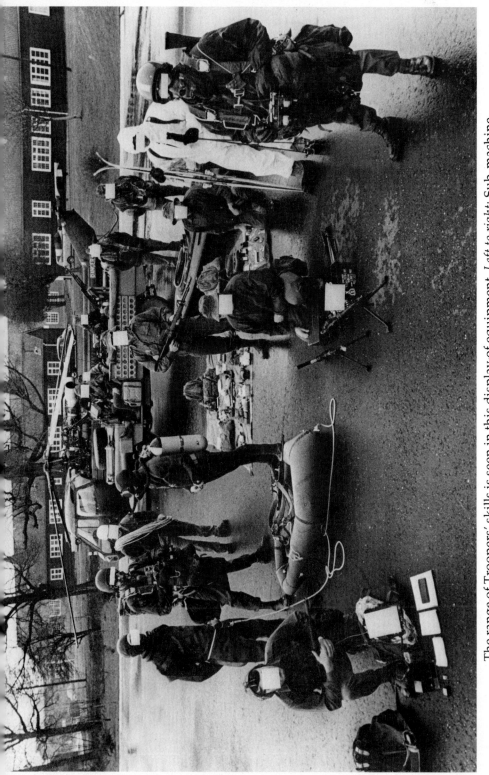

The range of Troopers' skills is seen in this display of equipment. *Left to right:* Sub-machine-gunner equipped for urban warfare. Swimmers and divers of Boat Troop with inflatable. Parachutist with leg bag. Mountain trooper with white snow camouflage helmet. Land Rover crew. Scout helicopter for recces. In front of the canoe team men in tropical rig. Mountain

Trooper equipped for free-fall parachuting with oxygen for breathing at high altitude and altimeter

A climber of Mountain Troop with his small ice-axe, two karabiners, climbing rope and Self Loading Rifle

Troopers demonstrating belt equipment

A Trooper's belt pouch with its animal snares and dried rations, signal panel, altimeter and tool kit, fish hooks, lock-picking tools and saw blades will enable him to survive without a normal issue of rations

Troopers firing the 84mm Carl Gustav anti-tank weapon, a man-packed defence against armoured vehicles

Camouflage, stealth and speed are the hallmarks of successful SAS patrols

Fast moving shadowy figures, men of the SAS

One SAS-led patrol successfully ambushed a Chinese party on the mountain ten kilometres west of the Bemban. Other patrols found all manner of activity but mainly military not Communist forces: one Indo platoon withdrew before it could be cut off; a fort with mortar pits and well-sited defences was found unoccupied; and in September a co-ordinated search mounted by twelve four-man patrols of A Squadron took three weeks to comb the area between the headwaters of the Bemban and Sempayang Rivers. De la Billière, who commanded 'A', co-ordinated this search on the ground, his Tactical HQ of four including his Squadron Sergeant-Major, moving as any other patrol did because Indonesian military forces were in the area. He redirected their routes in the light of reports on Indonesian activity, but the CCO camp eluded them. In September B Squadron waited a hundred strong in an ambush but were attacked by an Indo platoon on the Bemban track. The SAS had no casualties but killed at least eleven Indonesians before making a quick withdrawal. But the CCO camp was never found.

The decision to carry out cross-border operations had not been made lightly, because their implications in widening the conflict could have had unfortunate diplomatic repercussions. Therefore, when General Walker got clearance in June 1964 to carry a limited war up to 3,000m across the border, his senior Malayan staff officers were not told. The first of these 'Claret' raids, based on intelligence provided by SAS and their friends – whose headman had enjoyed electric light in his longhouse from an improvised 'gennie' – gave details of the Indo camp at Nantakor, south of Pensiangan. The Company of 1/2nd Gurkhas therefore knew, for instance, that the approach tracks were mined and that outlying machine-gun positions gave depth to the camp defences. They planned accordingly, and helicopters carried the company forward to LZs chosen by Phil Smith, as being not too close to the border to betray unusual activity, for they had to be large enough to land the company and quickly clear it on its way. Smith was not allowed to go on this raid, because an SAS prisoner would no doubt have been too political a capture for the Indonesians. (Other Troops, even Gurkhas, might successfully claim that they had crossed the border by mistake.) In the event, the Company was led by two Dyak Scouts who worked with Smith. The attack was completely success-ful. Although the Indonesians fought well, their Commander and five others were killed, after which the remaining twenty or so men extricated themselves from the battle, no mean feat, and withdrew down the valley.

SAS patrols would later cross the border (see Appendix II) but the experience could be nerve-rackingly frustrating on many occasions. Typical of this were the attempts to reach the Koemba River which ran for five kilometres parallel to the border of western Sarawak. This border from Cape Datu in the north crossed the coastal plain where Gurkha and

Royal Marines of the SBS patrolled across the border from time to time. It then ran north-south along the Pueh Range and turned south-eastward across the flat lands north of the Sentimo marshes. The Sarawak border then ran across trading tracks leading to Stass; the only major routes crossing the border for the next 50km of frontier ran along mountain ridges north of the Koemba and further eastward parallel to the Sentimo, before swinging north-east beyond Tebedu. In 1964 the obvious, if not easy, crossing for any Indonesian invasion was still through Stass and on to the Sarawak capital of Kuching with its population of 56,000.

SAS patrols in 1964 and the early months of 1965 had reached the edge of the Sentimo marshes and the headwaters of the Koemba but had been unable to penetrate the marshes north of this river. In February 1965 Sergeant D. ('Lofty') Large had spent over a week with his patrol trying to reach the upper part of this river from the mountain plateau separating it from the Sentimo. He found the western edge of the plateau's sheer cliffs offered no possible routes to the jungle 250m below the plateau. (Don Large, 6 foot 4 inches of gentle giant from Oxfordshire, was thirty-four and had been wounded when with the Gloucestershire Regiment in their epic battle on the Injon River in Korea, after which surgeons had needed four years to repair his paralysed arm. He felt the hunger of meagre rations more keenly than most, swapping cigarettes on his patrol for some spoonfuls of rice!) On their return across the border they had what might have been a tragic confrontation at the RV with a Guards' Patrol; then a second SAS patrol and the Guards' Dyak Scouts met unexpectedly at this RV. In a split second Large intervened to save any 'own goals', as he leapt from cover by the jungle path.

His and other patrols had been probing along the frontier to find access to these river lines-of-communication, which, if attacked – like the desert roads of North Africa – would have to be guarded, reducing the Indonesian strength from their Division available to cross the border near Stass and further east. However, to reach the rivers needed deeper penetration than 'Claret' raids had been allowed, and this range was increased to six kilometres in September 1964 and ten that December after General Walker had proved the need for such pre-emptive actions.

He left Borneo in the spring of 1965, expressing his tribute to SAS in saying that he regarded a Squadron (seventy men) from 22 SAS as being worth ten times their number of infantry. He was succeeded by Major-General George Lea, who as a Lieutenant-Colonel had commanded 22 SAS in Malaya in the mid 1950s. Lea made few changes to Walker's policies, but a small SAS command cell was set up in the theatre HQ on Labuan Island through which the new Director of Operations' staff could co-ordinate more readily the operations which he required to fit into the overall plan.

This scheme of operations in 1965 was aimed at preventing any

Indonesian occupation of a part of Sarawak or Sabah, but they were not expected to attempt a full-scale invasion because of diplomatic activity at the United Nations and the Malaysian government's negotiations to defuse the threat of all-out war. These negotiations also precluded at this time any major operation in company strength across the border, although a distinction was made between actions against the regular forces of Indonesia and the CCO. The Indonesians would quit when a political settlement was reached, while the Communists could be expected to continue their terrorism. Therefore, in the spring of 1965, while the search was continued for their Batu Hitam camp, no offensive action at all was being taken against the Indonesians opposite Stass. It was what SAS called 'a be kind to "Indos" period', one of the frustrating enforced lulls in local conflicts which can make them all the more difficult to bring to a military conclusion.

There seemed little point, however, in merely continuing the stalemate, and Lieutenant-Colonel M. (Mike) Wingate-Gray, commanding 22 SAS since the previous January (1965), used one of his visits to Borneo to persuade Lea – one doubts that he needed much persuading – that a few SAS attacks would be insufficient mayhem to cause diplomatic repercussions, yet would force the Indonesians to take account in any future plans of the need to deploy troops to protect their lines-of-communication. Patrols were, therefore, allowed to take offensive action on the last two days of a reconnaissance, provided that they were reasonably assured of success and certain that no incriminating pieces of evidence – including dead Troopers – were left behind. Actions in the Oman (see Chapter 7) had proved to diplomats that SAS could operate under such restricting conditions.

In Borneo the outcome was first seen that April, when Corporal Carter's patrol, having spent six days watching craft go up river towards Siding on the upper Koemba, shot two men and killed a third with grenades, as these soldiers paddled downstream. The Indonesians were armed but could not avoid the ambush from the jungle river bank. Large took in a patrol again which this time reached the upper river but could not find the expected Indo camp in this area.

On 9 May he made the final preparations for his patrol of D Squadron to make an attempt at reaching the Koemba near Poeri. Here the Indonesians were believed to have one of their main staging points for men and supplies going eastward to Seluas, a sizeable trading settlement where the Indonesian Division probably had its base. Six other patrols had attempted to reach specific points on the river near Poeri, but failed because the riverside marshes had proved too deep. Therefore Large was given his own choice of exactly where he might set up a river watch and cause a little mayhem near this town. He studied aerial photographs – not only foot patrols crossed the border, it seems – and found a spur of the low border hills pointed towards a broad bend in the river, a finger of dry ground which might reach the river, although it appeared to peter out a kilometre short of the bank.

His patrol – the No. 2 Pete Schooley, Paddy Millikin, the Signaller, and Kevin Walsh – checked their weapons and drew ammunition. This was limited to the amount they could comfortably carry in view of the fact that they did not intend to engage in any fire fights. Each man packed in his Bergen the clothing he considered essential for this patrol and his basic rations: oatmeal blocks, sardines, Oxo, small tins of cheese, biscuits, a little sugar, tea or coffee, milk in a tube, and twenty-four blocks of dehydrated meat – in all weighing less than half a kilogram for each day's meals. With these would be the little extras he personally preferred to add taste to the basic rations, such as curry powder, and cigarettes for the smokers, sweets for others; all men carried a piece of strong nylon cord, and most still carried a parachute silk sleeping-bag and a poncho to keep out the worst of the rain. Many patrols also took a camera, for photographs of likely interest to military intelligence, who could study a snap view at leisure.

The patrol also carried a large, empty waterbag, which they filled each evening, purifying the water with tablets when necessary, before carrying it away from the stream. (Since streams were obvious camp-sites, a patrol almost invariably made its hides some way from water.) Millikin had the heaviest load, and his rations were carried by the others, because besides the radio and spare battery, its aerials and the code books, he also carried on his belt the Sabre radio beacon. Helicopters could home in on this once the patrol was back across the border.

Large had been briefed at West Brigade's HQ, where as a trained aerial photograph reader he had been able, with the help of the Brigade's own specialist in this art, to spot that spur and other features that were equally obscure. His Squadron Commander, the neat Major Roger Woodiwise, had outflanked the billeting arrangements – hotel bills mounted and other quarters might be less expensive – with the result that his men lived in a Chinese merchant's house rented by the Army, while some other troops lived in converted warehouses and similar less homely surroundings. The Major, a soldiers' soldier highly thought of by his men, would follow the progress of the patrol with more than professional interest because he, like most SAS officers, was very close to them. But there was no fuss as they were driven from the Chinese house to Kuching's airfield and flown in twenty minutes by Twin Pioneer to Lundu. There a Whirlwind, its helicopter blades already turning, lifted them to an LZ near the border. That any Chinese Communist might have spotted that these four were something different to the normal run of reinforcements and replacements moving up to the border battalions seems unlikely, but the shorter time that they were in Lundu, the better their security.

From the LZ they moved off into the *ulu* that Tuesday (10 May 1965), along the first leg of the route that Large had chosen. This would take them roughly due south – the Sergeant knew the exact compass bearings – and several days later due west to strike the finger spur. They prepared to lay up this Tuesday night before dark, as was the usual practice, Large giving Millikin the evening's brief report which the signaller encoded before dark and transmitted to the Squadron HQ.

They moved on at first light next morning, Large acting as his own scout, followed by Schooley, a bright and usually cheerful man who had been in Borneo only ten weeks but had already been on patrols with Large. Each man on this patrol carried an SLR, for its hitting power was more likely to damage river craft than high-velocity lighter bullets from an Armalite. Millikin carried one, as SAS Signallers must be part of a patrol's 'sting' in action, following Schooley at an appropriate distance. The signaller came from Ireland and was regarded by Large as one of the best radio operators in the Regiment, having a Celtic intuition which some call 'second sight'. Kevin Walsh covered the rear of the patrol; a tough, down-to-earth soldier who had served six years with the Paras before joining SAS, he was exceptionally proficient even for an SAS Trooper; now he checked every few minutes that no Indonesians were stalking the patrol, for they were known to have men in this jungle.

Large was, therefore, quick to motion silently with his hand to stop his men when the distinctive noise of axe blows echoed through the trees. He slipped out of his Bergen and slid forward to investigate the woodman. At twenty metres from the sound of the axe blows, he could see a few Indonesian soldiers at work and heard more, perhaps a platoon in all, making jungle shelters. Large tracked quietly back to his men and led them in a wide detour, avoiding the clearer passages through primary jungle, edging their way noiselessly through chest-high tropical ferns and broad-leafed undergrowth – time-consuming work in which Walsh made sure that no signs of their passing, no awkwardly bent fern stems or upside-down leaves, might be noticed by any patrol from that Indo platoon. Thus it took all Wednesday to cover perhaps five kilometres towards their objective.

Next day they reached a broad track, running north-west from Poeri and no doubt used regularly by soldiers going to Achan. The Sergeant recognized it, for faint blurs – not as casually spotted on his map cover as anyone else might think – were reminders he alone understood. (SAS do not, as we have seen, make obvious even which 'fold' of a map they are using, and so do not plaster it with the bright chinagraph symbols the military usually rely on to indicate key points.)

They moved swiftly once they saw this track was clear and vanished again into the *ulu*. On Friday, Day 4 of the patrol, they came on a recently cleared track running compass-true parallel to the river – so straight, indeed, that it would not only give a cut-off party a quick route to some border ambush but itself provide a swathing lane of fire for Indo machine-guns. Again they crossed unnoticed, although, having passed such a clearing, there was always the nagging thought that some unseen OP had spotted them and that, even as they moved on, two observers had radioed in patrols to block both their advance and retreat.

— But no patrols appeared, nor, Large realized, were they likely to do so ahead of him, for the swamp began here, north-east of the river bend. Knee-deep at first, they were able to push on towards the finger-pointing spur, until in the early afternoon the water became too deep to cross, with 22kg of Bergen and 5kg of loaded SLR. Palm leaves floated on the swamp and lay on small islands of firm ground. Green-hard, they split with a loud crack if stepped on, and even as they were pushed gently aside in the water, they could split with what seemed in the stillness a very loud noise. Yet the small islands enabled Large to dump the Bergens, so that he and Schooley could swim forward, feeling their way westward. Now, as Large freely admitted later, they were in a frightening position. They had only one spare magazine apiece, their *parangs* (machetes) and their escape kit, for survival if they could not find their way back through this tangle of rank vegetation to their Bergens.

As he and Schooley waded forward, the Trooper always distanced himself from the Sergeant, so they were unlikely to be killed by a single burst of fire, as the water swished past them, leaving a tell-tale trail across the surface scum. Was an Indo gunner just waiting for them to get another five metres closer? The man who casually dismissed such thoughts would risk all in careless movement. Large knew the risks and conquered his fears, giving all his concentration to his compass – almost all, for part was needed to be sure each footing in the tangle of roots under water was reasonably secure. Break an ankle here, and there would be problems. Schooley, following his Sergeant, found time to see slimy marsh bugs with their many legs scamper across the weed-covered surface. He hoped, he whispered to Large, that they were both the 'goodies' in this scenario, because they always survived to the end of the film, a whispered gentle joke that eased Large's tension. How valuable a man with the right sense of humour can be in any crisis. As it was, that Friday night was grim enough as they bivouacked on a tiny island, not using hammocks so that they physically kept a low profile, and no cooking: the dry meat blocks must have been particularly unsatisfying for that main meal.

They spent Saturday and most of Sunday in the swamp, hearing from time to time the heavy throb of diesel engines of large launches, which they guessed were in the main channel. Yet they could see nothing beyond the green wall of tall plants which they could not break through because the water was too deep. Finally, Large decided to backtrack north-east to the firm ground where they had bivvied on Sunday night.

Next morning they swapped ideas, in the sensible way SAS NCOs and officers have of pooling the suggestions of Troopers on a patrol in what they called 'a Chinese parliament'. Out of this came the simple plan to continue westward but as close to the river as was practical.

They had gone some way, waist deep in river water, when a large boat (by the sound of its engine) swished by close to the swamp edge. Its wash lifted the flotsam of leaves so high that Walsh was submerged, but not his rifle, for they held their SLRs high over their heads when in deep water, a punishing test of physical endurance when you have been wading for hours. Large now changed direction to head into the swamp in case they might accidentally break out into the river just as a boat was passing silently downstream on the current. The change of direction was, however, a lucky break, for they came onto firm ground. Without doubt this was the fingertip of that spur.

Large took in the scene as they stood on the edge of narrow strip of jungle, looking at the broad sweep of the river bend through the well-spaced trees of a rubber plantation. On his left the strip continued to the river bank, an obvious OP; in the centre a large tree spread its branches above scrub and a bit of a ditch, but with open ground surrounding both – as open as it was to his right, where the plantation's ranks of trees spread along the river bank. These were, he could see, being rested, with no sign of recent tappings, although there were well-used paths through this rubber plantation. He plumped for the lone tree and its scrub-covered ditch; this was no place to hang about, however, and having made as sure as he could that no one was about, he put the patrol into this scrub.

They had not been there overlong, with two on lookout and two resting hidden in the ditch, when the first launch chugged past, crewed by six Dyaks. Two soldiers idly watched the banks and protected the tarpaulined cargo amidships from any thieving hands. The boat flew a red and white ensign – later they discovered that this must have been the Indonesian flag. No other military traffic passed that afternoon, and after nightfall they were able to fill a waterbag. Next morning there was a scare: two soldiers were paddling straight for the tree – a diversion move, perhaps, for an attack across the open ground behind? Large took no chances, and they took up firing positions without so much as shaking the scrub, ready for all-round defence. Then the tension eased: the soldiers emptied a fishtrap and went back down river.

Throughout that Tuesday they watched the waterway, logging the traffic. A stores launch passed and a little local traffic in the morning; in the afternoon a river-cruising yacht approached. She made a grand target, but fears of diplomatic incidents if they sank a senior civilian official rather than a military general discouraged a fleeting impulse to fire at her. As the yacht passed at fifteen metres, since the main channel swept near their OP, they could not be mistaken: a girl in a white sun-suit stepped out of the deckhouse. The yacht was followed twenty minutes later by a launch with seven soldiers relaxing under its fixed canopy. The patrol logged its passing. Their records had begun to show the pattern of river traffic.

That evening Large radioed for permission to fire on any suitable target next day and received approval early next morning. Soon after Millikin decoded this signal, two soldiers passed in a canoe and might have been snatched as useful prisoners, but sinking a launch would be more effective. Its loss might frighten the river community into not co-operating with the Indonesians, the other side of the hearts-and-minds coin. A sizeable craft for this river, about ten metres long, passed going swiftly downstream with the current pushing her along, but in the next five hours only the usual small boats passed the OP, although some carried a couple of soldiers. Then, just as the afternoon rains darkened the sky, a big launch came up river through the downpour.

Large had rehearsed his men in a plan which allowed their target launch – not necessarily the *Ark Royal*, which Walsh impatiently sug-gested the Sergeant was waiting for – to pass the OP. They would then fire on her in the fashion of the master gunners of an earlier age: raking her from stem to stern. This would guarantee the maximum kills as the SLR bullets smashed through the length of the craft, leaving its troops only the narrowest of fronts, the width of her stern, from which to return this fire. As she passed the OP in the steamy heat, the rain was lashing down so hard that the drops bounced off the river and her deckhouse roof. The canvas side screens were closed against this weather, but Large estimated she would be carrying as many men or stores as would be carried by a four-ton truck.

Walsh and Millikin came up from the ditch and spaced themselves three metres apart, with Trooper Schooley, while Sergeant Large moved to direct the battle from the left, on slightly lower ground. From there he had a clear view of the river bend as it swung to the right, up river. He fired the first round, which was the signal to the others to open fire at the stern of the launch. Walsh and Millikin hammered away at the transom's waterline, but Schooley's rifle jammed. He had not been issued with his own SLR for some reason and had complained – had 'honked', as SAS would say – about it. Now he cleared the stoppage in seconds, for, if another craft appeared, they would need all the firepower they could muster. In thirty seconds Walsh and Millikin had each put the twenty rounds into the launch, one magazine full, as Large had ordered. He had added ten rounds and Schooley had fired half a magazine before the Sergeant called 'Stop!' All four immediately reloaded, as was the standard drill, with a full magazine, for they might need twenty shots in the next immediate action, and Schooley did not want to be caught with only ten.

The launch had begun to list, men jumping over the side as they pushed aside the canvas screens. Smoke hung low in the heavy rain as it spread from beneath these screens. Large did not wait to watch the total effect but waved Walsh and Millikin to withdraw: they made a dash for the rubber trees, as the other two watched the river and peered into the rain to check that no enemy patrols were along the bank. Then, as the first two covered them, ready to fire if any Indonesians appeared, Large and Schooley ran for the trees. Suddenly Large darted back to the ditch; Schooley, fearful that the Sergeant had seen enemy riflemen in the plantations, followed him. But he had not seen the enemy but had gone back to retrieve the water-bag. They had a long way to go – or he did not want to leave incriminating evidence behind – or, the most likely, he just did not want to leave it for the Indos.

As they moved back into the strip of jungle beyond the rubber, they saw the flare of an explosion through the mist-heavy rain, and the launch rolled onto its side. Speed was of the essence now, but as Large led them along at a fast walk, each man still distanced from the one ahead, a king cobra suddenly reared its dinner-plate-sized hood in fright, ready to strike at Large's chest. He was quicker and had his SLR's foresight at its head before he froze motionless. To fire might give away his patrol's exact position, as Schooley knew five metres back as he aimed his rifle at the 'great, dirty yellow head'. A shot would certainly confuse the other two, who could not see the snake and might take evasive action, thinking an Indonesian patrol was ahead. But the snake, having no cause to strike the rock-still Sergeant, eventually retracted its hood before sliding away behind a log.

They could still smell the burning launch, a kilometre from the river, as they hurried on. Before dusk they had crossed the fire-lane track, and Large decided that they should lay up. The headlong dash ceased abruptly, for turning to the right off their route they moved without leaving any trace as they went into a thick patch of jungle. One man was left as the sentry between their old route and this jungle hide, just in case anyone tried to follow them. But there was no sign of the enemy, although sounds of distant mortaring suggested that they were searching elsewhere. No doubt what the Indonesians intended them to think, for they knew all the tricks. Once, as an SAS patrol was avoiding two enemy sections which had fired several times indiscriminately, the leading Trooper had caught a glimpse of a third section moving silently in the gap between the others.

On this Wednesday night – so much had happened in one day – Large allowed them to eat extra rations, as they were within a day's march of the border. They had been out for little more than a week but had carried enough for two; therefore they buried what they did not need, to lighten their loads on the last leg. This brought them next morning to a point on the border different from the one through which they had entered

Indonesian territory. Here the low hills, with no clear contour lines or outstanding features, made navigation especially difficult. And they were all feeling the effects of the speed at which they had made their withdrawal. Millikin, in particular, was showing signs of distress but would not let anyone else carry the radio: he was, as he stressed, the only one who could use it quickly in an emergency.

Late that afternoon, Day 10 of the patrol, Large was not certain of his navigation and told Millikin to radio for a chopper, as its pilot could then home-in on the Sabre and fix their position relative to the LZ. The pilot, intent on doing more than just fixing their position when he arrived overhead, lowered his winch wire with two harnesses attached, the 40m from the treetops. They piled the Bergens into one, and Schooley climbed into the second, before the wire was reeled in. The harnesses jarred against the winch coming up with such a jolt that the harness full of Bergens came loose, hurtling to the ground, leaving Schooley hanging in horror on the second one. But, as they were only 200m from the LZ, twenty minutes of jungle walking, two by chopper, Schooley was safely lowered on landing. That Tuesday night the patrol was debriefed in Kuching, and later 'Lofty' Large was awarded a Mention-in-Despatches.

Other patrols went to the bend in the Koemba River: one from 'A' found impenetrable swamps west of Large's OP; another photographed the fire-lane track before Indonesian patrols forced it to withdraw. Large's success had forced the Indonesians to step up their patrolling and improve their defences, before 'Claret' raids across the border were intensified in July, to underline Britain's continuing support for Malaysia when there were some who doubted whether the British still had the will to support her ally.

Major de la Billière brought A Squadron back to Borneo to take over from 'D' in late May. He had commanded it since the spring of 1964, taking over from John Edwards, and like him had walked long stretches of the border. That year he had introduced closer co-ordination of the Squadron's patrols with border-based battalions, putting in a senior NCO with the tact and self-assurance to advise battalion Colonels of SAS abilities and limitations. He had made improvements in the organization for supplying patrols in the field, and his prodigious capacity for hard work – he lived in the 'ops' room without a day or a night off when patrols were out – enabled him to know what was happening, the moment that reports were radioed to his HQ. When expedient, he led the Squadron in the field, as we have seen, showing that practical ability which he melded with a capacity to delegate and organize and which led ultimately to his appointment as the most senior officer serving with SAS, its Brigadier.

When he was commanding 'A' in the August 1965, he worked closely with the CO of 2/2nd Gurkhas, Lieutenant-Colonel 'Nick' Neill, in a series of cross-border operations. On one occasion, the Major took 1 and 3

Troops with his TAC HQ patrol to the headwaters of the Koemba, three days before two of the Gurkha Companies followed them separately but in force without attempting any secrecy. However, unseasonable rains and the loss of radio contact between de la Billière's HQ and 3 Troop made this 'Claret' raid a wash-out in more than one sense, although the Gurkhas ambushed some small craft and, having made their presence known, the British intention to continue supporting Malaysia was unmistakably clear. 2/2nd made other forays into areas west and south of Stass, for which SAS patrols provided detailed intelligence of Indonesian camps.

SAS raids in Borneo usually involved reconnaissance and/or ambushes, but there were several mounted with variations on these fundamental themes. One patrol trained vigorously – over-vigorously some might say! – to snatch a prisoner, with practical runs that bruised their victims in realistic rehearsals. Another patrol tapped an Indonesian telephone line fifteen kilometres across the border, bringing back the taped conversations recorded over five days. They were nearly caught, however, by a skilful Indonesian interception, the Troopers only getting back across the border because they moved too swiftly for the Indonesian paras, as they put in an attack on the eavesdroppers.

In one raid, mounted to snatch documents from a specific hut across the border, the SAS patrol became involved in a dawn skirmish but brought back those Chinese scripts, which apparently were of particular interest to the Special Branch. Quite a different operation was set up when there were too few patrols to cover a wide area of Sabah's uninhabited jungle: a series of minefields were laid, any one of which could warn of an incursion. The fact that none was triggered by the enemy was significant in itself, as it proved they had not intruded along these jungle routes. Had they done so, there is no doubt that these eight death-traps would have blasted a warning of their presence, for dish-like plates of 'Claymore' mines, each studded with ballbearings, were cleverly sighted chest-high on trees. Camouflaged from view but not obstructed by branches, a group of 'Claymores' would normally have killed all who were within twenty metres of them, but for good measure there were also grenades linked into the circuit of instantaneous fuse, which set off the group once the tripwire was touched. Setting these wires was an art in itself, for they had to be not only hidden but also positioned where a wild pig or other animal was unlikely to set off the minefield.

Plans were sketched for carrying the undeclared war deeper into Indonesian territory, should this prove necessary, but the confrontation eased after a military government replaced Sukarno in March 1966, and a treaty was concluded between Malaysia and Indonesia the following August. This ended an undeclared war which had lasted nearly four years, killed 114 Commonwealth soldiers (including seven of 22 SAS) and caused the death of over five times as many Indonesians. A decade later there was no ill-feeling between Indonesian paras and SAS (as is the way of battlefield soldiers), and the owner of that yacht with its girl passenger so nearly sunk by Large visited SAS headquarters. He had not known as he sailed up the Koemba River how close he had been to death, although at the time he commanded the Indonesian Parachute Regiment.

Confrontation in Borneo had shown the value of SAS in those difficult half-wars, when diplomatic constraints preclude British forces carrying the fight into the enemy's homeland. Yet the Troopers in Borneo had made friends in the jungle, helping to influence the successful outcome of this confrontation in far greater measure than such small numbers of Troopers might have been expected to do.

While the Borneo campaign was being fought in steamy jungles, the British had been embroiled in a desert campaign in southern Arabia. Here a Federation of Sheiks had a long-standing treaty with the British, who were committed to protect their lands covering an area of desert mountains with isolated oases, larger than the United Kingdom but with a population only the size of Manchester's. De la Billière served on attachment to the Sheiks' Federal Regular Army (FRA) in the winter of 1963–4 based in the small colony of Aden, which had been a bunkering port on the British trading route to India for over a hundred years. Its strategic value was also prized by the Russians, who in September 1962 engineered a revolution in the Yemen, to the north of the Protectorate, when a Communist military dictatorship replaced its ruling Imam. The stage was then set for pro-Russian forces to seize first the Protectorate and then the port of Aden.

The Imam escaped assassination and raised a Royalist guerrilla army which fought the Communists for the next eight years. His forces were financed by Saudi Arabia, which also organized a mercenary force which included a number of former SAS Troopers. These soldiers of fortune, secretly based in the Aden Protectorate, were discreetly helped by the British and, as explained in the next chapter, had been recruited in London and Paris to provide radio communications in the mountains of Yemen and some training teams.

In April 1964 the FRA forces had to be withdrawn from the rugged plateaus of the northern mountains in the Protectorate, known as the Radfan. Its tribes had warred for thousands of years among these hills, judging by the age of some of their stone-built defence works (their *sangars*) and the well-worn firing positions to be found guarding the entrance to some mountain caves. In 1964 they were actively supporting Yemeni-backed forces infiltrating south to Aden, against whose incursions the FRA were concentrated that spring along the Protectorate's northern border, leaving the Radfan tribesmen free to attack engineers building a road into these mountains. The Sultans of the Federation called on the British to redress the situation, and on 29 April 45 Commando Royal Marines with a company of 3 Para were poised to move into the mountains. A Squadron of 22 SAS had arrived in Aden a fortnight earlier for a period of desert training. At least that was their official reason for being in Aden, but they were looking for some action after nearly a year of inaction since their first tour in Borneo.

The chance for this came with the Commando's planned capture of two key mountain positions codenamed 'Cap Badge' and 'Rice Bowl' (since it overlooked a small, fertile valley) on one of the routes used by dissidents moving from the Yemen to Aden. A Para company were to drop at midnight that Saturday/Sunday 30 April/1 May to a DZ on 'Rice Bowl' while the Commando infiltrated through a wild wadi and up into the mountains to seize 'Cap Badge'. There were too few helicopters to lift this force into the mountains, and, as little was known of the whereabouts of the warriors who lived and fought there, any landing area would first have to be secured even for a parachute drop. A Squadron's 3 Troop undertook, therefore, the job of seizing a DZ on 'Rice Bowl', moving into a Troop base 4.5km east of Thumier before Friday 29 April.

That night two patrols led by Captain Robin Edwards were taken in armoured cars up the Wadi Rabwa, east of Thumier, when these cars with a platoon of infantry were clearing the tribesmen's pickets overlooking the wadi. The act was in part a diversion – not only to cover the insertion of SAS patrols – for the Commando were to advance the following night along a less accessible wadi to the north. The armoured cars would also clear the enemy from Wadi Rabood so that artillery could be brought forward from Thumier to be within range of 'Cap Badge' and 'Rice Bowl'.

Edwards, a young officer who had been with the Regiment for only a year, had a number of Malaya and Borneo veterans in his patrol. All were physically hard and fit, although Trooper Nick Warburton, the signaller, had stomach pains of which he made no complaint. They carried enough water for a day on 'Rice Bowl', where they planned to lay up so that on Saturday night they would mark a DZ with torches and an Aldis lamp for the para drop. Water was more important than ammunition in the heat of this desert, and de la Billière had told them that, if they did have a brush with the Arabs, they were to conserve all that they could of the two hundred rounds each man carried for his SLR, and the two thousand rounds they carried between them for their Bren-gun. Warburton carried the A41 radio, weighing twenty kilos and no doubt seeming a lot heavier as they moved by moonlight through the warm night.

The signaller's food-poisoning now slowed him down, and by 0200 on the Saturday morning they still had to cover nearly half of their planned route. To go on risked being in the valley at daylight, below the high ridge they had reached, and Edwards cast round for somewhere to lay up. He found two ancient *sangars* in which all nine of the two patrols could hide. At dawn they could see the village of Shi'b a thousand metres below them and their objective five kilometres to the north, across the Wadi Taym. Tribesmen were moving up from the village to positions where they could watch for any soldiers coming from Thumier, but none came to the patrols' *sangars*. The sun was burning down by mid-morning when a goatherd was seen coming up a path from the village; he was calling to a woman out of sight of the patrol. Could they grab the goatherd without his companion noticing? It seemed unlikely, and he was within metres of the *sangars* when his calls to the woman suddenly took on an urgency that boded trouble. He would not have needed to see the Troopers to know that someone was there, because his goats sensed the patrols and moved away. A single shot then killed him as he fled back down the hill. The game was up.

The armed Arabs soon came up the hill, moving heedless of any danger until several were hit 'to reduce the odds'. These Edwards would reduce still further, as he had been in radio contact with the Squadron head-quarters at Thumier since he first decided to hide in the *sangars*. Now he put the radio to deadly purpose over an improvised link by telephone and the radio of the Air Support Officer, to pairs of Hunter aircraft which would be guided onto targets. Just as the first Arab sharpshooters got into positions overlooking the *sangars* from the ridge top barely ten metres above the Troopers, Hunters strafed the ridge, avoiding the *sangars* now clearly marked by cloth panels originally intended to identify the DZ. By mid-afternoon the skirmish had become a stalemate, as the Hunters' cannon fire held off any attempt to rush the positions. Edwards's control of the aircraft had reached such a finely tuned pitch that a pilot's point of aim could be corrected as he swooped in towards the hillside. Artillery fire from British guns in the Wadi Rabwa also was directed by radio from the *sangars*, yet despite this close support Arab marksmen repeatedly hit them. Rock chippings from these shots cut the faces and hands of the Troopers, but no one was hit. Firing back effectively at these expert Arab marksmen proved almost impossible, because they moved their positions among the rocks and boulders in the heat haze on the hillside, so the Troopers held their fire – as did some of the tribesmen, although more had arrived as the afternoon passed, for both sides realized that at nightfall the Hunters would no longer be able to intervene in the battle.

During the afternoon de la Billière had sent a Troop towards the area but their helicopter, one of the 'fathers of grasshoppers', as the Arabs called the Wessex, was shot up and had to withdraw. The original plan to drop in the paras was also changed, since setting up the DZ had 'gone for a ball of chalk'. They were quite willing to drop to an unmarked DZ but this was considered too hazardous, and the objectives of the advance on Saturday night were limited to hill crests nearer Thumier.

The first SAS casualties came about 1630: Lance-Corporal 'Paddy' Baker accidentally exposed a leg outside one *sangar* wall and was hit by two .303-inch bullets. A second Trooper was hit when moving between the two *sangars*. They were less seriously wounded than they would have been by service bullets, because these warriors fired home-made ammunition, refilling used cartridges with an explosive they had concocted. Shortly after this two tribesmen rushed the larger *sangar*, hoping to push over its dry-stone walling. They died, each with a surprised look, as Sergeant Alf Tasker fired the Bren from his hip and Baker aimed at several others approaching the *sangar*. The sniping resumed for a couple of hours as the patrols and aircraft kept the attackers at bay until day quickly changed to night at 1915.

Already Edwards had the men briefed on a fighting withdrawal, but a little before nightfall Warburton, no doubt trying to get a better position for his radio in the second *sangar*, was killed after being hit several times and his radio destroyed. Edwards still had the small emergency radio used for morse signals but took out its crystal and destroyed it along with all that the patrols would not now need. Four men had taken up positions in the rocks outside the *sangars*. They would cover the second four as they leapfrogged, one party covering the other's movement along the ridge. Some minutes after they had cleared the *sangars*, an artillery bombardment drenched the area in explosives.

The first four were in position when Edwards called out to check that each man had taken his anti-malaria pill that day – a calming touch of routine which caused amusement in relaxing the tensions. Then they were ready to move, Edwards calling to those in the rocks: 'Right! We're coming out now.' Paddy Baker hobbled out first, followed by Edwards, then by Sergeant Tasker, the Bren at his hip, with a Trooper behind him. They were met by heavy fire from men behind two boulders, who seemed to concentrate on the young Captain: he was killed before he had gone far. The others dashed on, for there was nothing that they could do for 'the Boss', as they took up firing positions fifteen metres from the other four, who now followed. Moving so as to take every advantage of what cover there was, they joined Sergeant Tasker; all seven then climbed quietly up to the ridge, while two parties of Arabs seemed to be shooting at each other from around the *sangars*.

Fatigue and tension after nearly eight hours in action began to play tricks with the judgement of even these experienced Troopers. Baker, dimly aware that something beside his wounds was making walking difficult discovered that his field-dressings were flapping around his ankles only when the medic put fresh ones on his still bleeding leg. After the moon rose, shadows played tricks on their imaginations as they climbed to avoid some Arab tents which later were seen, at a different angle, to be large rocks.

They were weakly making their way west along a goat track, Baker and another wounded Trooper having fallen behind the others, when they sensed that they were being followed. They moved off the track and caught sight of an Arab's white dress. The man, moving silently, caught up with them. He was so intent on following the sound of the others moving along the path that he was dead before he realized he had been ambushed. Three others following him also died as Baker and his companion each emptied a magazine-full of rounds in the direction of the pursuers. Baker, confused through fatigue and loss of blood, continued to squeeze the trigger of his SLR after it had stopped firing, having to make a careful check in his mind as to why his gun had stopped firing before realizing that the magazine was empty. They caught up with the rest of the patrol, looping up hill just in case they were mistaken for pursuing Arabs, and Tasker fired a couple of bursts from the Bren-gun to discourage any further pursuit. They were again followed about 0200, by Arabs who had been in *sangars* along the Wadi Rabwa, and again they ambushed their pursuers.

They had covered over eight kilometres along the rocky hillside, tiring walking at the best of times but after thirty hours on the move or in nerve-taut action of battle they were exhausted. Yet, in the tradition of the Regiment, they still kept going, not only moving ever westward towards Thumier but doing so with military caution, for although the Arabs did not usually fight at night, there were apparently pickets on the wadi side. Sometime between 0400 and 0500 they knew they had only two kilometres to cover to reach the sentry posts covering the camp, but again their training enabled them to resist the temptation to rush these last few kilometres, although they were parched – their water had run out some way back most of it given to the wounded.

As they moved to the valley floor to wait for daylight, when the sentries would be able to recognize them, they had their first piece of luck on this patrol: a stream ran along the valley and they drank from its probably impure water, regardless of the consequences. Baker became unconscious from loss of blood, oblivious of the flies which swarmed round his wounds once the sun came up. Half-an-hour later an armoured car ground its way up the wadi on its first patrol of the morning, and the wounded were loaded into it. The other five marched into the base camp 'a weary but unbeaten little group straggling along the track'. Baker was awarded an MM for his part in the action. Alf Tasker is on record as saying of that day in the Radfan: 'When fighting for your life with a fifty-fifty chance, you have got to enjoy it . . . It was a good day.'

The Radfan tribesmen were never subdued but a Brigade gained control of the mountains beyond 'Cap Badge' and 'Rice Bowl'. Later actions were fought more often at 500m than fifty, with SAS patrols having their share of recces and occasional ambushes, more often bringing down artillery fire than using SLRs against unsuspecting dissident bands, not aware of hidden SAS observation posts.

There are no Geneva Convention rules in the savage cut and thrust of guerrilla warfare – the heads of the two men killed in the Radfan were displayed in a medieval manner on poles for a public show in the Yemen. In the back streets of Aden, among the close-packed mud-walled hovels with the corrugated-iron roofs, were a few highly trained and ruthless terrorists who would lob a grenade at a 'crocodile' line of schoolchildren or, with more selection in their choice of target, kill officers of the Special Branch. By 1966 there was every sign that the Federation could not sustain its authority and that Communist agents had infiltrated the joint military police headquarters. There were no hearts or minds to be won in this situation, for the British had declared their intention in February 1966 to leave Aden the following year. Several British regiments, therefore, formed their own undercover teams, 'keeni-meeni' as the Army called this work, from the Swahili phrase for the unseen movement of a snake.

De la Billière set up a Close Quarter Battle course for selected Troopers, men who could pass as Arabs or one of the many non-European peoples who lived in Aden. On this course a number of Fijians mastered the art of drawing a Browning pistol from the folds of an Arab *futah*, to such good effect that two of them killed would-be assassins, although these terrorists already held guns levelled at the Fijians. Although the SAS Squadrons each had a training spell in Aden between their Borneo tours, the Regiment at the time did not consider much had been achieved by these operations, except in gaining knowledge of the new techniques involved. Yet for the British services as a whole, this experience of fighting urban terrorists, with its many problems different from those of a purely military battlefield, proved useful. The SAS had been building up their experience of such delicate military actions with their difficult political implications, since the late 1950s. Although at that time some senior British officers felt that Troopers might be too quick on the trigger for such operations.

7. Teaching War and Winning the Peace – the Oman Campaign

In November 1958, D Squadron proved to any doubters that the Regiment was not only a competent military unit but well able to tackle those sensitive operations with diplomatic complexities which any major power has to face from time to time. The operation that month was in support of the Sultan of Oman, with whom the British had had a treaty since 1798; his opponents, however, were supported by another of Britain's allies. D Squadron's action in a few weeks that November ensured more than a victory for the Sultan: they made a major contribution to the continuing existence of the Regiment.

Oman is a Sultanate with a hereditary ruler who in the 1950s believed that the trappings of modern society would corrupt his people, therefore he would not allow even cameras or gas cookers to be imported, nor the medicines which could have cured some of his people's debilitating diseases. They lived as they had for centuries, by exporting high-quality dates and dried fish to India, from the mud-walled capital of Muscat and even smaller ports along the country's 1,500-km coastline in south-east Arabia. One of the most westerly of these ports is Salalah, capital of the province of Dhofar which bordered on the Aden Protectorate (the modern Democratic Republic of Yemen). Here, across 650km of desert from Muscat, the Sultan spent much of his time, as he was a recluse to whom the lusher nature of the Dhofar Hills, watered by monsoon clouds from June to September, had particular appeal. At the opposite end of his country was a detached small province which dominated the southern coast of the Hormuz Straits through which half the Western World's supply of oil passed in that decade. This gave the British a particular interest in the Sultanate. American oil interests wanted to gain exploration rights, however, and the Saudi royal family sought a more orthodox government on their eastern border, an alliance of interests which led to their indirect help for the Beni Hina tribe when they revolted against the Sultan in 1954. The revolt was defeated but one of its ablest leaders, Talib, led a series of raids against the Sultan's forces during the next three years.

Talib's men joined forces with a local tribe living on the great mountain plateau thirty by fifteen kilometres of the Jebel Akhdar (the Green Mountain), which could be approached only up towering cliffs, the dozen main tracks up clefts in these rock walls being guarded by machine-gunners with modern weapons. Attempts to defeat their tribesmen with bombing from the air failed to stop them blowing up 150 vehicles in the summer of 1958. Before this the British Foreign Secretary had declared that there would be no question of deploying British forces on any large scale, particularly in view of the high temperatures in the Oman deserts, although a small number of British troops had been acting as advisers and training teams for the Sultan's forces – teams which, in some cases, found themselves in a battle the day they arrived, commanding units of the Sultan's small army.

During October, the War Office considered various anti-guerrilla tactics, including bands of former guerrillas bribed to mix with a few British soldiers in order to scale the mountain. This mountaineering requirement was more suited to SAS than to other British Army troops, and, more importantly, there were to be no casualties, or at least none on a scale which might cause a public outcry. Yet there was not the time for any prolonged preparation, as there was a debate due in the United Nations at which the Middle East would be discussed, and for diplomatic reasons any British operation in the Oman must be completed before there could be public embarrassment over their support for a reactionary regime.

A number of senior British officers met in the Oman to review the situation: Major (later General) Frank Kitson, at that time one of the Army's top planning staff, who had pioneered counter-revolutionary warfare in Kenya during the Mau-Mau rebellion a few years earlier; Lieutenant-Colonel Anthony Deane-Drummond, Royal Signals, commanding 22 SAS; and Colonel David Smiley, on loan to the Sultan as his Chief of Staff. The upshot of these meetings was the deployment of D Squadron within a couple of weeks of their being brought out of the Malayan jungle. Such a move from jungle to desert mountains inevitably necessitates retraining, and during part of this fortnight the Troopers practised for sixteen hours a day with rocket-launchers and at long-range shooting, very different techniques from firing shotguns and other close-quarter ambush methods in the jungle.

The Squadron arrived at Muscat on 18 November 1958, and during the next week recce patrols gathered information on possible routes up the cliffs and learnt what they could of the enemy. Talib had 150 warrior sharpshooters and perhaps five hundred other armed supporters, most of whom could kill a man at four hundred paces, or even further when, at times, visibility was exceptionally clear on the mountain. Talib's sentries were therefore able severely to limit any movement below the cliffs, and

Corporal 'Duke' Swindells MM, an experienced SAS operator, was killed by one of them, when he must have considered he was beyond their range as he walked along a ridge. The Squadron thereafter patrolled at night, something the local forces considered impossible on the rough ground below the cliffs, and by moving at night the patrols also avoided the exhausting heat of daytime, a heat so intense that two British soldiers – not SAS Troopers – died of heat exhaustion that autumn.

John Watts, commanding 'D', made several recces alone in these probes to find a route to the plateau, one of which a local sheikh knew on the north side of the mountain. He was the only guide willing to lead SAS patrols, and two Troops led by 'Rory' Walker made the 2,000m climb following this route in a night. They were hidden only by darkness, as the narrow path led across rock faces which gave no cover or opportunity to move off this path had they been attacked. Indeed, they passed several *sangars* which were unoccupied since Talib's men considered the plateau impregnable at night. Before daylight thirty Troopers were in positions on the lip of the plateau, and the SAS held these positions despite many counter-attacks in the next few weeks. On one occasion forty Arabs armed with modern rifles and two Bren-guns were allowed to come within a hundred metres of the SAS *sangars* before the nine men holding them opened fire. Nine Arabs were killed or mortally wounded in the few seconds after the Troopers opened fire and the attack withered away, although the attackers returned on other days, once getting within fifteen metres of the defenders.

On 27 December Walker led a recce across the plateau to the twin peaks overlooking the SAS positions, known as 'Sabrina' (after a well-endowed lady who appeared on TV in the 1950s). He was climbing a hundred metres of ropes up one of these peaks when an English-speaking Arab taunted him with 'Come on, Johnny.' Walker climbed on up the rock, flung a grenade and enabled two Troops to get in position from where eight more Arabs were killed, before the Troopers withdrew.

Yet the toehold remained no more than a small lodgement of rock-bound *sangars*. Constantly buffeted by strong winds, with their water-bottles freezing solid at night, the Troopers suffered the discomforts of exposure, with cracked lips and wind-burnt faces. They were re-supplied by parachute drops, one of which failed probably due to the 'chutes being badly packed, with two out of three not opening properly. As these containers plummeted onto the rocks, several filled with mortar bombs exploded, injuring one SAS Trooper. The Squadron and the Life Guards (most of whose armoured cars had been damaged by mines) kept some thirty men in these positions, closely watched by a major part of Talib's tribesmen. There was, therefore, no practical means of expanding this tenuous hold on the plateau. Meanwhile, recces on the south of the mountain failed to find an alternative route, although one dawn de la

Billière's Troop 'shot up' a cave using 3.5-inch rockets in a daring twenty-minute action during which the rocket team stood exposed on an open stage, so to speak, in a natural amphitheatre whose hostile audience was kept at bay only by accurate machine-gun fire and strafes by Venom aircraft.

These aircraft were attached to the Sultan's forces which at that time included fewer than eight hundred regular soldiers, although British instructors had trained some of these as heavy machine-gunners for his Northern Frontier Regiment. There were also tribesmen who supported the Sultan, but their loyalties were fickle, and one of their leaders, given the job of keeping a track clear of mines, was himself laying them to help Talib. Colonel Smiley, the Sultan's Chief of Staff, knew that he could only advise the Sultan on how such problems might be dealt with, and in no way could the Colonel order events. He therefore asked for British reinforcements as the Sultan's forces needed to seize the plateau before the weather would seasonably deteriorate in February. He did not get all the forces he asked for but was given a second SAS Squadron: 'A' arrived from Malaya on 9 January 1959, after a week's intensive preparation. They spent their first few days in the northern toehold, from where they were later to attack but in what their Colonel called a 'training exercise' in the 'Sabrina' Hills (Aqbat Dhafar on their maps).

The CO of 22 SAS, Lieutenant-Colonel Antony Deane-Drummond, who was a veteran of World War II, flew back to the Oman, where he and the two Squadron Majors – Watts of 'D' and John Cooper of 'A' – found a possible route to the plateau up the south-west cliffs. Aerial photographs showed that this 3,000m of a steep climb would need ropes fixed along its last third on a sharp ridge top, if heavy equipment was to be brought up. There would also have to be some means of diverting most of Talib's men from this edge of the plateau as they had proved quite fearless in their attacks near 'Sabrina' and would sweep any assault Troops back down the cliff, unless heavy machine-guns could be positioned soon after the first men reached the plateau. The assault parties could also expect to need considerable firepower, and a reserve of ammunition and water would have to be parachuted to them at first light. Having made these decisions, the Colonel also decided to use not one but two diversionary attacks, from the toehold towards 'Sabrina' and at a point ten kilometres south of there, above the village of Tanuf. While these were being put in by 'A' and a reinforced Troop of 'D', the main force was forming up in an area held by the Sultan's forces east of Kamah village. Most of D Squadron, the Troop of Life Guards who had been serving as infantry for over a month, a Royal Signals detachment and a company of machine-gunners from the Northern Frontier Regiment would scale the Kamah route. The machine-guns and further reserves of ammunition (in case bad weather prevented an air re-supply) were loaded on donkeys, whose handlers had been told that they would be needed at Tanuf for the main attack – a piece of information which, as expected, they had passed to Talib.

As A Squadron made their attack, they were met by a hundred Arabs. A reinforced Troop of 'A' climbed 150m above Tanuf to find Talib's main force and, having engaged it, then skilfully withdrew. They reached the valley floor near the village and were taken in trucks to join the rest of the Squadron already on their way to the high ridge. De la Billière's Recce Troop led the way, moving quickly and silently past an unmanned machine-gun which could have held them in the moonlight a fateful hour at least had not the gunners been asleep in a cave nearby. When they did wake up, they found they were prisoners of the two Troopers left to guard them. The Colonel and Major Watts were with the Recce Troop when at 0300 there was still that high ridge to cross. Each man had been carrying thirty kilos of kit, including a good deal of ammunition, and with the progress of the reluctant donkeys needing a lift by SAS and Life Guard Troopers from time to time, the force were unlikely to reach the top by dawn. Deane-Drumond therefore ordered the leading two Troops to cache their Bergens and press on in belt-order – that is, with a few magazines for their SLRs and ammunition for the Brens.

The climb became a race led by the Troop Commander, the Squadron Commander and the Colonel, who all reached the plateau shattered by physical exhaustion that might have left them helpless had not the Colonel driven himself and the others on towards a nearby village. They surrounded this so quickly that the local sheikh, Talib's ally, escaped capture only by leaving behind a small armoury of weapons, chests of uniforms and some personal letters from his backers! Venoms attacked the enemy *sangars* further west, while isolated sharpshooters fired on D Squadron as they consolidated their hold. One of these did 'a spectacular Hollywood death-dive over a sheer cliff'. Others withdrew to the west, and by the end of January the plateau was clear of rebels or at least of their leaders, and those tribesmen remaining there became loyal to the Sultan. The victory was complete, achieved with such an economy in the use of forces as to make 22 SAS's reputation inviolate in Whitehall's corridors of power.

In 1960 A Squadron returned to the Oman for a training spell, using Land Rovers in the way David Stirling's men had crossed the North African deserts. But the major British military help for the Oman in the next decade came in the form of British Army Training Teams (BATTs) and the number of former British officers and NCOs who served as individuals on contract to the Sultan. Lawrence Smith, having retired as a Warrant Officer with an MC, was one of these contract officers in the 1970s; others came from the Regiment and various British services, the former officers commanding the Sultan's battalions and NCOs commanding companies in the Sultan's Armed Forces (SAF) which the British trained. Its regiments were recruited from northern Omani Arabs or from Baluchis, a hardy, disciplined people from Pakistan's province of Baluchistan on the northern shores of the Gulf of Oman.

The 'Kremlin' – that SAS HQ intelligence unit which keeps tabs on likely trouble-spots worldwide – had reports in 1969 of an Iraqi team training leaders among the tribesmen in Oman's northern province, that sensitive area dominating the Strait of Hormuz. An SAS Recce Troop therefore, in 1970, made a free-fall drop from 3,000m into the area, landing on a DZ in a valley surrounded by high mountains, but Trooper 'Rip' Reddy's heavy Bergen shifted its position, and his fall became a tumble to his death, as the lines of his parachute became entangled round his body. This Troop joined up with the rest of their Squadron landed by the Royal Marines' Special Boat Squadron (SBS), the Royal Navy's equivalent of the Army's SAS. The Troops had a minor brush with suspected dissidents, one of whom was wounded, and the potential threat to stability at that time in the Persian Gulf was removed. Some years later, this province of Oman was sold by the Sultan to Pakistan, but the SAS Squadron operation there in 1970 underlined their ability to snuff out trouble before it became a major rebellion which might conflict with British interests – actions which are possible only when men are in training with the sharpening of such 'exercises' as A Squadron's attack on Sabrina.

During the Easter holiday in 1970, John Watts, now commanding 22 SAS, and two other senior SAS officers were considering where the Regiment might next need to sharpen its training exercises, and they took a long hard look at Dhofar, Oman's southern province. An SAS Troop had been training the Sultan's forces since before the previous Christmas and were in Dhofar, where the Sultan's forces had been driven from the mountains near the coast by Communist-backed guerrillas. There had been many changes since Talib's men were defeated in 1959, as oil had been found in commercial quantities in 1964, but the Sultan's anxiety to keep his people free from western influence continued. Even agriculture on the fertile Dhofar Plain had been reduced to growing mainly dates, pomegranates and coconuts and selling the rare frankincense cut from bushes, although just over fifty years earlier wheat from this region had fed a British army in the Middle East. The nomadic Dhofars lived by herding a small breed of cattle which survived through the winter season by eating dried sardines when there was no pasture. These proud people had been subjected to a Communist tyranny mounted from the so-called Democratic Peoples Republic of Yemen, the military dictatorship which took over Aden on the British withdrawal in 1967.

Not surprisingly, therefore, the SAF received little support from the hill tribes, and in the spring of 1970 they were virtually bottled up in the

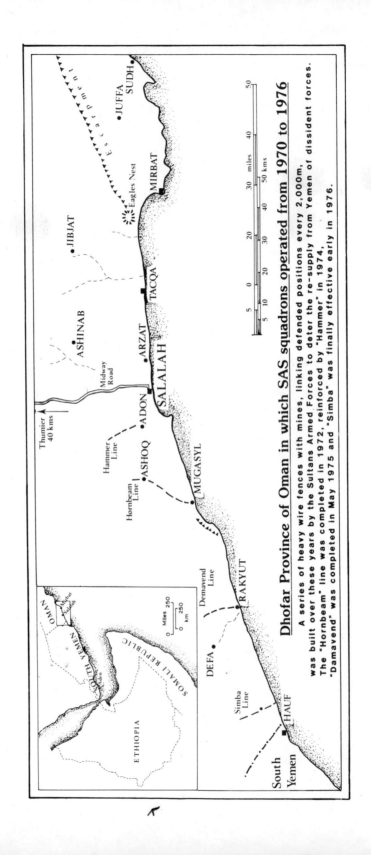

Dhofar Province of Oman in which SAS squadrons operated from 1970 to 1976

A series of heavy wire fences with mines, linking defended positions every 2,000m, was built over these years by the Sultans Armed Forces to deter the re-supply from Yemen of dissident forces. The "Hornbeam" line was completed in 1972, reinforced by "Hammer" in 1974, "Damavend" was completed in May 1975 and "Simba" was finally effective early in 1976.

Salalah, with its airfield and the little seaports of Rayzut to the west, with Tacqa and in Mirbat to the east. Johnny Watts knew that the only way to beat these Communist infiltrators was to gain the support of the Dhofaris in the mountains – the ingredient in what are called 'low-intensity' operations, at which SAS had become experts, and which Watts now formulated into a strategy for Dhofar. He wanted his Squadrons to provide medical services for fifty thousand people living in these mountains and to find vets who would help them to improve the breeding of cattle. On the military side he planned a comprehensive intelligence operation, while offering inducements to tribes to change sides in what had become a rebellion against the Sultan. If – and that Easter it was a big 'if' – the Sultan would allow a civil building programme, the results of these improvements would outbid anything which the Communists could offer.

The 'if' was removed that July, when the old Sultan was replaced by his son Qaboos. A progressive and level-headed young man who had been trained at the Sandhurst Officers' Training School, Qaboos was helped in this nearly bloodless *coup* by a young sheikh and others who will possibly never be named. No one was killed and the old Sultan retired to live in London for the last two years of his life. Qaboos's rule was faced with many difficulties in 1970, but, with British advice that included the loan of British Army Training Teams (BATTs), there seemed every chance that his enlightened rule would lead his people to a more prosperous life, although the British had no intention of maintaining even their training teams in the Oman once their Treaty obligations were fulfilled.

The first SAS Troop sent to Oman shortly after Qaboos came to power was to provide bodyguards for the young Sultan, among other duties. In Dhofar a Troop of the usual SAS size (in this case nineteen strong) set up an intelligence cell and an Information Team at Salalah. The former consisted of an SAS Warrant Officer and two Intelligence Corps NCOs whose detailed cross-referencing of every piece of information had built up an outline of the enemy's command structure within twelve weeks. But they would need considerably longer to get a fuller picture of the Communist influences on the mountain tribes, for these people lived on a remote plateau stretching from the escarpment by the sea, 75km east of Salalah, to the border, far to the west of his provincial capital. The high ground was gashed by great wadis which ran steep-sided into the plain, like Scottish glens, but after the monsoon they were choked with lush, lank grass, their many bushes providing good grazing for camels and cover for soldiers. Westward along the plateau towards the Republic of Yemen's border, these wadis were several hundred metres across at the mouths on the plain, their cliff sides running north – south. The valley floors had been natural routes for camel caravans over the centuries, following tracks along breaks in a wadi's wall up onto the plateau and down similar re-entrants at the next wadi. After the monsoon, water ran on the riverbeds in these otherwise dry valleys, making them unexpectedly beautiful with dragonflies and birds, sweet figs growing on large trees that shaded rockpools.

This water was essential for the Dhofari cattle herds, driven down each afternoon to drink their fill after the smaller pools near the plateau villages had dried out. These were usually of eight or so round stone-walled houses, with a domed roof of thin straw-thatch, supported on a central treetrunk, its dead limbs interlaced with smaller branches which were replaced every couple of years. The house itself might last twelve years, and although the tribesmen were nomadic in the sense that they moved their herds from one water-hole to another, they remained in their tribal areas. The Bait Kathir, on the other hand, one of the largest tribes on the plateau, lived mainly from their camels and goats, some of their clans controlling the Empty Quarter north of the plateau. This desert of sand dunes had been crossed by Wilfred Thesiger soon after he left the LRDG, but apart from a few explorers and Bait Kathir raiders, no one lived in this vast sand sea.

Before SAS patrols were allowed to work on the plateau, much had to be done to stabilize an uncertain situation of shifting loyalties in the late summer of 1970. Qaboos, having established his rule in the north, issued a general amnesty which the SAS Information Team in Salalah put over to the tribes on the plateau. At first the only means of doing this was by air drops near the villages, scattering leaflets of simple pictures which conveyed the message, for few Dhofaris could read. But a brief text on the back of one leaflet was read by an Omani, Mohammed Suhail, who had been trained by the British and had served in the Trucial Oman Scouts which policed one of the countries neighbouring Oman, before joining the rebel tribesmen after being disillusioned by the old Sultan's regime. Now he came back to serve Qaboos on his intelligence staff, which was organized by an SAS officer. He was among the first of many who would later come to work for a revitalized Oman, after fighting for the opposition.

Persuading these men who returned to the Sultan's support – the word 'surrendered' was avoided in this context – needed more than leaflets, as Corporal John Lane, heading the team, fully understood. This SAS Corporal's quiet and courteous manner enabled him to build wide-ranging contacts in the new Omani government, who knew him as 'Mister Lane' since his rank might be regarded by some officials as not weighty enough to warrant him a hearing, although Lane was extremely good at his job and later worked on contract for the Omanis. In the early 1970s, working with an expert on psychological warfare, 'psyops', and Dhofari advisers, Lane's team built an effective network of information rather than propaganda. The aim was to tell the truth without recourse to misinformation in 'black' propaganda planted as if it came from the opposition, although Omani victories were emphasized and their defeats explained as temporary setbacks on the way to ultimate victory.

The team was able to demonstrate their good news in practical ways, SAS being responsible for getting advice on equipment recommended by the Royal Engineers, to drill wells, and they also helped establish a model farm. Lane spread news of its developments and much else by radio broadcast, giving cheap transistor radios to men from the hills visiting Salalah. These sets the Communists confiscated as they were Government property, so Lane put them on sale in the *souk*: no one was going to let some political upstart part him from his personally purchased radio. The Information Team also published a weekly paper, but at the checkpoints where people queued to pass in or out of the Salalah perimeter wire noticeboards were seen by even more readers of pictures.

The British Government, not wanting to detract from the Sultan's Armed Forces, did not admit that SAS teams were in Dhofar until a Squadron arrived that September, not so much to fight SAF's shooting battles at this stage as to provide Civil Aid Teams for the war against disease and ignorance. As usual in such delicate political situations, they were told that they must not have casualties. Yet teams of four men would often work far from any SAF military garrison, with little chance of being extracted from trouble if it arose, as in 1971 there was only one helicopter working out of Salalah. Along the coast from this Provincial Capital, a typical SAS team, a 'Bat' team in the jargon of the time, lived at Tacqa, a fishing port with narrow streets and an all pervading stench of fish drying in the sun. The 'Bat' home and medical centre were in a small house identified by the Omani flag hanging from an improvised flagpole on one corner of its roof. There was a noticeboard outside for the townsfolk to read pictures which made clear the danger of allowing flies to cluster round a baby's eyes, or the newest civil development the Government had undertaken.

The balance of military threat and government promises had to be finely tuned. Too many threats only stiffened the resolve of those fighting the SAF, who were clearly not winning the shooting war, while too many promises suggested that the government was weak and needed to 'bribe' the people. Lane and his successors would develop to a fine art the balance of threat against promise, but in the autumn of 1970 much depended on the SAS teams' individual skills on the ground in facing the dangers of sudden ambush while delivering the promises of better health for the people.

The Troopers in Tacqa, a sleepy town, moved instinctively in pairs five metres from each other, each man carrying his Armalite, easily identifiable as 'Bat' Troopers by their olive green shirts and shorts, if not by

their fair hair. Some men elsewhere had stones thrown at them occasionally, but here they were the only authority the people could turn to, as
there was no government representative (no *wali*) in the town. There was
an *askar* band of armed tribesmen, however, manning the town's fort,
who kept watch on the perimeter wire. Some of the townsfolk had helped
the 'Bat' to erect this fence, but the *askars* were less trusted in the town
than the SAS team, who found that the people were cheerful enough but
eerily afraid to talk to the Troopers. Clearly the opposition had men and
women living in the town, a dusty place of lethargic old men and bubbling
children with their veiled mothers always shyly distancing themselves
from the 'Bat'.

The medical corporal with the team ran a clinic each morning at the Bat
house for the old men and children, the young men having gone into the
hills with the opposition, but women's illnesses could be diagnosed only
by asking questions, for no Dhofari would allow another man to touch his
womenfolk. This led to one pregnancy being diagnosed as constipation,
but fortunately only with happy results: a baby boy for the family and a
goat, given in thanks, for the Bat's supper. The Corporal visited the
bedridden in the evening, and what little information the Bat gleaned
came from occasional conversations with patients. Yet much of the
people's sickness needed no magic nor the sophisticated drugs in the
medic's pack. Children would eventually be persuaded to clean their
teeth – although not in 1970, for all the efforts of the medic, and many of
their eye troubles would later be cured when a regular clinic was set up in
the town. The Bat medic's work did wonders that winter – and he cured a
few camels' injuries as well.

Such work established belief in the practical results of the government's
promises despite the presence of the opposition. This in 1970 had
developed from a minor local rebellion of 1962 against the old Sultan's
refusal to allow any modernization. His troops went onto the plateau, and
failing to catch any guerrillas, harassed the local tribesmen. Some of them
had seen service in various Arabian armies during the 1960s and were
well aware of the benefits of modern living which they had seen in Saudi
Arabia, Kuwait and Bahrain, if not in Europe. They had formed the
Dhofar Liberation Front but this was absorbed by the Chinese-sponsored
People's Front for the Liberation of the Occupied Arabian Gulf, based in
the Republic of Yemen. Its young men, with fanatical conviction in the
Communist cause, first established cells within tribal centres on the
plateau and then began to break down tribal loyalties, organizing their
fighters into village militias and the more seasoned men into battle
groups. Children were sent away from their parents for schooling in the
PDRY, and young men to guerrilla warfare schools in Russia and China.
All religious practices were banned; old men had their eyes put out for
refusing to deny their god; their daughters were deflowered by young

Communists as of right; and with their customary arrogance the Communists laid down how individuals must behave.

But the leaders of the original Dhofari rebellion began a counter-revolution. In September 1970 a hard core in the eastern area of the plateau fought their way out of a Communist encirclement, and twenty-four of their best fighting men left the mountains. Meanwhile, the Communist cells in Tacqa and other towns of the plain did not take an active part in this civil war, as the Communists were being supplied to some extent with food from these centres, although their arms and weapons came by camel train from the Republic of Yemen, across the border and up onto the plateau.

The split between the Communists and the Moslem factions on the plateau helped the SAS concept of turning rebels into fighters for the Sultan, as did Qaboos's amnesty for the rebels, although this meant that for some months the Communists' camel trains passed unmolested through the great wadis and into the mountains. However, by March 1971 over two hundred rebels had 'returned' to the Sultan's support, many bringing their Kalashnikov rifles, for which they were paid £50.

Major (later Colonel) Tony Jeapes arrived in Salalah that January, later to be followed by his Squadron, and had the responsibility not only of forming counter-revolutionary bands from the Dhofaris but also of selling this idea to the authorities in Dhofar. A few days after he arrived, he was visited in Salalah by Salim Mubarak, who had led the Dhofar Liberation Front's two dozen fighters out of the mountains the previous September. A lean man, used to command, with a quick intelligence, he had been trained in China and on returning to the plateau was appointed second-in-command of the Eastern Area. He proposed forming an anti-guerrilla band, a *firqat* (literally, a company), drawn from men of several tribes, to be called the *Firqat Salahadin* after the great Moslem warrior who had fought the Christian Crusaders of the twelfth century. Salim's knowledge of war in its widest sense surprised the Major, who was later to discover how much the Dhofari had learnt in China of ways to influence society by speeches as much as by firearms.

Jeapes visited the British Brigadier in Muscat who was the Sultan's Chief of Staff, explaining that the proposed *firqat* would be more than guides, even more than *askars*, and that SAS would provide not only training teams but also the radio communications needed for the company's air and artillery support. Brigadier Graham liked the concept and later helped Jeapes convince the British Consul of the soundness of this scheme, but there were some doubts over whether a full SAS Squadron could be committed. Yet within forty-eight hours there was confirmation that all Jeapes's Troops would arrive on 14 February. There would then be a whole Troop available to train the *Firqat Salahadin*, and other Troops to train several tribal *firqats* for a number of tribal leaders who now wanted to offer companies to fight for the Sultan. Jeapes also visited the Sultan's governor of Dhofar, whose support would be essential in matters of pay and administration of the *firqats*. There were inducements of better pay than for service in SAF.

Recruiting men for the *firqats* (the 'firqs' or 'firkins', as the Troopers called them) would be a slow process, for these fighters were used to electing their own leaders. On the plateau a chief would be elected on merit and even then was not paramount but must listen to all the men of his tribe, who made collective decisions on any matter of importance. These recruits, like others who had changed sides, had not been interrogated with any rough handling; indeed it would have been counterproductive as it usually is in stiffening men's resolve not to talk. But questioned over a cup of tea with a cigarette, their initial suspicions were usually broken down, and if they did not tell all that they knew on their first questioning, most of them did so in a day or two.

Training the 'firqs' became a major role for SAS over the next six years, many Troopers being first sent on a ten-week course in colloquial Arabic before going to Dhofar, and some picking up sufficient Jebeli to be able to make themselves understood to non-Arabic-speakers. By the early spring of 1971 there were sufficient Arabic-speakers in the Troop training the *Firqat Salahadin* at Mirbat, a larger and busier port than Tacqa, but isolated on the coast, 65km east of Salalah. A Civil Aid Team continued to work in the town, separately from the Troop giving instruction.

There were no distractions here, for the *firqat* trainees and supplies could be brought in by sea, and there were plenty of training grounds out of the view of all but the opposition's cell in the town. This was in turn watched by Salim's friends in the town, and not long after training had begun there, Salim had all four members of this Communist Directorate in custody. After they had given him more names, he announced that he knew all those who had helped the opposition and that if they signed a confession next day they would not be arrested. Forty signed.

Captain Chester's Troop had found the thirty trainees reasonable pupils, sensitive to criticism and not to be laughed at. They wore 'sort of field grey' uniforms (sari fluorescent green dye, washed out by sea-water) and carried FN rifles, from which most of them could get all the rounds from a full magazine onto a training target. Changing sides appears to have given Salim's men no problems, although one *firqat* sentry shot at an SAF patrol, having momentarily forgotten that Baluchs were no longer his enemy.

Salim's *firqat* were blooded in a night landing at Sudh, 30km to the east of Mirbat, where the enemy, the *adoo*, had pickets on headlands either side of the port, but seldom in the town. This opposition numbered about fifty but could not be quickly reinforced as the port was some way from the mountains, and – as Jeapes had expected – the whole *firqat* got ashore without opposition north of the enemy pickets to a beach secured by an SAS Troop. By 0100 hours on 24 February they were huddled in their forming-up position in a *wadi* north of the port, trying to catch some sleep in bright moonlight, but it was 'too cold to do more than dose fitfully'. At 0530 they began to advance down the *wadi*, approaching the town from the landward side when the opposition might have expected them to land from the sea. With two sections on high ground to the east and west and most of the company with two SAS Troops on the *wadi* floor, they passed through the early morning mist and took up positions a hundred metres short of the town, while a scouting party of ten Dhofaris slipped into it. Its fifty or so houses remained shuttered as all was quiet after two shots had warned one townsman to halt. The scouts reported that there was no opposition, as did patrols to the headlands.

At 1000 hours the *firqat* rounded up all the men, whom Salim addressed, answering the questions of bolder spirits among the seventy or so sitting around three sides of the town square. Suspicion turned to friendliness: the Sultan's forces would not be leaving the town. *Firqat* men then went back to each household and spent most of the day explaining to families how the government would improve their lot – interrupted only by a few bursts of long-range fire from enemy scouts, one of whom must have had a horrific tale to tell his fellows, after the SAS Carl Gustav anti-tank weapon blew off the hilltop beside his firing position.

Two weeks after Salim had died of a heart attack, his second-in-command led the *firqat* in a night climb to a position of caves and ridges on the edge of the escarpment. This Eagle's Nest had been recced by an SAS patrol the previous week, when they established the correct route to the top, lay there hidden all day and left no tell-tale signs of their visit, not even footprints, for they kept to bare rock. Their *firqat* had made the first move of the counter-revolutionaries into the plateau, and the training of their SAS Troop now paid off.

When the company advanced westward from the Eagle's Nest, they moved in a military, if not exactly a disciplined, formation; four or five groups of scouts trotted well ahead of their main body, checking possible ambush positions, waited at each of these till the company passed through, and then came up for fresh orders. Twenty *firqats* screened the front of the main force, followed by SAS with the GPMGs and heavy loads mostly of ammunition, while more *firqats* covered the SAS Troop's rear. They fought off enemy attacks for over a week, although the water supply proved almost impossible to reach and quite impossible to hand up by bucket, an action which made clear that any permanently held *firqat* or SAF position would need an airstrip nearby, although the Sultan's Air Force 'had been superb', to quote Colonel Jeapes, flying strikes against the enemy and once landing supplies on a rough but level strip near the *firqat*. Thirty-five men of a second *firqat* had joined the *Salahadin* on the third or fourth day of the battle, and more *firqats* were in training by May.

The initial numbers in each company were small, thirty to forty men, but grew in strength as their successes attracted more volunteers, although Dhofari politics also played a decisive part in recruitment. The *Salahadin* company sixty-eight-strong by late April, was suddenly reduced to twenty-eight when forty men decided they would prefer to follow Qartoob, once an important DLF leader who had joined this company sometime after the night landing at Sudh. But the total strength of the *firqats* was by now about 450, and most of the men who left the *Salahadin* company joined their tribal *firqat* of the Bait Kathir. This was formed from the clans of both the west and east, who took several weeks to decide which of their leaders should command the *firqat*. In addition to this tribal company of irregulars, three others were being formed that summer, and the port of Sudh had its own local defence company trained by a SAS team.

There were those in SAS who felt that these companies might someday prove an embarrassment to orderly government in Dhofar, for their commanders were strong-minded individuals. They had, as others have done in the undeveloped world, intended to use Communism as a means to gaining an independent Dhofar, but few if any were true Communists. One former political commissar, who later died fighting for the Sultan, regarded Warrant Officer Birrell of the SAS 'Int' section as a 'Communist', merely because the WO had spoken of giving people a voice in their own future. Yet for all the stresses of competing modern ideology, the fundamental politics of the Dhofar were based on the family and the clan. A *firqat* sergeant-major was once murdered by a picket from a neighbouring company in the continuation of a long-standing blood feud.

After the SAS Troops were withdrawn, control of the *firqats* depended entirely on how closely integrated their British Liaison Officer became with his Company. Many of the best of these LOs were former SAS officers and NCOs, but even then the companies had understandable limitations. They were at their best moving swiftly to search a wadi, while regular forces held the high ground, and in passing into the opposition's territory to learn from a distant cousin, perhaps, or a wife's brother, things no regular military recce might discover. On the other hand they were not much use in conventional battles, although at times they were used as a screen of troops forward of an SAF battalion, intended to bump the enemy like beaters in a shoot for game birds.

There were many other actions in which SAS became involved over the years in Dhofar, after the summer of 1971 when they were allowed to send patrols onto the plateau (see Appendix II). The most decisive, however, fell to the Bat Troop training a *firqat* in Mirbat, a year after the *Salahadin* company trained there.

The opposition this misty morning, 19 July 1972, broke the long boredom of random shelling with half a dozen mortar bombs one day, followed by three 75-mm shells the next that kept a Troop of B Squadron aware of the opposition's presence beyond the wired perimeter of the town but did not interfere with the training programme. The Troop's Bat-house here was both a strongpoint, with two machine-guns in sand-bagged emplacements on its roof, and their HQ, in a single room below with its radio. To the west, overlooking the cattle-fence wire, for the perimeter was little more than that, was the fortified house of the *wali*, to the west a gun-pit with a 25-pounder and a fort nearby manned by *askars* and armed police.

On 17 July 1972, an *adoo* raiding party trailed its coat before the town, or at least near enough to it to draw the forty men in training out on a realistic exercise into the hills. Their departure left Captain Mike Kealy, aged twenty-three, with eight of his Troop and the *askars*, to defend the town. What no one in the military command – and less still young Kealy – knew was that the opposition had assembled secretly 250 of their best fighters to strike a blow for their cause by overrunning Mirbat. That raiding party had been a decoy, and now, with the 75mm ranged on the *askars*' fort, they were ready to launch a dawn attack.

About 0515 Corporal Bob Bradshaw and two SAS machine-gunners stood-to on the Bat-house roof. At 0530 the first shell exploded, then a second shook the house, and Kealy was up the bamboo ladder onto the roof. The Bat 81-mm mortar began returning fire, and the Fijian Corporal Labalaba raced over to help the Omani gunner fire his 25-pounder. *Adoo* came in small groups determined to cross the wire, one being shot as he straddled the fence, encouraging others to cross it. Several got through and were hit by carefully aimed machine-gun bursts as they made for the fort. Others crossed near the *wali*'s house and took cover in dead ground – safe from aimed fire – beyond it. Kealy radioed Salalah, calmly describing what was happening, although the mist hid a hilltop overlooking the town. He asked for Strikemasters to support his small defence force as soon as the mist cleared, and a helicopter to evacuate the wounded. The helicopter flew in during a lull, but its landing was aborted after Lance-Corporal Chapman had flung a red smoke canister of warning as the *adoo* machine-guns opened fire again.

Radio contact with the gun-pit was lost before then, and Kealy made a daring run with one of his medics, Corporal Tobin, across 400m of open ground to find out the situation there. The Fijian corporal had been wounded, as had Trooper Savesaki, who had gone to join him after Labalaba had radioed that he was wounded. In the next half hour, as Tokin dressed their wounds in turn, the Fijians continued to fire at *adoo* infiltrators. They got close enough to fling grenades towards the pit; one got around the sand-bagged wall but was shot by Kealy before the Arab could aim his Kalashnikov. A grenade fell at Kealy's feet but failed to explode. Labalaba had loaded and fired one or two 25-pounder rounds without help before he was killed. Tobin took over but was also hit. The Captain radioed his machine-gunners and mortarmen to fire at the fort wall just beyond the pit. Then, at 0900, with the weather clearing, two Strikemasters flew in, Kealy helping to direct them onto targets by a radio link through the Bat-house Sabre manned by Corporal Bradshaw, who also gave them targets. One 500-pound bomb caught the *adoo* on the east side of the fort, and they began to fall back towards the hills, giving Savesaki, an Arabic-speaker, the chance to call to the fort 'How are you?' Omani troops still held it.

About 0915, as a second pair of Strikemasters took over the strafing of the *adoo*, the first of three helicopters came in, carrying twenty-three men of G Squadron. 'G' was in the process of taking over from 'B', and most of its Troop commanders had left Salalah to join *firqats* in the hills, but by good fortune the Squadron's commander, his Sergeant-Major and these men had been paraded that morning to test-fire new weapons. They carried therefore nine GPMGs, four M79 grenade-launchers and Armalites or SLRs, formidable firepower as the *adoo* discovered. They probably looked a diminutive reinforcement as the helicopters landed south-east of the town after flying up the coast at sea-level, but in two ten-man battle groups, controlled by the Tac HQ, they began moving in leapfrog bounds towards the town. While the trainees who were not out in the hills moved out of the town to take their toll of *adoo*, the others in their *firqat* were caught by the retreating enemy but got back to the town carrying their dead and wounded. Kealy had been out to look for them, carrying a Sabre in the hope that he might direct the Strikemasters in their support, but the monsoon mists had persisted and he could see no further than 300m from the hill beyond the wire.

Throughout the battle Kealy had shown not only great courage but a cool judgement, despite the hammering noise of battle and the imminence of death. He was so tired that he had to cudgel his brain for the right decisions, yet he made them. His men, all experienced soldiers like Corporal Bradshaw, had also to make decisions on their own initiative. Kealy was awarded a DSO, Tobin a posthumous DCM, Corporal Bradshaw an MM and Corporal Labalaba a posthumous Mention in Despatches. There had been 'an unusually large number of gallant actions at Mirbat' as a senior SAF officer concluded in his despatch soon after the battle.

The opposition never again attempted such an attack, and in the terror which followed this defeat several Communists were executed as scapegoats for their collective failure. If these deaths are included, over a hundred of the enemy's best fighters had been killed or died of wounds as a result of the Mirbat action. For the Communists, it was the beginning of the end, although they fought on for another four years. During this time more *firqats* were raised, given support by SAF to seize a bridgehead in their tribal area, and patrolled from this base. A deep well would be drilled for a water supply to this centre, a Civil Aid Team would set up a clinic, a government shop would sell subsidized rations. Within a month herdsmen were using the water for their cattle, and relations of the *firqat* would bring in intelligence and see at first hand the Government's ability to provide for their people. Not surprisingly, *firqat* leaders then began to control their areas more as politicians than warlords, seeking new clinics, pre-fabricated schools and all the essentials for local government.

In October 1975 the SAF's British Chief of Staff, Brigadier (later General) John Akehurst, exploited what was intended to be a diversion. When the enemy did not oppose an advance by the Muscat Regiment, Akehurst reinforced it and within twenty-four hours SAF forces held a five-kilometre line cutting the camel caravan routes close to the Republic of Yemen's border. Thereafter Communist bands fought isolated actions in the eastern hills, the last of their leading supporters from the Bait Gatum 'coming over' early in 1976, after SAS Bat-Teams moved back into this area. Shelling from beyond the western border continued until April, and the following September the last SAS Squadron handed over its civilian aid work to the government's Civil Aid Department, run by a former SAS officer.

SAS concepts and ideas had proved far more influential than might be expected by so few soldiers – there had never been more than seventy to eighty officers and men of 22 SAS in Dhofar at any one time. Yet, as Colonel Jeapes has written after commanding the Regiment from 1974 to 1977, 'Persuading a man to join you is far cheaper than killing him. Words are far, far less expensive than bullets let alone shells and bombs . . . [and] by killing him you merely deprive the enemy of one soldier. If he is persuaded to join the Government forces . . . [there is] a gain of plus two.'

8. Internal Security

In 1969 D Squadron were sent to Northern Ireland for a few weeks in the late summer. Parading in uniform, with no attempt to hide their presence, they laid a wreath on Paddy Mayne's grave, searched fishing boats for possible Protestant gun-runners and returned to Hereford without any particular comment by the British or Irish Press. In the next few years, however, Press hostile to British attempts to bring peace to Ulster began implying that SAS were there in various guises. One of these, to quote Tony Geraghty, was as 'someone able to speak six languages while disguised as a bottle of Guinness'. Individual officers and men were seconded, as they are from time to time, to the Intelligence services and worked in Ulster after the spring of 1972, but a Squadron was not deployed there until 1974, although some Troopers – posing as having been returned to their original units – served in the Military Reconnaissance Force which had men in civilian clothes on the streets of Ulster. During 1974 the Squadron reinforced the MRF for a period and were then withdrawn since, by the 1970s, the knowledge that SAS Troops were deployed in any region suggested to some Press and politicians alike that there was an escalation of trouble or that one was expected by the British Government.

Prime Minister Harold Wilson astutely turned this respect for SAS to political advantage in January 1976, announcing in Parliament that SAS was to patrol the remote border territory of South Armagh. This 'escalation' of British commitment helped to satisfy Protestant feelings that not enough was being done to counter the Provisional IRA's successful forays into Armagh during which forty-nine soldiers had been killed. Yet only a few men, perhaps sixty, began the SAS patrols in Ulster. Some of these were made in unmarked cars by teams well armed to meet terrorist threats and intended to rout out local IRA leaders: within a year, four were killed or captured and six had moved south across the border. Certainly there were only two of the Security Forces killed in South Armagh that year, both men of the Ulster Defence Regiment shot while off duty. The strength of the SAS commitment was apparently raised by 1977 to two full Squadrons, although this would still be only 160 men.

There were mishaps: eight of the Regiment were brought to trial in

Dublin, having inadvertently crossed the border. Or had they broken the Regiment's Standard Operating Procedure and crossed it chasing a stolen car? There seemed every likelihood that this crossing was accidental, and after due process of Irish law the men were released. Then, just over a year later, in July 1978, a youngster came back to look at some explosives he had reported to the police the previous day. He was killed by an SAS Sergeant waiting, with a Corporal, to arrest anyone collecting this cache of arms from its graveyard hiding-place. There seems no doubt that Sergeant Bohan acted on reflex, as any trained soldier must do as he stands only ten metres from a man who appears to be about to aim a rifle when challenged. But the Court cases dragged on, for both men were accused of murder, charges on which they were eventually acquitted – although, to quote Geraghty again, one cynic in the Regiment remarked: 'Letting the opposition shoot first is what we call the "Irish Dimension".'

In March 1978 the then Minister for Defence announced that patrols from British Regiments would be deployed in Ulster trained for SAS-style undercover operations. Courses of instruction for these soldiers who would operate in plain clothes were no doubt organized by the Regiment, and the Minister's announcement points to a successful record for SAS patrols working undercover, although no details have been published, for obvious security reasons. The Regiment did give a hint at its methods or at least an indication of the quality of its patrols in answering a journalist's enquiry on SAS activities in Northern Ireland: 'The SAS,' the reply read, 'is a regiment of carefully selected, highly motivated and professional specialists.'

There is no doubt that these specialists are as competent in their use of modern surveillance techniques as they are in radio communications and other technical skills. They must therefore make good use of image-intensifiers (the 'shuftiscopes' which they have used since the 1970s), the portable radars on which a skilled operator can distinguish the blip reflected from the movement of a cow from that which indicates reflections from a man or woman. Modern infra-red detection devices and the tremblers of electronic sensors which react to all but the lightest footfall, they can not only sense when men or vehicles are using a route but relay up to seven kilometres a silent warning of their presence – more effective than the 'Claymore' minefields of Borneo, although not as immediately lethal. A single patrol, therefore, could cover a much wider area than might be expected, as they monitor the relays from these silent ambushes at illegal crossing-points along the border.

Patience, allied to such technical sophistication in these and other listening devices, must enable a patrol to watch and even to eavesdrop on meetings in the opposition's 'safe' houses or what they believe to be secure meeting places. This patience, of which SAS Troopers have an abundance when necessary, allowed some of their patrols to spend three weeks undetected in the Falklands during the 1982 campaign to recover the islands; there is, therefore, every reason to believe reports that they have at times stayed hidden for such periods in the countryside of Ulster.

The Regiment enjoys no special privileges in matters of discipline or command, being answerable through its Directorate at Hereford to the Ministry of Defence. Although their critics may wish to claim otherwise, no one has substantiated any more wayward actions than a bank robbery by two Troopers, who had abused the Regiment's training. It does not claim to perform more than a part of the total Security operations in Northern Ireland, the Oman or elsewhere. SAS authorities have stated that in Ulster the Regiment 'is conscious that the main burden falls on the uniformed elements of the Security Forces', although they appear always to have contributed a good number of effective ideas for any operations in which they are deployed. In matters of life and death, the SAS is the only Regiment in history which can claim with justifiable pride to have saved or delivered into this world more babies than the number of enemies it has killed, for the medical services it has provided in remote regions of the world far outweigh the extent of its lethal use of firepower. That is not to say that SAS do not regularly run more risks of death than most soldiers, but with their skill at arms they can be precise in hitting targets, an essential criterion for operations in heavily populated areas.

In 1973 a Counter Revolutionary Warfare Team (CRW) was formed by the Regiment, when they were given an official anti-terrorist role. This was added to their commitments for deep-penetration raids in Europe in the event of a major conflict and their training teams' work in Dhofar. Speculation on precisely how Standard Operating Procedures might be laid down for the CRW would be foolish and no doubt inaccurate, for Hereford must have access to equipment, methods and ideas which even a producer of a James Bond film has never dreamt of. They also have close links with British Intelligence services, judging by the few facts which journalists have uncovered and which common sense suggests would be essential in any operations far behind a main battlefront in Europe.

Hostility in the late twentieth century, however, has never involved a shoot-out between European armies. What it has produced is a series of terrorist acts to achieve ends which often turn out, on examination, to be criminal rather than ideological. Certainly in Europe the terrorist tends to rob banks to finance his or her activities, which can only then be rationalized by trumping up some cause, while the public rightly support the SAS as a force which protects them from such criminal elements.

In April 1980, for example, seven terrorists of unknown nationality flew into London from Iraq. Their briefing, by whoever sent them had painted a misleading picture of the irresolute stand a British government might take when threatened with the death of hostages. These were to be seized in the Iranian Embassy with a view to forcing the Iranian government to release several men in their custody who wanted independence for the rich Iranian oil province at the head of the Persian Gulf. The terrorists' paymasters allowed them a month in London, when they bought all manner of Western luxuries, from toys to video recorders, and arranged for them to be airfreighted to Baghdad. Only their leader spoke English, and not fluently at that; nor were his men properly trained in the use of the Soviet RGD-5 grenades, automatic pistols and carbines with which they were armed, no doubt because their paymasters expected that there would be no need to resort to violence. A quick threat, publicity for their province's independence, and even if the Teheran authorities failed to release any prisoner, the terrorists would be allowed to put their arguments for independence to three selected Arab diplomats, before being deported to Iraq. But there was to be no free flight 'home'.

On the morning of 30 April 1980, a Tuesday, the terrorists entered the Embassy in Prince's Gate, London, held up the security staff and gained control of what was a large building with fifty rooms, threatening to blow it up, with the hostages, if the demands were not met. There were twenty-one hostages, including Police Constable Trevor Lock of the small section of Metropolitan Police trained to guard embassies, Sim Harris, from the BBC, who was visiting the Embassy, the Iranian Press Attaché and other Embassy staff, including five women. The Metropolitan Police began the psychological and highly skilled negotiations by which the terrorists come to identify themselves with a single negotiator who speaks of 'us' and 'them' – the Security Forces. This process of talking the terrorists into surrender needs time, days if not weeks. Always provided no hostage has been murdered.

On the fourth day, at about 1300 hours, the terrorists sealed their own fate, when they shot the Press Attaché, Abbas Lavasani, and dumped his body on the front steps. Their leader then told the negotiator that one hostage would be killed every thirty minutes until he was allowed to negotiate with the three Arab ambassadors in London. For the British Government there was no option but to refuse this blackmail, not only because once governments allow such terrorists' threats to succeed there would be no end to such demands but also because the Teheran government had decided the whole affair was an Anglo-American plot. Americans had been held in their Teheran embassy for months, and an American Special Force's attempt to rescue them had come to nothing that April. Now in Teheran there was the sort of misunderstanding which stems from suspicious minds. At Hereford CRW teams were on standby as the 'Kremlin' monitored events and teams were sent to West London six hours before a formal order to move them was received that Tuesday from the Ministry of Defence. They then spent five days planning the operation, which they expected would be violent in view of the terrorists' stated determination to die if they did not achieve their objectives. Neither Press nor public knew that the teams were in London until they appeared about 1900 hours the following Sunday, a fine summer's evening, when marksmen began to cordon off the building. They would ensure that no terrorist escaped from the scene, not only at ground level but by way of the sewers or over the roofs. The assault group would break into the building, an operating procedure in which they were well rehearsed. They could detect which rooms were occupied by scanning a building from the outside with a thermal imager: use of fibre-optic equipment threaded into a room from next door maybe, to view much that was going on without the occupants noticing the tiny intrusion, or the CRW might overhear conversations on various types of listening devices.

Each man was dressed completely in black, from his Balaclava helmet to his gloves and boots ; some carried Heckler and Koch MP5 submachine-guns, with a special ammunition that ensured great accuracy and modifications to the magazine to minimize, if not eliminate, stoppages. The 'HK' fires ten 9-mm rounds a second but has only a relatively short lethal range which ensures that any bullets which fly out of a window do not cause damage to innocent neighbours; some HKs had powerful torches attached. They also probably had a Remington shotgun to blast open doors locked by terrorists; other means of entry might need a prepared charge of plastic explosive, such as the armoured glass windows of the Embassy would require. A frame of PE could cut these, whereas most bullets would not break them. Each man also carried a personal radio so that the operation could be controlled in the smoke and dark of the building.

The sole objective of the CRW is to rescue hostages alive. If they have to kill the terrorists to achieve this, then the terrorists die. There are times when distinguishing who is hostage and who his or her keeper must be extremely difficult, but no doubt SAS has developed some tricks for this. Certainly they can stun everyone in a room or in the confines of an aircraft fuselage with the XFS grenade devised in the back rooms of the Hereford Headquarters. This cardboard carton of explosive, with its two-second fuse, sheds its only hard metal mechanism in flight before exploding with such an intensity of light and noise that anyone within a few metres of its blast is temporarily blinded and stunned. They also had CS (Canister Smoke) gas against which they wore respirators (gasmasks) throughout any operation in which it might be needed. The rest – and it is a lot of skills – entails that agility and training by which SAS Troopers have mastered Close Quarter Battle techniques described earlier.

The CRW is not directly involved in the 'bore them to death' conversations of police negotiations, but the responsible officers are kept in touch with their progress. Quite properly, the police have absolute control at the scene during this stage of any counter-terrorist operation, but in the case of Prince's Gate and other cases of political blackmail, direction of the operation is in the hands of the Home Secretary, who has overall political responsibility for security matters in the United Kingdom. He has a small committee to advise him, on which sits an SAS representative among others, giving the CRW direct access to the top decision-making, as well as liaison with the police at the scene.

When the CRW were told that they could proceed, they knew exactly what they would do, because they undoubtedly had done their 'homework'. From the day the siege started, if not before, SAS planners must have known the layout of the Embassy, how its rooftop might be reached from neighbouring buildings, the direction which the drains followed beneath it, and the strength of its walls and ceilings. All they needed to check, minutes before the assault, was the latest information on the position of the terrorists in the building. Fifteen hostages, all men, had been taken to the Telex room on the second floor at the front of the building, with three terrorists guarding them, although from time to time one or other of these would walk into other rooms to check them, for the terrorists were growing tenser as an assault seemed likely. Five women members of the Embassy staff were in a room opposite the Telex room, across a landing and at the back of the building. One floor below, on the first-floor landing, PC Lock and the man from the BBC, Harris, were by the telephone on which the terrorist leader was talking to the police negotiator.

The SAS plan was to blow in the first-floor window, a team crossing from a neighbouring balcony to one opposite the first armoured window, while pairs of Troopers abseiled down the back of the building to the first- and second-floor windows and others would blow open the back door. When the front window was blown in, the terrorists could be expected to be distracted in that direction, and the blast of this explosion was the signal for the abseil parties to break into the back of the building.

As they set off down their ropes – the timing in the operation seems to have been immaculate – they had their only mishap, when a man accidentally put his foot through an upper-storey window. As this glass broke, the terrorist leader put down the phone and went to look out of the back window. If he saw anything at this stage, it was a brief glimpse of men hurtling down the back wall at a frightening speed. They could not now rely on surprise nor wait for the front window explosion. Two began hacking out the second-floor window, and a team coming from behind a garden wall reached the back door. They were unable to use their explosives because one man was snarled up on the rope opposite the second-floor window. They therefore smashed down the doors with sledgehammers, ignored possible booby-traps and fanned out into the building, behind a screen of SMG fire and stun-grenades. The main power switch was cut at this time, throwing all the shuttered and curtained rooms into darkness.

Inside the building the terrorist leader now took aim at the SAS, who were hacking through the windows, but before he could fire, PC Lock brought him to the ground with a rugby tackle. At the front, with the charge set against the armoured window, the two Troopers clambered back across a short alloy ladder laid horizontally to the neighbouring balcony, one pausing first to set the fuse to this frame of explosive. Millions of TV-viewers later saw that explosion on their screens, the two men then disappearing into the smoke. Lock was struggling with the terrorist, the policeman drawing his .38-inch revolver which he had concealed throughout the siege, waiting for just such a moment. A cry from the first 'Trooper' – no doubt an officer or senior NCO – through the window on the first floor parted the struggling pair, and the terrorist was killed by a brief burst of fire before he could fire at Lock. Harris had moved towards the front of the building, to be met with a sharp command to 'get down' as the team who had come through the window passed him before flinging a stun-grenade. They had come up the stairs and on up towards the Telex room. Above them one of the terrorists had run into a fourth-floor room at the front, been heard or seen on some device no doubt, and was chased out by a canister of smoke with its 'tear gas' effect. The three terrorists in the Telex room had begun shooting their hostages, but the man guarding the women threw away his weapons and hid among these ladies.

The team which broke into the Telex room, the first one SAS cleared, found that the terrorists had killed the assistant press attaché but failed to kill two more, whom their shots had missed. Now they too were pretending to be hostages; they gave no sign that they had surrendered; no one had his hands up or was offering to submit to the Troopers. They demanded to know which the terrorists were, for they had claimed to have the embassy wired up with explosive. A hostage pointed them out and both were shot.

By now the heavy curtains on the front windows were on fire, and the building had begun to burn. This fire spread to the back, and the man still snarled up on his abseil rope – no doubt this nylon had sprung like elastic to trap his equipment – was being singed by the heat. Someone cut the rope and he dropped a storey. None the worse for falling five or six metres, he went into the building and shot the fifth terrorist as he tried to dodge out of a back door. The man on the upper storey was killed but the seventh man, who had been hiding among his women hostages, was tied up and bundled outside, as were all the hostages. Trussed up, the terrorists had no chance for suicidal heroics, a precaution justified as it turned out, for the women had not identified the seventh as a terrorist; Harris did this in the courtyard. He was later tried and sentenced.

Some have questioned whether the deaths of these terrorists might not have been avoided, but there is no doubt in this author's mind that they were bound to be shot when they failed to surrender – otherwise why hide, if not to blow up the building at the first opportunity? Had they done so, not only would the hostages have been killed and the SAS operation have been a failure but the implications of future terrorists' threats in London would have been open-ended. As the terrorists had died, others of any persuasion would be less inclined to use London as a battleground.

9. South Atlantic Victory

On Friday 2 April Lieutenant-Colonel M. (Mike) Rose OBE, QGM, the commanding officer of 22 SAS, heard on the BBC news that the Falklands had been invaded. He immediately put D Squadron on three hours' notice to move, men being brought back from leave, from training courses and from other duties, and they were given a general briefing that Sunday. Meanwhile the 'Kremlin's' staff had gathered together all the information that they could find about the islands in the MOD map-room, from the British Antarctic Survey's headquarters in Cambridge and no doubt from a few other, more confidential sources. But there were no contingency plans in SAS files or elsewhere in the British services for a recovery of the Falklands, because any of the long-term planners who had considered it had realized that it would be almost impossible to sustain such a campaign. The nearest feasible base from which to launch an amphibious assault was Ascension Island, nearly 7,000km from the UK ports and airfields, while the British garrison of forty Royal Marine commandos in Port Stanley, capital of the islands, was a further 6,250km from Ascension. These distances put Port Stanley as far from London as Rangoon, but with only open ocean, apart from Ascension, between the UK and the Falklands.

Early on Saturday the Navy's equivalent of the SAS, the Royal Marines' Special Boat Squadron, asked for two divers – one a former Marine – to complete a team flying out to Ascension and no doubt on from there to join a British submarine in the South Atlantic. (The SBS have released few details of their operations in 1982, and therefore a number of aspects of their activities can only be surmised.) Two of G Squadron joined 2 SB Section at the RAF airbase at Lyneham, Wiltshire, but there were no movement orders for D Squadron. Mike Rose therefore took initiatives to get the Regiment into action which its CO has to take from time to time, as Woodhouse did in Borneo. Rose telephoned the senior officer who would command the operation, Brigadier (later Major-General) Julian Thompson OBE, who commanded 3 Commando Brigade RM which was at seventy-two hours' notice to sail for the South Atlantic. Naval and Royal Marine staffs were working round the clock to arrange the embarkation of the men and war stores needed by the Brigade to spearhead any re-conquest of the islands in an operation that was codenamed 'Corporate'.

A small advance party from 'D' flew to Ascension that Sunday as approval had been given for the Regiment to join the Task Force. Reference has been made to the Sabre Squadrons' tendency to work to Hereford rather than to local force commanders but in this operation the work of all Special Forces, both SAS and SBS, was co-ordinated through a command cell in Rear-Admiral 'Sandy' Woodward's flagship, HMS *Hermes*. Although she carried mainly Sea Harriers, she also had twelve Sea King HC4s of 846 Naval Air Squadron equipped to land commandos with whom they normally trained. There were few opportunities for comprehensive training on Ascension, however, as this small island can barely sustain its civilian population of a thousand, and the Royal Navy severely limited the numbers of commandos and other forces who could be ashore at any one time. Nevertheless, when D Squadron arrived by air, they were billeted in a disused school, the eighty or so Troopers sweating out the tropical days, keeping as fit as conditions allowed and test-firing their weapons on the improvised ranges, while in London the first steps in the recovery of the Falklands were being planned with more diplomatic than military activity. Yet the British had to show that they were able to send more than submarines into Falkland waters, strengthening diplomatic initiatives which outweighed purely military considerations on a number of occasions as the campaign developed, although in April it seemed to almost all the members of the Brigade and SAS that there was unlikely to be any major conflict, even though they made every preparation to face one.

Colonel Rose and the officer commanding 'D', Major Cedric Delves, were keen to get the whole Squadron embarked when there was a request for an SAS Troop to sail for an undefined assignment. No doubt with the help of Hereford, the Navy were persuaded to take the whole Squadron in the fleet auxiliary *Fort Austin*, of 23,600 tons with facilities for four helicopters, as her assignment might lead to action which at that time seemed likely to be the only battle in this war. She sailed in company with the large destroyer HMS *Antrim* (6,200 tons), the frigate *Plymouth* (2,800 tons) and the large fleet tanker *Tidespring* (27,400 tons).

Aboard the tanker were M Company of 42 Commando RM, who, Delves learnt, were to be landed in South Georgia. This island lies 1,300km east-south-east of the Falklands and, as the main base of the British Antarctic Survey (BAS) teams, was particularly important to the British. More significantly, its recapture would be a clear indication to the world's diplomats that the British intended to fight if necessary to recapture occupied territory.

The second-in-command of 42 Commando, Major Guy Sheridan RM, was in command of the landing forces including the SAS and would work with Cedric Delves aboard *Antrim* in planning their assault on the island. In addition to 'D', Sheridan had some 120 men of M Company and about twenty-five swimmer-canoeists of 2 SBS, and there was a small detachment of Marines aboard *Antrim* with M Company's Recce Troop, a mortar section and the company's OC, Captain Chris Nunn RM: in all about 235 all ranks. Nobody could be sure how many Argentinians held the island, although three weeks earlier fifty or more of their Marines, supported by a Corvette, had seized the island after a four-hour battle with half their number of Royal Marines.

Sailing in radio silence, *Antrim*'s amphibious flotilla received a signal, no doubt dropped from a maritime reconnaissance aircraft, authorizing Sheridan to carry out covert recess on South Georgia, and plans were made for the Mountain Troop of D Squadron to land north of Leith, where the Argentinians had been collecting scrap from an old whaling station. 2 SBS would land about the same time in Hounds Bay, south-east of the island's main settlement of Grytviken, and move up the coast in their inflatable boats to establish OPs which could watch the settlement from across five kilometres of open water.

D Squadron had transhipped from *Fort Austin* to the ice-patrol ship HMS *Endurance*. Her crew were familiar with the harsh conditions on this island, with its bare rock mountains, swept by sudden gales, their intensity increased as the wind funnelled down valleys with gusts of over 150mph. Nor was the weather here predictable: what appeared as a 'window' of clear weather could be closed in minutes by whirling snow storms.

All this information the Troopers noted but since they included at least one man with Himalayan experience, they did not consider it would cause them undue difficulty. They prepared themselves with the usual SAS thoroughness. Arctic cold-weather kit was drawn from *Endurance*'s stores, as were four sledges (*pulks* hauled by hand), and detailed plans of the buildings on King Edward Point were carefully traced from drawings. These buildings had housed the Survey HQ and were now the Argentinian headquarters at the mouth of a cove a thousand metres from Grytviken. The Mountain Troop commander, Captain John (Gavin) Hamilton made sure that nothing was left to chance, although when he and the Troop flew to *Antrim*, the choice of Fortuna Glacier as the Troop's starting point was questioned. Major Sheridan, a mountaineer of considerable experience in high snows and ice, advised against it but was impressed with the whole Squadron's 'get up and go' attitude. Because of his RM rank, which, as a major, equates to that of an Army lieutenant-colonel, he was senior to Delves, but this was not a time to debate finer points of authority, and Hamilton was allowed to attempt his landing on this difficult LZ.

At midday local time on 21 April, three Wessex made an attempt to reach the LZ 500m above sea-level on the glacier. They were met by a 'white-out', with wind-driven snow making the earth and sky indistinguishable, conditions in which even a man on skis may lose not only his sense of direction but also his balance. The helicopters were not able to land until their third attempt later that afternoon, and then the wind was blowing at 80k.p.h., driving fine ice particles before it. These stung the men's eyes if they were not wearing goggles and more dangerously choked the mechanisms of their GPMGs.

They made the best that they could of the conditions, Sergeant 'Lofty' Arthy leading them down the glacier ice in arrowhead formation. They had intended to split up into four patrols, one to watch Leith, one Stromness and one Husvik, seven rugged kilometres from the LZ, while the fourth went down the opposite west slope to recce Fortuna Bay for boat and helicopter landing-points. Each man carried over 35kg of equipment including his weapons, and they hauled the heavily loaded *pulks* with their dead weight each of 300kg, equivalent to hauling a couple of bodies across the ice. After five hours they had covered 800m, continuously probing the snow layer to check for crevasses in the ice.

There would be no patrols that night, as in the gathering gloom of a southern 'autumn' evening they attempted to make camp and find some protection from the piercing cold. They were putting up two small tents in the slight shelter offered by a rock outcrop when the wind swept one away; five men climbing into the second one were hard put to keep its canvas from being buffeted across the ice. The rest of the Troop snatched what sleep they could 'in bivvy bags with their boots on'. Hurricane Force 11 winds howling over the mountains that night meant inevitably that the Troop would have to be withdrawn as soon as possible. Otherwise cold weather injuries, when hypothermia and frostbite disable a man, could become so severe that the men risked losing one or more limbs should frostbite become acute.

Next day, Wednesday, three Wessex helicopters ('helos' as the Navy call them) made several attempts to land on the glacier. The lead aircraft was equipped for anti-submarine warfare (A/SW), its radar navigation and other electronics being used to guide the helos to the Sabre beacon. When the weather cleared, they could see the green smoke from one of the chemical canisters set off by a Trooper, but this must have been quickly scattered down the wind, which was so turbulent in the glacier valley that flying was extremely difficult. Delves came in with the helicopters for this recovery – if not rescue – of his Squadron's Mountain Troop, and all of them were soon in the aircraft. The A/SW helo, stripped of some of its gear to enable it to carry a few of the Troopers, lifted off, followed by the second and third Wessex, which were troop-carrying helos. They were barely airborne when the second aircraft flew into a 'white-out', hitting the ice just after the pilot managed to 'push up' its nose. In the resulting crash an SAS Corporal was the only person injured from the seven aboard, including the pilot. They were then redistributed between the other aircraft, and the men ditched all but their weapons and belt equipment; the A/SW helo was also lightened by leaving part of its special equipment on the ground.

They took off again, but this time, when the pilot of the A/SW Wessex, Lieutenant-Commander Ian Stanley RN, was airborne, he saw through the white flurry below his rotors that the other Wessex had crashed. As much of his fuel had been used, he had no option but to fly back to *Antrim* after noting the position of the crash. He refuelled, but when he was back over the glacier much of it was hidden beneath a blizzard. The men on the ground radioed that they were 'making themselves comfortable', as comfortable, that is, as possible with only one survival tent and what kit they could salvage from the crashed aircraft. Stanley returned later that Wednesday and in a sustained piece of superb flying not only landed but took off with fifteen survivors besides his navigator and himself in the helo. It was so overloaded that, coming into land on *Antrim*, it flopped onto her tiny flight deck rather than making the Commander's usual elegant touchdown.

Thursday was a day for reassessing the position, and next evening 'D's' Boat Troop was launched, with the intention of setting up OPs on the north-west coast of the island. They had persistent trouble with the outboard motors of their three-man inflatable dinghies and set off to cross the 750m from *Antrim* to their landing point on Grass Island, with only two engines working, one craft towing two others and the second powered craft towing the fifth inflatable. They were making steady, if slow, progress in relatively calm water until they were some 400m from the beach, when a blasting gust of wind off the mountains tore apart the towlines of two dinghies, which were swept away westward. The crews of the other three craft got ashore and set up their watch on Leith and Stromness. These whaling stations were now virtually deserted, but thirty years earlier there had been twelve hundred men working in the blubber factories at various stations around the island.

This same Thursday night the SBS teams were flown in and, having launched their boats on the shores of the eastern arm of Cumberland Bay, which leads to King Edward Point, found that chunks of glacier ice floating in the bay were being driven ashore by the wind. So sharp-edged were these small floes that they punctured the buoyancy off the SBS craft and their recce had to be abandoned. They were brought back aboard *Antrim* in the early hours of Saturday.

Later that day an Argentinian reconnaissance plane flew over the area, no doubt looking for *Endurance* but – the British later learnt – the Argentinians' initial fears of landings had been disarmed, probably because this plane saw no signs of men having got ashore. Reports of the presence of one of their submarines, however, scattered the British ships away to the north of the island. In searching for her that morning Commander Stanley spotted one of the missing SAS inflatables, lifting its three men to safety after a corporal had made sure that the dinghy would sink. There was no sign of the second craft that was missing and which was possibly blown clear of the island into the vastness of the southern ocean. While the other ships sailed north, *Endurance* tucked herself out of radar contact and sight, in the steeply sided Hound Bay, from where no doubt she monitored Argentinian radio signals and probably heard the signal reporting that the submarine had landed reinforcements on the island, bringing its garrison strength to 140.

That Saturday night the British ships moved back into their patrolling positions off the coast, although *Tidespring* remained well to the north as she refilled her tanks from another fleet oiler. Not long before dawn Stanley re-inserted the SBS teams and was flying back from this mission when he spotted the submarine on the surface as she sailed over the shallows of Cumberland Bay, heading out to look for the British ships. He straddled her with two depth-charges, and soon afterwards she was attacked by *Endurance*'s Wasp and the Lynx from HMS *Brilliant*, a Type 22 Destroyer of 4,000 tons. These helicopters forced the submarine to run for King Edward Point, her conning tower damaged and listing after being hit by missiles.

Twenty-four hours earlier, just before the British ships scattered north, Sheridan had been giving his final orders for an immediate landing to seize Leith and Stromness, although the recces were incomplete. No doubt there was pressure from London to retake the island quickly, as further indication of Britain's political resolve, so he was keen to get his men ashore. But with M Company still six hours or more away from the coast, as *Tidespring* was still replenishing her tanks, a landing force would have to be improvised if he and Delves were to exploit the Argentinians' set-back. The Majors decided on a bold stroke, and a quick reaction force of three composite Troops was formed aboard *Antrim*. Delves would lead the Mountain and Boat Troops, 2 SBS and commando recce Sections of '42' would form a second composite Troop, and a third was made up from commando mortarmen with ships' Marines, in all totalling seventy-five all ranks and little over half the strength of the island's garrison.

Some hours elapsed before the Navy were ready to execute the plan, but at 1435 a Wasp helo landed a Royal Artillery commando officer, to direct the fire of *Antrim*'s two 4.5-inch (114mm) guns in a shoot that would ensure the landing area and Brown Mountain which dominated it were clear of Argentinians. The SAS composite Troop then landed in a high valley two kilometres south-east of the British Survey buildings on King Edward Point. They were followed by the other composite Troops. Already Sheridan had been in contact through *Antrim*'s radio with the

Argentinian headquarters in the Survey buildings. Fearful of the naval firepower, they were ready to surrender and warned that there were minefields laid in defence of their weapon pits.

Meanwhile, unaware of these mines, Delves was leading his men across Brown Mountain. They shot up some elephant seals, easily mistaken for men in woollen Balaclava helmets among tussocks of grass. A couple of similar confusions occurred, but when the Troop reached the top of Brown Mountain, they could see only an apparently deserted settlement with white flags flying from several buildings, although the Argentinian flag still flew from its mast near the headquarters. Sheridan had been unable to contact Delves on the radio but the SAS Major moved his men quickly down to the shore where there were unlikely to be mines, and the Troop arrived at the buildings as the garrison paraded for surrender. Next morning SAS and SBS teams flew into Leith and took the surrender of its garrison. That morning a Sabre radio signal was received from the three men in the second dinghy, which had been blown westward. They had been lying low after paddling ashore on the north coast of Stromness Bay, four kilometres from their intended landing point, and survived three bleak days on this icebound shore, keeping radio silence so as not to compromise the other recce parties. A helicopter answered their signal and picked them up 'still fit to fight'.

The importance of this swift operation was the recapture of a base much closer to the Falklands than Ascension, where ships could anchor beyond the range of Argentinian fighter-bombers, although it had no major airstrip. Its capture was also another turn of the diplomatic screw as the British government tried to avoid the need for a possibly bloody assault on the Falkland Islands.

While D Squadron were fighting the elements and the Argentinians on South Georgia, 'G' were sailing south in a fleet replenishment ship, the RFA *Resource* (22,890 tons). She had a helicopter flightdeck from which Troopers could be flown to other ships, including HMS *Hermes* leading the naval battle group towards the Falklands.

No amount of diplomacy now was going to take the islands back from the Argentinians, so, in a classic use of sea power, the British first posed a threat to the occupation forces and then put a landing force ashore.

Before any landing could be made, however, confirmation was needed of the exact disposition of the garrison's defences. Some sensible – and, as later proved, correct – conjectures were made by the British staffs when considering these in April. At that time they assessed the likely Argentinian strength to be around Port Stanley, with the heaviest concentration of their forces facing south-west to prevent any advance along a motorable track from Fitzroy. Apart from the fact that a number of the defences were well camouflaged, there were no aerial or detailed satellite pictures available, so old-fashioned 'eye-ball' recces were needed. This was a job given to the SAS and SBS, Special Forces trained in deep penetration raids which suited them ideally for this role. They would have to cover not only the two main islands of East and West Falkland but also some of the smaller islands around their 15,000km of coast line.

The two main islands have a total area nearly equivalent to that of Wales, with a terrain not unlike windswept Dartmoor, rough pasture with no trees. On the Falklands, however, there were many bogs and rock runs of slippery, moss-sided boulders which in some runs are a metre or more across. Although the hills along the northern half of East Falkland – the island's so-called mountains – rise to only 450m on Mount Kent, their climate is equivalent to that on English hills of twice this height or more. The Special Forces' teams faced a daunting task in surviving in such conditions for many days at a time, never mind their doing so without being detected by the Argentinians.

Much has been written about the lax military manner of these enemy forces, yet in April and May they were far from being defeated, especially in their regular, as opposed to conscripted regiments, which, for example, included an airfield defence unit that fought bravely at Goose Green. In another action a patrol of Argentinian Marines successfully directed the bombing runs of Argentinian fighter-bombers against British ships in San Carlos Water, until the patrol was captured. The Argentinians also had effective radio direction-finding equipment by which they located several British officers landed on the islands to direct naval gunfire by radio. Against such opposition the Special Forces' success in maintaining patrols on the islands from 1 May until the British landings three weeks later, without any of these soldiers and Marines being captured, was confirmation indeed of their professionalism. Later, when the SAS and SBS teams continued to patrol areas dominated by the enemy in East Falkland, they also maintained their close observation of the garrisons on West Falkland, which lies twenty kilometres and less in the north, across Falkland Sound from the eastern island.

The British plan in broad terms was to land on East Falkland sufficiently far from Port Stanley's airfield and large garrison, to enable a beach-head to be established before it could be heavily counter-attacked. From there the main thrust of the attack would cross the mountains, where, as the British rightly believed, the Argentinians would not be expecting any major force. Once across these uplands, the back-door to Stanley, so to speak, would be open. This proved to be the case, but in April hard military intelligence was needed to reinforce the theory of this plan, if the landing force were to be put ashore without undue risks.

Some examples of these recces by both G and D Squadrons are briefly summarized in Appendix II, and one of the most daring on East Falkland can be reconstructed on the assumption that it followed the general pattern of these operations, always with the proviso that no two patrols were alike. But with that in mind, the story of Captain Aldwin Wight's recce of Stanley can be recounted.

Wight's mission began on *Resource*, where the G Squadron's operations room was housed – if that is the word – in the ladies' lavatory. His team took off in a Sea King HC4 of 846 Naval Air Squadron, to fly over 200km to an LZ in the centre of the island. They followed a route over the north-west coast of the island, flying the last twenty kilometres up a valley that led to the uplands well inland from the coast. The noise of the Sea King's rotors being dispersed on the wind, her arrival over the LZ drew no enemy attention, in part perhaps because they would not expect helicopters to land at night without lights. Yet the pilot was able to put them down on the LZ almost as easily as he would land in daylight, because he wore Passive Night Goggles, which gleaned every scrap of starlight and residual moonlight that filters through clouds even on a dark night, intensifying this light in a way that enabled the pilot to see the countryside, albeit in shades of blue. At that time there were only a dozen or so sets of PNG with the helicopter squadron, and these had been borrowed only a day or two before they sailed, when scientists evaluating them realized that they might be invaluable in the South Atlantic.

The navigator of the helo was able, using its electronic aids, to pinpoint the LZ which had been chosen by Wight as the starting point for his long approach march to the intended sight of an OP overlooking Stanley. The importance of landing at the exact LZ cannot be too strongly emphasized, for a day or more might have been wasted on foot in finding the correct start of a route, had the helo not put them down at the correct LZ. Movement over this rough terrain would prove a slow process at night, and by day the teams must lie hidden as Argentinian helicopters and patrols moved over the hills. Enemy foot patrols might even have been about at night, and therefore the team wasted no time in off-loading their kit, as one man moved away from the LZ to act as sentry. The helicopter would be gone in seconds rather than minutes, hovering perhaps for ninety seconds over the LZ with its wheels half a metre from the turf.

The team set out with the lead scout periodically scanning the ground ahead of them through the night sight of his rifle, as they moved along a compass bearing on the first leg of their route. This, like each future leg, had been carefully chosen, and on later nights, as they neared known Argentinian positions – identified by the camp fires that they had lit – a leg might be recced by Wight before the team set off. They would be making good progress if they covered fifteen kilometres in a night, as they had to move silently in case there were Argentinian sentries watching and listening. Men seldom spoke, even in a whisper, but passed on directions

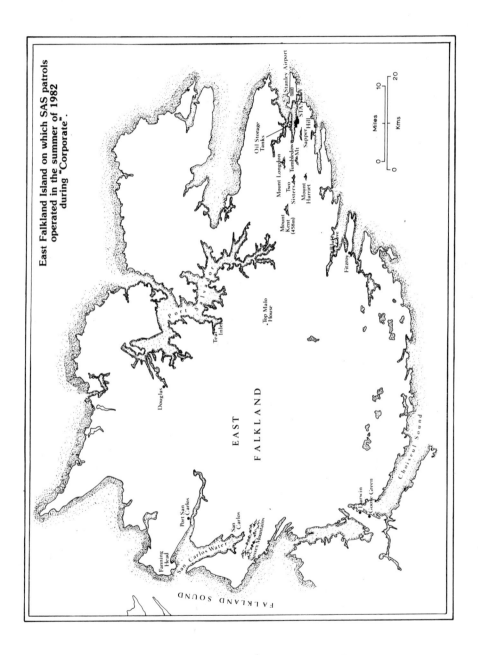

East Falkland Island on which SAS patrols operated in the summer of 1982 during "Corporate".

and signalled warnings by a grip of a Trooper's arm and a finger pointed in the direction of possible danger. At times when minefields might be expected, they had to tread even more warily.

Three nights of such movement brought them to Beagle Ridge, after lying hidden in scrapes each day. They had passed through areas constantly patrolled by the Argentinians, which must have meant particularly stealthy movement at night and effective camouflage to their 'hides' during the day. From Beagle Ridge they moved to set up their OP on Beaver Ridge, where 'there was little cover from view or the elements', to quote Wight's citation for gallantry. Their observation post must nevertheless have been cleverly camouflaged with a roof of turf that melted into surrounding ground and possibly some form of additional cover which hid them from the view of thermal imagers which helicopter crews might use in their sweeps over the hillside.

The hide was always damp, despite its lining of plastic sheets, poorly ventilated if ventilated at all, and with only a small aperture through which a powerful telescope gave them a view of Stanley airfield on a clear day. This small opening did not provide any more than a glimmer of light, and therefore there seems to have been no chance to read any paperback during the more tedious hours. On alternate days, or on most of them, the port and surrounding countryside were enveloped in fog during these early weeks of May. But when they could observe the town, spending a couple of hours watching through the telescope, a man's eyes would be red-rimmed with fatigue. For the eight hours of daylight every day, he was cramped and uncomfortable, his boots damp and his limbs numb as his blood circulation became constricted. Only at night could he move out of this hole and stretch, so that, gradually, with some pain, the circulation was restored to numbed feet. There was a chance also for warm food, cooked on the tiny hexamine stove shielded from view; this meal was the only source of warmth, as all day the men ate mere snacks of cheese, biscuits and chocolate. Wight's men may, like some SBS teams, have cached spare clothing and food some distance from their hide, although even a change of socks left one's feet damp and cold, leading to the uncomfortable foot-rot known as 'trench feet'.

After the first few days, even this stark pattern of life became a routine, and there was time to take stock of the situation. Listening to the BBC World Service radio over muffled headphones, the team kept abreast of developments in the councils of the United Nations. They learnt of setbacks and occasional triumphs perhaps but pondered their own position should they become involved in a shoot-out when war had not been officially declared. If they did become involved in any fighting, there was no quick-reaction force to fly in to their rescue. Being men of the character they are, however, they did not dwell on the difficulties but got on with their job of watching and reporting, their information 'giving a clear and accurate picture of enemy activity in the Stanley area', to quote again from Wight's citation.

Among these reports were the locations of Argentinian helicopter-parks, for by mid-May, some of these aircraft were being flown each night into the hills away from the airport, which the British bombed from the air and bombarded from the sea on several nights. The dispersed aircraft were seen by SAS patrols and attacked by Harriers, although there was always difficulty in getting reports back to *Hermes* since the patrols could not broadcast even short messages without the risk of being D/F-ed, as they had few, if any, so-called 'burst' radios. (These first recorded an encoded message in morse and then squirted it out in fractions of a second.) Wight's operator may have had one of these or, in the long-established practice, using a one-time pad (see p. 71), have sent a brief few groups of letters which were a pre-arranged signal to indicate particular events. Some patrols had to be lifted out for debriefing or sent reports back with the helos that flew in to re-supply them. Whatever method was used took time to reach the Special Forces' command cell unless it could be sent on a 'burst' radio. Once, reportedly, Wight's team sent information on a target, but due to the scarcity of Harrier aircraft and to the foggy weather no doubt, three days passed before it was attacked.

Any temptation for the patrol to emulate Paddy Mayne on such occasions had to be resisted, in part because the British did not want to reveal the extent of their recces before D-Day on 21 May, while any skirmish could only further compromise what little hope there was of achieving a settlement by diplomacy. Wight's team avoided these temptations, enduring for twenty-six days the frustrations of cramped conditions and the risks of detection by the Argentinians, not being relieved until at least four days after the landings. Their achievements were remarkable but by no means exceptional, for Sergeant Mather's team watched Bluff Cove and the track from Fitzroy to Stanley for twenty-eight days.

Besides their recces, SAS made three major offensive raids, the first of which was to destroy aircraft that were within range of the intended landing beaches of San Carlos Water. They were based on a grass strip near the only settlement on Pebble Island and included IA-58 Pucara ground attack planes built in Argentina for use against lightly armed forces. Each carried two 20mm cannons, four 7.62 machine-guns and bombs or rockets, all of which they could use when flying slowly, the better to strafe troops on the ground. There was also believed to be a radar station on the island, although electronic checks showed that, if there was one, it was not being operated. In the cut and 'blip' of this type of warfare, however, the British could not chance possible detection of their amphibious ships as they neared this island on their passage to San Carlos

Water. Therefore, as this war in the South Atlantic was to prove in other aspects, the 'look see' of less sophisticated times was still necessary even in the electronic age.

In an operation preliminary to this raid, D Squadron's Boat Troop, the men who had landed on South Georgia, again had their difficulties but managed to get a recce patrol on the edge of the grass airfield. This lies on the narrow waist of the island with the sea each side, open and exposed without natural cover anywhere along the two-kilometre field where the aircraft were dispersed. These were also protected against attacks from the sea by an estimated hundred Argentinians. Their sentries were not particularly alert but, a four-man SAS patrol, having made their approach to the airstrip in the dark, found at daylight they had to hug the ground in a slight depression if they were not to be seen. They crawled along this but were obliged to leave their Bergens, since these would have been seen had they tried to carry them, so slight was the depth of the fold in the ground. The men nevertheless reached their boats on the beach to report that there were eleven aircraft on the field, but Argentinian patrols were likely to find the Bergens, warning them that a landing was likely.

The main assault was planned for early on 21 May, leaving only eight days from the time of this recce (on the 13th) for not only the attack on Pebble Island but also the re-supply of patrols elsewhere. The dozen troop-carrying helos were available for only ten hours of flying each day, as they had to be serviced, and since the nights of 16 to 19 May were scheduled for the re-supply and debriefing of recce patrols, any landing on Pebble Island would have to be made before the 16th. In the event, it was completed in five days from the decision to make this raid to the destruction of the aircraft in the early hours of the 15th.

The operation was not 'all plain sailing', however, as *Hermes* took longer to reach the launching point than expected, as she steamed into strong headwinds, which prevented the helos being prepared on the flightdeck during her passage westward; and there were then further delays as the aircraft were brought on deck to be made ready for flight. When they were eventually airborne, G Squadron had only thirty minutes and not the intended ninety minutes in which to destroy the planes, their ground crews and the rest of the island's garrison. Therefore the attack was limited to destroying the aircraft, ensuring that the raiders' helos were back aboard *Hermes* before full daylight, in order that she and her escorts could be well to the east of the islands before the Argentinian Air Force might attack them.

The Regiment, flexible as ever in meeting crisis situations, revised their original plans: the Mountain Troop, now fully recovered from their night on the glacier, would attack the planes, using LAW 66mm one-shot anti-tank rockets and small arms fire, much in the way Stirling's men had shot up aircraft with K-guns. A second Troop would seal off the approaches to the strip, with a third Troop in reserve. Demolition charges, made up for the more certain destruction of the aircraft under the original plan, were taken and an 81mm mortar as well as *Glamorgan*'s '4.5s' would bombard the defences, her fire being directed by a gunner officer landed with the SAS Squadron.

The helos touched down on an LZ marked by the Boat Troop, whose captain quietly briefed the other Troop officers, while over a hundred mortar bombs, the explosive charges and LAW rockets were off-loaded from the helicopters. The bright moonlight must have made the Squadron feel vulnerable, but quickly and quietly the Troops each moved off, guided by one of the Boat Troop to show the way over six kilometres of moorland to the airfield. Others in the Boat Troop formed a protective screen for the mortarmen and the gunner, as each man moving forward left two bombs for the mortar. Hamilton, accompanied by the captain of the Boat Troop, reached positions that gave a clear view of the aircraft, while air-burst shells from the warship and bombs from the mortar forced the Argentinians to take cover, only occasional bursts of machine-gun fire coming Hamilton's way.

As this was inaccurate fire, Hamilton took his men on to the dispersal areas in clear sight of the enemy, and coolly they fixed explosive charges to the planes. The base's petrol store and magazine – hit by naval gunfire – went up in a blaze of light at this time, revealing that one plane was as yet undamaged. Trooper 'Paddy' Armstrong, a demolition expert, went forward and placed a charge on it as Hamilton covered him out in the open. Between them they destroyed four aircraft that night. Colonel Mayne would have appreciated this score. Within fifteen minutes all eleven aircraft had been destroyed, with only one SAS casualty, a man hit in the leg by a piece of shrapnel. He later fired a grenade from the attachment on his Armalite to wound – judging by the screams – men in a slit trench who had been calling out to their commander during the battle.

As the Mountain Troop withdrew, the Argentinians fired a remotely controlled mine which hurled one Trooper three metres into the air; he was concussed but there were no other injuries. The helos then returned on time and the Squadron were lifted back to *Hermes* as she and *Glamorgan* steamed eastward. No radar station was found during this raid or on later searches by the SBS. Those Bergens were still lying in the shallow depression four weeks later when the Troop captain returned to the island – an indication of the less than competent opposition Rear-Admiral Woodward had in mind when he later commented that the 'time-scale [for such raids] will usually be longer and the assets needed . . . will be considerable'.

The second major fighting patrol to be made by D Squadron was by way of a diversion on the night of the landings. But the last helicopter, cross-decking them in a five-minute flight from *Hermes* to *Intrepid*, had to make a second circuit while a flightdeck spot was cleared for it to land. Flying at 180m in the dark, there was a sudden bang and the engine cut, causing the helo to drop into the sea. It rolled over and sank within minutes, only ten men managing to swim clear of the fuselage. They clung to one of her rescue dinghies, its automatic search-and-rescue beacon transmitting while the pilot and co-pilot let off flares. Look-outs on the ships had heard a double bang, and a searching helo found the dinghy, winching a corporal to safety; one of *Brilliant*'s cutters picked up the rest, and her crew revived the men suffering from hypothermia after thirty minutes in these icy waters.

This was the heaviest loss the Regiment had suffered in a single day, with twenty-one killed, including one of the helicopter crew and a number of specialists attached to SAS. Among them were Flight-Lieutenant C. Hawkins RAF, a forward air controller, and Corporal Douglas McCormack of the Royal Signals, who had worked together for a number of years, guiding aircraft onto ground targets. The survivors were flown back to the UK and their replacements parachuted into the sea from a Hercules to be picked up by the Navy.

The Sea King had probably hit a giant petrel with a two-metre wing span, but the cause of the accident has not apparently been proven. Whatever the cause, such events underline the hazards faced by SAS and others in going about routine military movements.

Not much more than twenty-four hours later, sixty men of D Squadron landed near Goose Green with GPMGs, Milans, mortars and rifles. Their task was to create the impression that a battalion, ten times their number, had landed. It was one of several diversions that night which distracted the Argentinians' attention from the main landings on the opposite coast, far to the north of Goose Green. 'D', supported by *Ardent*'s single 4.5-inch gun, created such a barrage of fire, seemingly in a long defence line as Troopers moved their positions between firing GPMG bursts or other weapons, that the defenders stayed in their trenches and did not attempt to probe these 'battalion' positions.

The main landings were effected with only three fatal casualties after two light helicopters of the Commando Brigade Air Squadron were shot down. By mid-morning 2 Para had advanced onto high ground south of San Carlos Water, from where they saw 'D' moving north in open formation. A Pucara attacked them but was shot down by a Trooper, the plane exploding before the pilot could eject. This shot, with an American Stinger missile, was the only success the Squadron had with this weapon, a number of which had been brought from America by a team training there early in April. Results might have been better but the expert on Stingers had been killed in the helicopter crash.

During the next fortnight SAS patrols ambushed Argentinians on the snow-covered hills, continued their deep-penetration patrols and landed five patrols on West Falkland on 5 June. There both SAS and SBS patrols made extensive use of naval gunfire support, but the garrison was more aggressive than the defenders of East Falkland and made better use of their D/F equipment. John Hamilton was killed soon after dawn on 10 June, when he and his signaller were surrounded 2,500m from Port Howard with its garrison of eight hundred men. Hamilton could not withdraw to the coast because the position from which he had been controlling naval gunfire against the port was overlooked from high ground. Argentinian patrols here covered every avenue of escape, forcing Hamilton to try to break out of their cordon and escape into the hills. He was wounded as he covered his signaller on the first leg of this bold move, telling the Trooper to make good his escape. The Captain was killed soon after this, and his signaller, out of ammunition, was captured – but he was released four days later when the Argentinians surrendered.

Long before then, Colonel Rose had been in radio contact with the Argentinian headquarters on East Falkland, working on their weaknesses and highlighting British strengths in a masterly piece of psychological warfare. In this he was helped by a young Royal Marine, Captain Rod Bell, who spoke Spanish as his first language and understood the mentality of his enemy – an understanding which, when linked to Rose's aggressive arguments, brought matters to a successful conclusion. Although earlier in the campaign the Colonel's Oxford graduate thinking was for a time probably outweighed by SAS traditions of lethal raids against enemy headquarters, on this occasion he probably decided such a *coup* was impractical because of the risks of causing civilian casualties should the mainly wooden buildings of Port Stanley take fire.

To reinforce the 'psyops' and stretch the Argentinian defences, the third and last major raid was mounted on the night of 13/14 June. That night SAS and SBS teams attempted to set fire to oil storage tanks in Stanley's harbour installations. They came ashore from high-speed raiding craft but were unable to breach the defences before withdrawing without serious casualties. Yet their raid succeeded in convincing the Argentinians that they were likely to be attacked from the sea as well as across the mountains.

SAS's war in the South Atlantic in 1982 proved that the modern Trooper is as professional a soldier, as daring and as resourceful as any in the Regiment's forty years' history. To quote one example of a gallantry award shows the measure of these men who serve in the Squadrons in the 1980s. The citation for John Hamilton's posthumous award of the Military Cross includes reference to his 'outstanding determination and extraordinary will to continue the fight in spite of being confronted by hopeless odds and being wounded'. He had been with the Regiment five months.

This study of SAS operations cannot include some secret ventures in which they may from time to time have been involved, such as the intriguing question of who was flown to where by a Sea King burnt out by its crew, no doubt, on the southern shores of Chile. All its crew were later given gallantry awards usually associated with exceptional bravery. Who they landed and for what purpose has never been revealed, and historians' conjectures on such matters are not helpful to British interests.

The examples of other operations have explained the development and continuing ingenuity of SAS techniques, while the outstanding courage and individual feats of arms, by men serving in the Regiments before and after 1946, show clearly throughout these actions, in which some paid the supreme penalty for their courage. To them this book is respectfully dedicated.

Appendix I: Abbreviations

AE	Assault Engineer
AS/W	Anti-Submarine Warfare
BATT	British Army Training Team
'Cdm'	Camouflage
CAT	Civil Action Team
CCO	Chief of Combined Operations
Cdo	Commando
D/F	Direction-Finding (radio)
DZ	Dropping Zone
ELAS	*Ellenikos Laikos Apeleftherotikos Stratos* (Greek Popular Liberation Army)
EMFFI	*État-Major des Forces Françaises de l'Intérieur*
FOO	Forward Observation Officer
GHQ	General Headquarters
GPMG	General Purpose Machine-Gun
HE	High Explosive
helo	helicopter
HDML	Harbour Defence Motor Launch
IS	Internal Security
L Detachment	forerunner of SAS, 'L' probably from 'Layforce'
LAW	Light Anti-Tank Weapon
LCA	Landing Craft, Assault
LCI(L)	Landing Craft Infantry, (Large)
LCS	Landing Craft, Support
LCU	Landing Craft, Utility
LRDG	Long-Range Desert Group
LSL	Landing Ship Logistic

LST	Landing Ship Tank
LZ	Landing Zone
MAS	Motor Anti-Submarine (Italian boat)
NAAFI	Navy, Army and Air Force Institute (canteens)
OG	Operational Group (of OSS)
OSS	Office of Strategic Services
RASC	Royal Army Service Corps
recce/recon	reconnaissance
RFA	Royal Fleet Auxiliary
RTU	Returned-to-Unit
RUC	Royal Ulster Constabulary
RV	rendezvous
SAF	Sultan's Armed Forces (Oman)
SAM	Surface to Air Missile
SABRE	Surface to Air Rescue Beacon
SAS	Special Air Service
SBS	Special Boat Squadron or Section
SD	*Sicherkeitsdienst* (Secret Police)
SHAFE	Supreme Headquarters Allied Forces Europe
SMG	Submachine-gun
SOAF	Sultan of Oman's Air Force
SOE	Special Operations Executive
SIG	Special Interrogation Group
SLR	Self-Loading Rifle
SS	Special Service

Appendix II: Summary of Operations

Mediterranean, Italian and related theatres 1941–5

Date	Location	Targets destroyed and/or outcome
1941		
16/17 Nov	Gazala area	failed only 22 of 60 men returned
12/13 Dec	Sirte	fuel tanker vehicle; Tamet 23 aircraft El Agheila road park shot up
c. 18 Dec	Agedabia	37 aircraft
25/26 Dec	'Marble Arch'	300km withdrawal on foot
25/26 Dec	Nofilia	1 aircraft
27–29 Dec	Sirte	over 12 trucks
27/29 Dec	Tamet	27 aircraft
1942		
22/23 Jan	Buerat	fuel destroyed but no ships to attack
8 Mar	Benina	aerial torpedo dumps; Berka Main failed to find airfield; Barce 1 aircraft and 8 trucks; Berka II 15 aircraft; Slonta defences too strong
24 Mar	Benghazi	recce
c. 25 Mar	Benina	5 aircraft
28/29 Mar	Benghazi	stores and fuel, but ships not reached
21–22 May	Benghazi	stayed 48 hours but no major targets
13/14 June	Benina	2 aircraft and workshops; Berka Main 11 aircraft; Berka II 9 aircraft; Barce fuel and stores; Derna East and Derna West betrayed by German agents; associated raids on Crete – Heraklion 21 aircraft; Kastelli 8 aircraft and 4 dumps of bombs; Timbaki no targets; Maleme defences too strong – French patrol captured
c. 16 Jun	Benina	road vehicles
2 Jul	Cairo	52 all ranks leave for desert base
7/8 Jul	Fuka Main	8 aircraft; Fuka II 6 aircraft; Bagush 37 aircraft by machine-gun fire; Fuka road 3 trucks and took 3 POWs; Sidi Barrani road vehicles (?)

Date	Location	Targets destroyed and/or outcome
12/13 Jul	Fuka	22 aircraft
12/13 Jul	El Daba	3 jeeps lost through air attack
26/27 Jul	Sidi Haneish	*c.* 40 aircraft by machine-gun fire
26/27 Jul	Bagush	diversion raid took 3 POWs
11–14 Aug	Sicily	raiders captured
1 Sep	w of Alamein	raids aborted
13 Sep	Benghazi	lost 50 men and many jeeps
7 Oct	Cairo	A Sqdn. left to set up desert base
14–23 Oct	Tobruk–Derna	cut railway almost daily
23 Oct	nr Daba	fired on by British armoured cars
c. 4 Nov	nr Daba	took 6 POWs
28 Nov	w of Alamein	A Sqdn. completed four weeks of raids on coast road
12 Dec	nr Buerat	coast road traffic, telephone lines, an HQ
16 Dec	Misurata	20 loaded trucks and telephone lines
18 Dec	nr Misurata	road mined as it was on other occasions
c. 20 Dec	Zliten	capture of 4 Italians
23–24 Dec	nr El Fascia	B Sqdn's base surrounded after ten days' raiding 275km of coast road from Tripoli to Buerat; base surrendered
1943		
5 Jan	Buerat–Agheila	A Sqdn. completed five and a half weeks of recces and some raids on coast road
15–18 Jan	Bir Soltane	recces of Mareth line from this base and some roads and railways mined
23 Jan	Tripoli	patrols entered port
23–24 Jan	Gabes–Sfax	roads and railway mined
25 Jan	nr Gabes	French patrol captured
c. 27 Jan	Gabes–Gafsa	Stirling recaptured after initial escape near this road
late Jan	Gafsa	survivors of Stirling's patrol reach First Army
Feb	Tunisia	SAS guides for Eighth Army's advance
Mar–Apr	Pinchon & Gafsa	patrols of 2 SAS found enemy defences too compact to infiltrate
28 May	Pantelleria	recce of island
30 May	Sardinia	east coast airfields recced
23 June	Lampedusa	recces (and raids?)
23–27 June	Kastelli	several aircraft
10 Jul	Brenner Pass	raiders captured
10 Jul	Heraklion	petrol dumps
10 Jul	Timbaki	airfield not in use
7–25 Jul	Sardinia	aircraft, petrol dumps, telephone lines

Date	Location	Targets destroyed and/or outcome
		in N of island by two patrols – one operated 17 days from 7 Jul and second for 11 days from 14 Jul before capture
10 Jul	Sicily	two patrols one raiding SE coast defences and second attacked bridges, mined roads and cut telephone lines in rear of defences
10 Jul	nr Syracuse	SRF captured 3 coast boatyards and 1500 POWs
12 Jul	Augusta	ashore 24 hours disrupting port
3 Sep	Bagnara	SRF seized port and held 24 hrs till relieved
7–14 Sep	Spezia–Bolognia–Florence	patrols derailed 14 trains
9 Sep	Taranto	mopped up German rear parties
9 Sep	Rhodes	SBS (at that time part of SAS) provide negotiator parachuted to Italian HQ
9 Sep	Kastellorizon	island seized and later anchorage for SBS schooner close to neutral Turkey's coast
10–17 Sep	Taranto–Ginosia–Riverella	jeep patrols broke SW to link with main Allied advance
15 Sep	Kos	Island seized, Allies held till 3 Oct
15 Sep	Samos	island seized, Allies held till Oct
15 Sep	Leros	island seized, Allies held till mid-Nov
17 Sep	Simi	island seized, Allies held till 11/12 Oct
19–30 Oct	from Bari	jeep patrols with armoured brigade
c. 19 Oct	Rhodes	recce
c. 20 Oct	Kalino	island seized but SBS later withdrew
c. 21 Oct	Stormarella	patrols from Bari in street fighting
late Oct	Lucera	12 men of jeep patrol capture town
24 Sep–15 Oct	Rhodes	three-week recce
2–9(?) Oct	Ancona–Pescara	jeep patrols cut railway at 16 places etc
3 Oct	Termoli	with Commando force seized and held town
19/20 Oct	Simi	recce
27 Oct	Pescara	railway cut in two raids
20 Nov	Simi	boatyards, installations and inter-island telephone destroyed, garrison attacked
18–25 Dec	Ancona–Pescara	railway trucks, line cut in three places
1944		
7 Jan	N of Rome	railway cut in two raids
7 Jan	Ancona–Rimini	important bridge
12 Jan	San Egidio	several aircraft

Date	Location	Targets destroyed and/or outcome
c. 22 Jan	Kastellorizon	schooner *Tewfik* anchored as SBS base
27 Jan	Pesaro	railway bridge
28 Jan – early Feb	Patmos, Archi & Lisso	in series of recces and raids on these islands 1 caique sunk, 2 captured, garrisons attacked
31 Jan	Khalki	German HDML captured
31 Jan	Stampalia	seaplane, 4 caiques, telegraph and billets
Feb	nr Perugia	11 aircraft on Italy's west front
Feb	Simi	staff in HQ killed
Feb/Mar	various of Dodecanese	small parties as coast watchers reporting movements of ships and aircraft
March	Nisiros	2 large supply barges, 27 Germans killed; Piscopi (Tilos) garrison attacked after raiders ashore 20 days; Kalimnos fuel store, garrison attacked; Stampalia recce results of earlier raids, two naval officers captured; Kalino 25 SBS and Greeks had casualties
Apr	Patmos	Italians handed over arms; Piscopi recce of results of March raid, ambushed German patrol; Amorgos one German captured; Nisiros 4 Germans killed; Khalki raiders betrayed and captured
19–29 Apr	Cyclades	raids on island garrisons including: Ios; Amorgos (see above); Mykonos; and recce to Anidhros – caiques, etc . . .
22–29 Apr	Santorin (Thira)	14 men successfully attacked garrison of 48 Germans and Italian Fascists
May	Paros	several Germans killed and officer captured
16–19 May	Naxos	contacted partisans and made joint attack on billets of garrison
c. 22 May	Siphnos	captured caique and one German
late May	Samos	1 caique captured, fishing crews warned not to co-operate with Germans
mid Jun	northern Sporades	recce for potential targets including those on Pelagos, its garrison then captured
mid Jun	Kithira	weather prevented landing on island then raiders held by Greek partisans on mainland
17–18 Jun	Leros	2 destroyers and 3 small escort ships
Jun	Kalimnos	recce found strong defences on island
1 Jul	Kalimnos	25 men attacked garrison

Date	Location	Targets destroyed and/or outcome
13/14 Jul	Simi	major raid with Greek Sacred Regiment – captured garrison coy, destroyed boatyards and port installations
23–? Jul	Crete	7 main fuel dumps, garrison attacked
Aug–Sept	Karasovici	SBS with Yugoslavs breakout of German encirclement in one of several operations supporting the partisans
Aug–Oct	Albania	S Sqdn with partisans in operations to harrass Germans' withdrawal
early Sept	Piraeus	recce in force by L Sqdn
24 Sept	Aroxas on Gulf of Corinth	M Sqdn parachuted to aid Greeks; 30 Sept Patras garrison of 2,465 surrender to 62 men of Sqdn; *c.* 3 Oct several POWs taken from German force hunting Sqdn and RAF Rgt troops with it; 7 Oct part of Corinth garrison surrender to Sqdn
Oct	southern Greece	M Sqdn part of 'Pomp' Force harassed German retreat from Athens through Lamia, Kozani and Florina to Albanian border
early Oct	Sporades	mopping up ops by SBS
Oct	Salonika	German demolition parties killed or captured
Nov	S Italy	Sqdns of SBS concentrated at Monte St Angelo
3 Dec	Crete	Sqdn based on Heraklion to help partisans contain German garrison in Malme area
Dec	Zara	base for raids in northern Adriatic
27 Dec	Spezia	patrols attacked road transport in this area of NW Italy killing over 130 Germans
1945		
Feb	Lussin	attacked strong point on island, cleared buildings but took casualties
Feb	Cherso	captured 12 of island's garrison and code books
18 Mar	Cherso	unable to capture bridge to Lussin as island's garrison resisted strongly
6 Mar – 13 Apr	Spezia – Reggio – Bologna	raised partisan battalion and successfully harassed German retreat ('Tombola' and related operations)
mid-Mar	Istria	recce for bases

Date	Location	Targets destroyed and/or outcome
2–15 Apr	Comacchio	recces and fighting patrols in flooded area north of Ravena
12 Apr	Istria Peninsula	operations frustrated by political considerations but several coast-watching teams established and some captured

North-West Europe 1944–5
(Numbers in ( ) after locations refer to map pages 72–3)

Date	Location	Targets destroyed and/or outcome
5/6 Jun	Normandy	Two of four diversions with dummy parachutes west of Dieppe (8) and at Isigny (?) with small teams, caused some confusion
6 Jun – 6 Sep	nr Dijon in E Central France (36)	'Houndsworth' base with patrols covering half a department of France, cut railways (derailed 6 trains), road transport ambushed, escorts attacked, armed *c.* 5 bttns *maquis*
6 Jun – 2 Jul	NW of Massif Central (39)	'Bulbasket' base with patrols covering Haute Vienne-Indre area, cut railways, ambushed roads etc before being betrayed
6–12 Jun	N Brittany (14)	'Samwest' base French SAS armed *maquis*, ambushed trucks, cut railways before being attacked and having to regroup
6–17 Jun	nr Vannes (18)	'Dingson' base French SAS armed *maquis* but attacked and had to regroup
7–15 Jun	Brittany (16)	jeep patrols in 'Cooney' dropped blind to DZs and then covered 75km cutting railways, ambushing roads etc
14 Jun – 15 Aug	SW of Paris (25) (and map p 83)	'Gain' bases for patrols in Orleans 'gap' between Seine and Loire ambushed roads, cut railways, reported targets for air bombing before several teams killed or captured
20 June – end July	several locations in central Brittany (19)	'Grog' bases for survivors of 'Dingson' where several 1,000 *maquis* were trained and French SAS with a few men from 1 and 2 SAS also sabotaged railways, laid ambushes, etc.
23 June – 18 Jul	Brittany (17)	large-scale French operation to link up SAS units in Brittany, armed *maquis*

Date	Location	Targets destroyed and/or outcome
		with eventual strength of 25,000, caused over 2,000 German casualties
8 Jul – 11 Aug	nr Le Mans (20)	recce for potential targets for Allied airforces and liaison with *maquis*
16 Jul – 7 Oct	Vendée (35)	'Dickens' base of French SAS closed railway between Saumur and Nantes by 26 July, destroyed 200 vehicles, killed 500 Germans
19 Jul – 23 Aug	Normandy (13)	infiltrated German lines, for recces
23 Jul – 10 Sep	Meuse (12)	limited success against railways as close to battle areas and many Germans
25 July – 13 Aug	Rambouillet area (24)	failed to capture Rommel or his staff but harassed road transport
27 Jul – 18 Sep	Plateau de Langres (31)	jeep patrols against withdrawing Germans in eastern France, 'Hardy'
27 Jul – 15 Aug	nr Le Mans (22)	Belgian SAS on foot attacked rearguard as most Germans had withdrawn
31 July – 15 Aug	nr Le Mans (23)	Belgian SAS rescue 150 Allied airmen with direction from SOE's MI9
3–15 Aug	Chartres (26)	Belgian SAS attacked road transport and reported targets for bombing
3–24 Aug	Maine (21)	limited success as much of patrols' area reached by American's on 4 Aug
3 Aug – 5 Oct	Poitiers (41)	French SAS attacked road and rail transport with marked success, targets reported led to many vehicles being bombed
5–18 Aug	Finisterre (15)	French SAS prevent demolition of viaducts in assisting American advance
10 Aug – 27 Sep	Limoges (43)	French SAS assist *maquis* in road ambushes and other attacks
10 Aug – 23 Sep	Loire et Cher	assisted *maquis* causing many German casualties
11–24 Aug	Corrèze (44)	French SAS stiffened *maquis* in successful ambushes
13 Aug – 21 Sep	Vosges (28)	patrols from this 'Loyton' base with ambushes and target reports help *maquis* to embroil two German divisions
13–24 Aug	Creuse (44)	French SAS (details not traced)
13 Aug – 19 Sep	Massif Central (39)	French SAS cut bridges and railways
14 Aug – 25 Sep	NE of Orleans (29)	jeep patrols of this 'Kipling' operation moved from Orleans to N of Dijon at end of Aug, there in Sep ambushes of roads successful despite limited supplies due to weather preventing air drops

Date	Location	Targets destroyed and/or outcome
15 Aug – 19 Sep	Upper Loire valley (43)	five patrols of French SAS make attacks that inspire *maquis* to bolder resistance
16 Aug – 13 Sep	Ardennes (5)	Belgian SAS recces for important intelligence and bombers' targets, with *maquis* in ambushes of German rearguard
17–26 Aug	NW of Paris (9)	Belgian SAS but results limited by Allies' rapid advance to this area
19 Aug – 11 Sep	Burgundy (33)	French SAS successful reinforcement of *maquis*
19 Aug – 19 Sep	Burgundy (30)	patrols of this op 'Wallace' drove over 550km to Plateau de Langres ('Hardy's area) caused heavy casualties, moving further eastward on 2 Sep; target reports exceptionally useful
26 Aug – 3 Sep	Compiègne (11)	target reports led to successful air attacks
27 Aug – 22 Sep	Lorraine (34)	French SAS base 'Abel' with patrols leading *maquis* in ambushes
28 Aug – 1 Sep	S of Amiens (10)	Belgian SAS road watch, valuable intelligence collected
29 Aug – 14 Sep	E of Bourges (36)	French SAS destroy over 100 vehicles in disrupting German crossing of Loire
2–18 Sep	Ardennes (6)	Belgian SAS liaise with resistance forces
2–12 Sep	W Belgium (4)	drop dispersed by high wind, aborted
6–11 Sep	NE Belgium (1)	Belgian SAS dispersed by high winds but had limited success against rearguards
9–18 Sep	Vosges (N of 28)	dispersed on dropping two SAS shot
16 Sep – 3 Oct	Alsace (27)	4 trains derailed, road ambushes
16 Sep – 14 Mar	Arnhem (G)	Belgian SAS intelligence recces and aid to British airborne troops in escapes
27 Sep – 17 Mar	N Holland	Belgian SAS useful intelligence recces
24 Dec – 25 Jan	Ardennes (3)	French SAS in 31 jeeps for series of recces
27 Dec – 15 Jan	Ardennes (2)	Belgian SAS recces for counter-offensive to German breakthrough
1945		
25 Mar – 10 May	E of Rhine (H)	jeep patrols as recce screen ahead of Canadian and other units' advances
3 Apr – 6 May	N of Arnhem	forward recces for Canadian units
6 Apr – 6 May	Meppen (D)	spearhead force in advance towards Oldenberg
8–16 Apr	NE Holland (C)	ambushes etc ahead of Allied advance
12 May – 25 Aug	Norway	helped to disarm 30,000 Germans

Date	Location	Targets destroyed and/or outcome
		Malaya

1950

Oct	Johore	formation of Malayan Scouts (SAS)
Nov	Ipoh area	A Sqdn patrols in Perak jungle to ambush known guerrilla routes
Dec	Johore	B and C Sqdns in jungle training
Dec	various	patrols to deny food to terrorists

1951

Jan – May	various	patrols to ambush terrorists including one of 103 days
June – Nov(?)	Johore	working as infantry with other security forces on jungle fringes and from jungle forts
Dec	Johore	Sqdns reorganized on more regular military lines

1952

Jan	–	Malayan Scouts redesignated 22 SAS
Feb	Belum valley	first use in major operation of technique for parachuting to jungle tree canopy, terrorists' jungle farm destroyed by security forces including SAS but no contacts with enemy
Summer	various	deep penetration patrols to ambush terrorists; first patrols that established contacts with aboriginal *sakai*
Nov–Dec	Negri Sembilan	patrols with Gurkha and Fijian infantry to deny terrorists food from a wide area, security forces killed or captured 16 terrorists

1954

Jan–Dec	various	mainly hearts-and-mind patrols to win support of aborigines (*sakai*)
Sep–Dec	various	deep penetration patrols dropped to DZs cleared by aerial bombing; captured 15 terrorists and encouraged *sakai* not to supply enemy with food

1955

Jan	various	five Sqdns in the field including one from Para Rgt and a New Zealand Sqdn which had replaced one recruited from Rhodesians

Date	Location	Targets destroyed and/or outcome
15 Sep – mid Dec	N Malaya	typical patrol of this time with constant movement, wearying searches for an elusive enemy and medical aid for aborigines
1957 July		cut to two Sabre Sqdns as part of British cuts in military spending but jungle penetration patrols continued
1958 9 Feb – *c.* 20 Mar	Telok Anson	killed or captured 10 hard-core terrorists

Southern Arabia

Date	Location	Targets destroyed and/or outcome
1958 Nov–Dec	Jebel Akhdar	operations by D Sqdn in support of Omani Sultan's Armed Forces (SAF); mainly recces but small lodgement on plateau held by dissidents
1959 26–7 Jan	Jebel Akhdar	night infiltration by A and D Sqdns established firm base on plateau
31 Jan	Jebel Akhdar	all insurgents captured or left plateau
1960–70 annual	Oman	Sqdns trained each year in Oman for periods of about three months and provided training teams for SAF from time to time
1964 29–30 Apr	Radfan	patrol lost two killed in trying to set up DZ for paras
13–19 May	NE Radfan	recces of enemy supply routes on one of which 2 of enemy killed in ambush
summer	Radfan	established hidden OPs from which artillery fire could be controlled, recces including those for security forces' major operations against dissidents
1965–7 various	Aden and Aden Protectorate including Radfan	continued to mount recces as in 1964 but also provided undercover teams to search out terrorists in urban slums,

Date	Location	Targets destroyed and/or outcome
		while in the Radfan the technique was developed for calling up commando/infantry units in helicopters to ambush enemy seen from OPs
Nov	Aden	British forces left

1970

not known	Straits of Hormus	patrol parachuted into area to be joined reportedly by a squadron for operations against possible dissidents
autumn	various in Oman	SAS training teams instructing SAF with an intelligence section and others in 19 men at Salalah (capital of Dhofar Province)
winter	Dhofar	full squadron deployed as British Army Training Teams instructing SAF and as Civil Action Teams (CATs) to aid local communities in coastal towns, both BATTS and CATs continued their work until final withdrawal in 1976
Dec	Salalah	first company of irregulars recruited as *firqat Salahadin*

1971

Jan/Feb	Mirbat	*firqat Salahadin* under training from SAS
23 Feb	Sudh	two Troops with *Salahadin* occupy this port
spring	Barbezum	*firqat A'asifat* formed
13–14 Mar	Eagle's Nest (see map p 154)	*firqat* and SAS Troops night infiltration onto Dhofar plateau
14–26 Mar	Tawai Atair	actions on plateau
Apr	various in Dhofar	further *firqats* raised with 500 men in training although numbers later fluctuated as men returned to their tribes for various reasons
May	Jebel Aram	two Troops with *firqats* and SAF in action to capture rebels' 75-mm gun but this withdrawn although ammo captured
1 Oct–2 Sep	E of Jibjat	two Sqdns with 250 of SAF and five *firqats* fought successfully to establish firm base on plateau

1972

| Jan–Dec | various in Dhofar | BATT and CAT deployments but Omani administration began to take |

Date	Location	Targets destroyed and/or outcome
		over much of the medical and allied services
19 Jun	Mirbat	eight men repulsed major attack but 2 killed before 23 others counter-attacked with such success that this action a major set-back for Yemeni backed forces
summer	various in Oman	government agencies established by this time co-ordinated intelligence among other work taken over from BATT
1973		
Jan/Feb	Hornbeam line (*see* map p 154)	BATT in operations with Iranians
summer	various in Dhofar	BATT in action in support of SAF and *firqats*
Dec	Salalah to Thamrait road	BATT with strong force of Iranians that cleared this area of enemy
1974		
Jan–Feb	Jibjat	BATT here on NE of plateau one of seven SAS teams supporting *firqats*
summer	central Dhofar plateau	*firqats* with BATT support clear valleys of enemy
by autumn	central Dhofar plateau	government agencies had taken over in this area from CATs
1975		
Dec	nr Rakyut	SAS patrol heavily engaged after setting up forward OP for artillery as SAF withdrew but successfully extricated
1975		
4–19 Jan	Shershitti	SAF Bttn with SAS BATTs seize airstrip at Defa north of this main Yemen supply base 20 km from Yemen Republic's border but after heavy engagement withdrew (Iranian Bttns capture Rakyut in associated op)
Feb	Wadi Ashoq	*firqats* and SAF destroy enemy regiment
Mar	Rakyut	SAS provide CAT
May	east Dhofar plateau	dissidents broken up isolated bands continued to resist government forces
Jun/Jul	Al Hallaniyah 200km E of Salalah	CAT found many islanders in ill-health but brought them medical aid and guidance on hygiene etc

Date	Location	Targets destroyed and/or outcome
15 Sep	Defa	SAS patrol into wadi but heavily engaged, two wounded before withdrawal
Oct	west Dhofar plateau	Yemen Republic withdrew all its regular troops who had been helping dissidents
1 Dec	Dhalqut	entered by SAS
mid-Dec	west Dhofar	logistic support by Yemen ceased
1976		
Feb	east Dhofar plateau	SAS BATTs returned to area with *firqat* rounding up dissidents
Sep	Oman	Sqdns withdrawn
1983		
May	Oman	newspaper reports of SAS training Omani Special Forces

Borneo with deployments mainly along borders with Kalimantan

1962		
Jan–Apr	Sarawak's 1st, 2nd and 3rd Divisions ('counties')	A Sqdn's patrols contact border villagers to establish intelligence sources
Apr–Aug	W Sabah in Pensiangan area; The Gap (W Sabah); and 3rd Division	D Sqdn patrols, as above and exploration of uninhibited jungle known as the 'Gap'
Aug–Dec	1st and 3rd Divisions and 'Gap'	A Sqdn patrols as above including 6-week east to west patrol of Gap
1964		
Dec '63–June	Sarawak; S of Pensiangan: and Kelabit Highlands	D Sqdn long patrols as above and first cross-border recces
May	1st Division of Sarawak	training of Border Scouts for recces into Kalimantan
June – Oct	mainly on border S of Pensiangan	A Sqdn patrols as above and first 'step up' OPs in mid-July with Gurkha coys in helos responding to reports of enemy incursions
13–27 Aug	Sembakung River	A Sqdn cross-border recce followed by others to this area
Sep(?)	Pa Raya	A's second cross-border recce

Date	Location	Targets destroyed and/or outcome
1 Oct	Long Pa Sia	Six ambushes of mines set from this date but no intruders caught by them
late Oct	Pa Fani (S of Long Pa Sia)	7-day cross-border recce and fighting patrol but no suitable targets fround for this deterrent strike
Nov	S of Pensiangan	B Sqdn patrols included guiding Gurkha coy to ambush but Indos warned by villagers; further mine ambushes set
late Dec	1st Div	B Sqdn moved to patrol W Sarawak border
29 Dec–14 Jan	Kaik-Babang	B Sqdn patrol found area too populated for hidden OPs
1965		
Jan	Bemban River	B Sqdn cross-border recces in search of Communist staging camp
late-Jan	S of Stass	B Sqdn cross-border recces
Feb	Koemba River	B Sqdn patrols unable to cross swamp
late Feb	nr Serik	patrol of B hunted by Indonesians but evaded pursuit
Feb–Mar	S of Stass to Koemba River	D Sqdn cross-border recces
?	Sidut	One of D's patrols capture documents
Apr	Koemba	D's first recce with offensive action as deterrent in last day or two before withdrawal, similar patrols mainly for recces followed
Apr	upper Sekayan	Patrol from D found large Indo camp before evading attack
Apr–May	Sentimo Swamp	recces by D Sqdn including one of 9 days in which Indo river craft sunk
10–19 May	Koemba	patrol of D recced river and sank large troop launch
late May	Koemba	patrolled by A Sqdn
May–June	Bemban	A's patrols recce W of river
July	Sentimo	A's recces for major cross-border op
Aug	Doemba and Sentimo	2/2nd Gurkha coys lay successful ambushes on these rivers using SAS maps but SAS not in op
Aug	Poeteh and Sentimo	co-ordinated Gurkha/SAS ambushes on these rivers
10–29 Sep	Bemban area	A Sqdn less 2 Troop search for communist camp Batu Hitam (as in Jan '65)
Oct	Bemban area	patrol from B attacked but killed 20 Indonesians before withdrawing

Date	Location	Targets destroyed and/or outcome
Dec–Jan	Bemban area	B Sqdn recce patrols only
1966		
mid-Jan	Koemba	Troop from B found little traffic on river sank 2-man boat
Jan	Sentas	B Sqdn crossed Sekeyan successfully attacking outer defence of this base
Aug	Borneo	British forces withdrawn

Other Areas

1953–4		
various	Kenya	patrols from 22 SAS briefly deployed
1959		
summer?	Birmingham	HQ of 23 SAS moved here shortly after formation of this Territorial Reserve Rgt
1969		
Aug	N Ireland	specific details of deployments from this date to mid-1980s not available
1975		
Dec	London	teams reported to be present during siege of terrorists in Balcombe Street apartment
1977		
Oct	Mogadishu, Somalia	2 men helped German Special Forces to rescue hostages from German aircraft
1980		
6 May	London	rescue of hostages held in Iranian Embassy
1982		
6 May	Hereford	Sqdns briefed for South Atlantic OPs
9 Apr	Ascension Island	D Sqdn embarked for S Georgia
21 Apr	S Georgia	D's Mountain Troop on Fortuna Glacier evacuated after severe snowstorms
23–25 Apr	S Georgia	recces by Boat Troop of D
25–26 Apr	S Georgia	D Sqdn and Commandos capture Argentinian garrisons
1–4 May	E Falkland	eight patrols inserted by helo at night for recces of several days or more
5 May–14 Jun	E and W Falkland	recces continued on both islands with

Date	Location	Targets destroyed and/or outcome
		OPs manned throughout campaign, one reportedly for 28 days
10 May	Pebble Island	recce by Troop from D Sqdn
15 May	Pebble Island	raid by D Sqdn destroyed 11 aircraft
18 May	NE of F Islands	20 of SAS killed in helo crash
20–21 May	Goose Green	diversions by D Sqdn during time of main landings in San Carlos Water
25–31 May	Mount Kent	D Sqdn patrols in a number of fire fights with Argentinians
3 June	Stanley	several patrols established on hills overlooking port
5 June	W Falkland	D Sqdn patrols (some replacing those of G already on this island) in extensive recces
13/14 June	Stanley	raid against oil installations landed from raiding craft but withdrew before reaching targets nevertheless led Argentinians to reinforce coast defences

Sources

Histories

Barzilay, D., *The British Army in Ulster* Vols I-III, Belfast 1973, 1975 & 1978

Dickens, P., *SAS: The Jungle Frontier*, Arms & Armour Press, London 1983

Ehran, J., *History of the Second World War: Grand Strategy*, Vol V, HMSO, London 1956

Foot, M. R. D., *History of the Second World War: SOE in France*, HMSO, London 1968

Geraghty, Tony, *Who Dares Wins* (2nd edition), Arms & Armour Press, London 1983

Hampshire, A. Cecil, *The Secret Navies*, William Kimber & Co, London 1978

Howard, M., *History of the Second World War: Grand Strategy*, Vol IV, HMSO, London 1972

James, H., *et al*, *The Undeclared War*, Leo Cooper, London 1971

James, M., *Born of the Desert*, Collins, London 1945

Ladd, J. D., *SBS: The Invisible Raiders*, Arms & Armour Press, London 1983

Lansborough, G., *Tobruk Commando*, Cassell, London 1956

Pitt, B., *The SBS*, London 1983

Playfair, L. S. O., *History of the Second World War: The Mediterranean and Middle East*, Vols I to IV, HMSO, London 1957–66

Strawson, J., *A History of the SAS Regiment*, Secker & Warburg, London 1984

Swinson, A., *The Raiders Desert Strike Force*, Parnell's Paperback, London 1968

Warner, P., *The SAS*, William Kimber & Co, London 1971

Warner, P., *The SBS*, Sphere Books Ltd, London 1983

Memoirs and Biographies

Cowles, V., *The Phantom Major*, Collins, London 1958

Farran, R., *Winged Dagger*, Collins, London 1948
Farran, R., *Operation Tombola*, Collins, London 1960
Harrison, D. I., *These Men are Dangerous*, Cassell, London 1957
Jeapes, Tony, *SAS: Operation Oman*, William Kimber & Co, London 1980
Lodwick, J., *The Filibusters*, Methuen, London 1947
McLuskey, J. F., *Parachute Padre*, SCM Press, London 1951
Stuart, M. Crichton, *G Patrol: the Story of the Guards Patrol of the LRDG*,
    William Kimber & Co, London 1958
Verney, J., *Going to the Wars*, Collins, London 1955

Articles and other references

Various papers and documents in the archives of the Royal Marines'
    Museum
Articles in *Mars and Minerva*, the journal of the SAS Regiment
Articles in *The Globe and Laurel*, the journal of the Royal Marines

Index

Abbott, Tpr D., 130
'Abel', 72
aborigines, 113
Aden and Aden Protectorate, 142, 143, 202–3
Adriatic, 79
Aegean, 55, 56, 58, 61
aerial photographs, 84, 151
Agedabia, 9, 16, 17, 193
Agheila, 12, 29
Ah Hoi, 111, 112
Ain Dalla, 8
Akehurst, Maj-Gen John, 165
Ancona, 195
Antelat, 22
Antilla, 21
Antrim, HMS, 175, 176, 179
Archi, 196
'Archway', 72
Ardent, HMS, 188
Ardennes, 200
Argentine and Argentinian, 181–90
Arnhem, 200
Arthy, Sgt J. 'Lofty', 177
Ascension Island, 175, 207
Astor, Maj J. J., 69
Astronavigation, 10
Athlit, 69
Auchinleck, Gen Sir Claude, 7, 19, 21, 29
Azzib, 45

Babang, 206
Bagnara, 195
Bagnold, Brig R., 9
Bagush, 40
Bait Gatum, 165
Bait Kathir, 156, 162
Baissac, Claud de, 82
Baker, L/Cpl 'Paddy', 145, 146

Barbezum, 203
Barce, 22, 27
Bari, 97, 195
'Barker', 72
Bateman, Lt, 87, 93
Battalione Alleata, 98
Batu Hitam, 128–30
Beagle Ridge, 184
Bell RM, Capt, R. D., 189
Belgium and Belgian, 69, 83, 100, *see also* SAS units
Bellegarde, 86
Belum Valley, 110–13, 201
Bemban, 130, 206, 207
Benghazi, 9, 12, 22, 23, 40, 193, 194
Benina, 22, 27, 193
'Benson', 72
'Bergbank', 72
Bergé, Comdr, 19, 28
Berka, 22, 27
Berets, 69, 115
Bifurno, 62
Bigglestone, Cpl, 128
Bir Chalda, 30
Birmingham, 207
Birrell, WO RAF, 162
Bir Zalten (Soltane), 42, 194
Bizerta, 62
Bohan, Sgt A., 167
Bologna, 66, 67, 195, 197
Bond, Maj A., 100
Bonnington, Lt C., 6
Borneo, 118–42, 205–7
Bourges, 200
Bourgoin, Comdt P., 78
Bourmont, Cpl, 25, 26
Bradford, Capt R., 96
Bradshaw, Cpl R., 163, 164
Brenner Pass, 194
British Antarctic Survey teams, 174, 175

British Army Training Teams, 152, 155–65, 203–5
British Military Forces, 106, 126, 179 – *see also* Long Range Desert Group, SAS units, War Office
  Commandos, 7, 43 *see also* Royal Marines
  62 Cdo, 62
  Far East Land Force, 106
  GHQ Middle East, 11, 12, 22, 40, 48
  Guardsmen, 11, 126, 150, 151
  MO 4, 50
  Parachute Rgt's Depot, 114
  Royal Engineers, 157
  Royal Signals, 151
  Special Interrogation Group, 23
  Supreme HQ Allied Forces Europe, commanding British units, 68
  Territorial Reserve, 104, 114 *see also* 21 SAS
  Yeomanry, 11
  Armies and Army Groups:
    Second, 99
    Eighth, 11, 13, 29, 30, 41, 42, 43, 47
    Twenty-first, 76
  Corps:
    XIII, 30
  Brigades:
    Rifle, 105
    West (in Borneo), 134
  Regiments and sub-units:
    Artists Rifles, 104
    GHQ Recce (Phantom) Rgt, 69, 70, 77
    1/2 Gurkha Rgt, 126, 131
    2/2 Gurkha Rgt, 140
    Gurkha Indep. Para Coy, 126
    Parachute Rgts, 113
    56 Recce Rgt, 62
  RAF and aircraft of RAF, 1, 17, 21, 66, 75, 76, 77, 83, 87, 97, 99, 110, 144
  Royal Marines, 7, 58, 175–80, 189
    in SAS, 55
    Commandos, 65, 174, 175, 179
    SBS (RM), 132, 174
  Royal Navy, 7, 58, 175, 176, 179 *see also* ships by name
Brittany, 78, 198
Brough, Sgt, 14–5
Browning, Gen A. F. M., 68, 69
Brunei, 118, 122, 125, 127
Brunt, Tpr, 66
'Brutus', 72
Buck, Capt, 22, 23, 24, 25

Buerat, 19, 43, 193, 194
'Bulbasket', 72, 76, 77
Bunfield, Sgt, 90
'Bunyan', 72
Burgundy, 200

caiques, 58, 59
Cairo, 30, 34, 193, 194
'Caliban', 72
Calvert, Brig. J. M., 99, 104, 106, 107
Campbell, Brig 'Jock', 21
Cape Batu, 131
'Carte', 82
Carter, Cpl M., 133
Challenor, Sgt 'Tankey', 66
Chambon-le-Foret, 92
Chapman, L/Cpl R., 163
Chartres, 82, 83, 199
Châteauroux, 77
Châtelhérault, 77
'Chaucer', 72
Cherbourg, 83
Cherso, 197
Chester, Capt, 160
Churchill, Sir Winston, 41
China and Chinese, 103, 123, 125
'Chinese parliament', 137
Civil Aid Teams, 157, 160, 165, 203
clandestine warfare, 68
'Claret' ops, 121, 131, 132, 140
Clark, General Mark, 98
Clayton, Maj P., 10
Close, Lt, 90
close quarter battle, 147, 170
Clynes, Capt, 59
codes, 71
Collins, Lt-Col I. G., 76
Comacchio, 198
command and control, 69, 140, 155, 168
  command cells, 132
communications including radios, 10, 11, 48, 50, 70, 71, 116, 118, 124, 126, 127, 135, 141, 143, 144, 159, 167, 170, 185
  'Biscuit' receiver, 71
  Sabre Beacon, 134
Communists, 23, 133, 147, 153, 158, 160, 162, 164
Compiègne, 200
Confrontation (Borneo), 141
'Cooney', 72, 79
Cooper, Maj J., 27, 31, 44, 110, 151
'Corporate', 175–89

Corrèze, 199
Cosne, 95
counter-measures to raids, 89
Counter Revolutionary Warfare Teams,
    168, 169
Crete, 46, 197
Cross Border Scouts, 130
Cumper, Capt W., 45, 59
Cyclades, 196
Cyrenaica, 3, 75

Dale, Sgt, 61
Davis, Lt P., 101–2
Deane-Drummond, Lt-Col (later Maj Gen)
    A., 149, 151, 152
Defa, 205
'Defoe', 72
de la Billière, Maj Gen P., 131, 140, 141,
    142, 143, 144–7, 151, 152
Delves, Maj C., 175, 177, 180
Dempsey, Lt Gen Sir Miles, 67
Dennison, Capt A., 128
Derna, 22, 23, 25
'Derry', 72
Devine, Craftsman J., 96
'Devon', 62
Dhalqut, 205
Dhofar Liberation Front, 158
Dhofar and Dhofari, 148, 153, 155, 158, 162,
    203–4
'Dickens', 72
Dijon, 76, 77, 198
'Dingson', 72, 76, 78, 79
Direction-Finding (D/F), 11, 181
Dodecanese, 55, 196
Doemba, 206
Dudgeon, Capt, 66
Due, M. le, 74
Duffy, Cpl, 92
Duggan, Mne, 46
'Dunhill', 72
Dunkley, Sgt, 92
Durnford-Slater, Col J., 62
Dutch Resistance, 99 see also Holland
Dyaks, 106, 122, 123, 125, 126

'Eagles Nest', 161, 203
Edwards, Maj J., 122, 127, 140, 143, 145
El Daba, 30, 32, 194
El Fascia, 42, 194
England, Capt R., 123, 124
equipment evaluation, 116

Esser, 23
Esterwegen, 100

'Fabian', 72
Falkland Islands, 174–89, 207–8
Farrar-Hockley, Gen Sir Anthony, 125
Farran, Maj R., 62, 67
Fenwick, Maj I., 84, 85, 87
Ferret Force, 105, 106
fire power, 39, 40, 58, 80, 151
firing ranges, 107
Field Security Sections, 98
Finisterre, 199
Fijians, 147, 167
Firqats, 159–64
Florence, 66, 195
Fontainebleau, 87
Fortuna Glacier, 176
Forward Observation Officers, 63, 189
Fort Austin, 175
Fourdan, 88
'Franklin', 72
France and French: 23, 32, 44, 76, 78, 87, 99,
    103
    Forces of the Interior, 76
    Military Forces, 19, 43, 92, 95 see also
        SAS units
Franks, Lt-Col B. M. F., 64, 102, 104, 105
Fraser, Lt W., 6, 16, 17, 18, 19, 31, 77, 96
Fuka, 30, 193, 194

Gabès and Gabès Gap, 43, 194
'Gaff', 72
Gafsa, 43, 194
'Gain', 72, 76, 79
Gap, the (Borneo), 128, 205
Gap, Orleans, 79, 81, 82
Garstin, Capt P., 80
Gazala, 3, 21, 192
Geneifa, 7
Geneva Convention, 147
Genoa, 66
Germany and German, 98–102
    military forces, 3, 7, 16, 17, 21, 23, 26, 54,
        62, 63, 77, 83, 84, 88, 94–8
Gerry, Sgt A., 128
Ginosia, 195
Goddard, Lt 'Monty', 96
Goose Green, 188, 208
Gottlieb, SIG, 25, 26
Graham, Brig J., 159

Greece and Greek, 56, 196–7
    Sacred Sqn, 43, 58, 59, 61, 196
Greaves, Cpl S., 50, 51, 52
'Grog', 72
Gubbins, Maj Gen Sir Colin, 22
Guild, Lt, 24
Gurdon, Capt the Hon R., 23, 28, 30, 32–4
Gun (Kalimantan), 124

'Haft', 72
Hackett, General Sir John, 43, 68
'Haggard', 72
Hallaniyah, Al, 204
Halliman, Capt G., 12, 13, 14, 15, 18
HALO, 116
Hamilton, Capt J. (Gavin), 176, 189
Harding, General Sir John, 106
'Hardy', 72
Harris, Sim, 169
Harrison, Capt D. I., 94, 101
'Harrod', 72
Hart, Maj L. E. O. T., 104
Hasledon, Col J. E., 41
helicopters, 125, 128, 131, 157, 163, 175,
    182, 188 *see also* RAF and RN
Henquet, Capt R. R., 80, 81, 82
Heraklion, 28, 194
Hereford, 116, 118, 169, 207 *see also* SAS
Hermes, HMS, 185
'Hermit', 81, 82, 88
Holland, 99, 200 *see also* Dutch
Holmes, L/Cpl L. R., 50
Hornbeam Line, 204
Hormuz Straits, 148, 153, 203
'Houndsworth', 72, 97, 103
'Howard', 72, 100

Ibans, 106, 130
Indonesia and Indonesian, 123, 124
    Marine Corps, 119
    Para Rgt, 142
Intelligence, military, 10, 97, 125, 155, 160
Ipoh, 106, 201
Iranian Embassy, 169
Istria, 197, 198
Italy and Italian, 3, 17, 18, 33, 34, 197–8

Jacquier, Lt, 22, 27
Jakarta, 121
Jamieson, Tpr, 96
Jalo, 8, 9, 11–13, 16, 17, 18, 41
Japan, 99

Jeapes, Maj-Gen Tony, 159, 165
Jebel Akhdar, 149, 202
Jebel Aram, 203
Jedburgh Teams, 77, 78
jeeps, 34, 79, 84, 87, 100
Jellicoe, the Earl, 28, 30, 32, 46, 47
Jibjat, 203, 204
'Jockworth', 72
Johore, 106, 107, 201
Jones, Gunner R. W., 50, 51
Jones, Tpr, 80
Jordan, Capt, 23, 25, 26, 31, 32
jungle, types of, 108–9

Kabu, 128
Kabrit, 7, 19, 34
Kahane, SIG, Karl, 27
Kaik, 206
Kalabakan, 128
Kalimantan, 118, 119, 124
Kalino, 195, 196
Kalimnos, 196
Karasovici, 197
Kastelli, 50, 194
Kastellorizon, 55, 195, 196
Kealy, Capt M., 163, 164
'Keeni Meeni', 147
Kelabit Highlands, 205
Kennedy-Shaw, Maj W. B., 10
Kenya, 149, 207
'Keystone', 72
Khalki, 196
Kidd, Sgt K., 110
Kieffer, H. J., 88
Kithira, 56, 196
Kitson, Gen Sir Frank, 149
Kochinoxes Cape, 48, 49, 54
Koemba River, 121, 128, 131, 133, 206, 207
Korea, 105, 132
Kos, 56, 195
Kuala Lumpur, 111
Kufra, 8, 9, 29, 41, 42

Labalaba, Cpl, 163, 164
Lamonby, Lt K., 49, 50, 54
Lampedusa, 194
Lane, Cpl J., 156
Langres, 199
Langton, Maj T., 46
Lapraik, Maj I., 46, 56, 58, 59, 61
Large, Sgt D., 132, 135, 136

'Larkspur', 72
'Larkswood', 72, 100
La Spezia, 66
Lassen, Maj A., 49, 51, 61, 69
'Layforce', 6, 7, 8, 69
Lea, Gen Sir George, 132
Leigh, Lt D., 96
Leith, S. Georgia, 176
Le Mans, 199
Lewes bomb, 2, 7
Lewes, Lt J. S., 6, 7, 12, 18
Lilley, Sgt, 18, 19, 27, 97
Lillico, Sgt E., 128
Limoges, 77, 199
Lisso, 196
Lock, PC T., 169, 172
Loire, 199, 200
London, 169–73, 207
Long Jawai, 124, 125, 128
Long Pa Sia, 206
Long Range Desert Group, 3, 6, 8, 9, 11, 13, 28
Lorraine, 200
'Lost', 72
'Loyton', 72
Lucera, 195
Lundu, 128, 134
Lussin, 197

MacArthur, Gen D., 105
Macbeth, Capt J. S., 59, 60
McCormack, Cpl D., 188
McLeod, Gen Sir Rodrick, 68
McLuskey, Rev J. F., 103
Maas River, 99
Maine, 199
Malaya and Malaysia, 105–18, 201–2
Malayan Scouts *see* SAS
Malta, 28, 29
Malvern, 114
Manners, Col J. C., 65
Manchuria, 103
Mao Tse-Tung, 105
Maquis, 77 *see also* France
'Marshall', 72
Martin, Lt (Free French), 42
Martuba, 22, 25
Mascarrah, 70
Massif Central, 198, 199
Mather, Sgt, J., 185
Mayne, Col R. B. (Paddy), 7, 15, 18, 20,
27–8, 30–4, 37, 40, 41, 43, 45, 62, 64, 69, 100
Mechili, 22
Medical Teams, 116, 123
Menginou, L/Cpl, 92
Meppen, 200
Mercer, Maj H., 110
Merryvaux, 87
Mersa Matruh, 29
Meuse, 199
Military Reconnaissance Force, 166
Millikin, Tpr 'Paddy', 134, 135, 138, 140
Mirbat, 155, 162, 204
Misurata, 194
Mitford, Maj E., 10
Mogadishu, 207
Mohammed Suhail, 156
Montgomery, Field Marshal Viscount, 41, 43
Moor Park Golf Club as HQ, 75
Morvan, 77
'Moses', 72
Mountain, Arctic and Cold Weather Warfare, 116
Mount Kent, 208
Msus, 22
Murphy, Cpl 'Spud', 125
Muruts, 122, 128
Muscat, 148, 149
Mycock, Lt, 95
Mykonos, 196

Nantakor, 131
NATO, 115
navigation and navigators, 10
Naxos, 196
Negri Sembilan, 201
Neill, Lt-Col N., 140
Nevers, 77
Newell, Maj C. E. 'Dare', 106, 108, 114
'Newton', 72
New Zealand and New Zealanders, 11, 113, 126
Nicholson, Sgt J., 50, 51, 52
Nisiros, 196
'Noah', 72
Nofilia, 193
Norman, Maj R. H. D., 125
Normandy, 43, 56, 72, 198, 199
Northern Ireland, 166–7, 207
Norway, 103, 200
nuclear warfare, 118

'Oasis' Force, 8
Oates, Lt, 90
Oldenburg, 100, 102
Oldfield, Maj P., 42
Oman, 113, 142–7, 148–51, 202–5
    Sultan's Air Force, 161
    Northern Frontier Rgt, 151
Orleans, 83, 86, 199
'Overlord', 71, 76 *see also* Normandy

Padawan, 124
Pantelleria, 194
Panzerfausts, 101
parachutes and parachuting, 1, 79, 81, 110,
    150, 188
    HALO, 116
Pa Raya, 205
Paris, 198, 200
Paros, 56, 196
Patmos, 196
Parsons, Lt, 87, 93
Patterson, Maj I., 69
Pebble Island, 185, 208
Penny, L/Cpl J., 130
Pensiangan, 122, 128, 131, 205, 206
Persia, 43
Persian Gulf, 153
Perugia, 196
Pesaro, 196
photo-reconnaissance, 84, 109, 133
Pinchon, 194
Pinkney, Capt P. H., 66, 67
Piraeus, 197
Piscopi, 196
'Pistol', 72
Pithiviers, 84
Plymouth, HMS, 175
Poeri, 133, 135
Poeteh, 206
Poitiers, 199
political aspects, 79, 113, 131–57, 165–6,
    171
Poole, Lt, 74
Port Howard, 189
'Portia', 72
Port Stanley, 180, 181, 189, 208
Prendergast, Lt-Col G., 10, 29
Princes Gate, 171
Prestwick, 69
'Prosper', 81, 82
'psyops', 156, 169, 189
Punans, 122, 123

Qattara Depression, 8, 29, 34
Qaboos, Sultan of Oman, 155

Radfan, 142, 202
Rakyut, 204
Rambouillet, 199
Rayzut, 155
recruits *see* training and selection
Reid, Brig D. W., 8, 9, 17
Reddy, Tpr, 153
'Regent', 72
Reggio, 197
returned to unit, 46
Rhine, 200
Rhodes, 195
Rhodesia and Rhodesians, 12, 13, 106
Riding, Capt 'Jock', 82, 87, 89, 91, 92
Rimini, 195
Ritchie, General Sir Neil, 9, 41
Riverella, 195
Robinson, Sgt, 66
Rome, 195
Rommel, Field Marshal Erwin, 13, 21, 29
Rooney, Maj M., 97
Rose, Lt-Col M., 174, 175, 189
Royal Air Force *see* British Forces
Royal Marines *see* British Forces
Royal Navy *see* British Forces
'Rupert', 72
Russians, 142

Sabah, 122, 205–6
'Sabrina', 150, 151
Sadler, Maj M., 12, 36, 38, 44, 92
St. Brieuc, 78
St. Lô, 74
St. Malo, 79
Salalah, 148, 157, 203, 204
Salerno, 66
Salonika, 197
Samos, 195, 196
'Samson', 72
'Samwest', 72, 76
San Egidio, 195
Santorin, 196
Sarawak, 119–41, 205, 207
Sardinia, 47, 194
Saudi Arabia, 142
Saumur, 83
SAS Troopers and units, 12, 75, 79, 106
    casualties of, 103, 125, 141, 188, 208
    date founded, 6

HQ and 'Kremlin', 116, 153, 174
individuality of, 104, 114
pay, 115
skill at arms, 80
strength in 1944, 71
tributes to, 44, 67, 132, 189
value of operations, 44
Brigade, 68–9, 99
Regiments:
    1st, 20, 41–4, 45, 69, 71–97, 100, 103,
      195–200
    2nd, 62–7, 69, 96, 97, 103, 197–200
    3rd (French), 69, 70, 103, 198–200
    4th (French), 69, 70, 93, 103, 198–200
    5th (Belgian), 69, 70, 100, 103, 199–200
    21st, 61, 105–6, 113, 201
    22nd, 109, 113, 117, 118–82, 201–8
other units:
    L Detachment, 1–41, 96, 193
    Information Team (Dhofar), 155, 156,
      157
    Malayan Scouts, 106–9, 201
    Special Boat Squadron, 43–62, 195–8
    1st Special Raiding Squadron, 45, 62,
      195–6
Schooley, Tpr P., 134–6
Scotland, 70
Scratchley, Maj R., 37, 64, 69
Secret Services *see also* SOE and US Forces,
    9, 75
Security Forces, 110, 112, 127, 128, 166, 169
    Police Field Force (Borneo), 128
Seekings, Cpl R., 16–27, 31, 97
Sekayan, 124, 128, 206
Sembakung River, 205
Sempayang River, 130
Sentas, 207
Sentimo, 121, 132, 206
Sfax, 194
'Shakespear', 72
Sheridan RM, Maj G., 175, 179, 180
Sicily, 47, 62, 194
Sidi Barani, 32
Sidi Haneish, 36, 39, 194, 195
Sidut, 206
Simi, 58, 59, 195, 196, 197
Sinarca, 63
Siphnos, 196
Sirte, 12, 13, 15, 18, 193
Siwa, 8, 9, 12, 23, 28, 29
Sloane, Lt-Col J., 108
Smiley, Col D., 149, 151

Smith, Sqn Sgt Maj L., 122, 123, 152
Smith, Sgt P. (Gipsy), 123, 131
'Snelgrove', 72
South Armagh, 166
South Georgia, 180, 207
Sousse, 44
Special Branch, 128, 147
Special Operations Executive, 75, 76, 88, 97
'Spenser', 72
Spezia, 195, 197
Sporades, 56, 196, 197
Stainforth, Cpl G., 124, 126
Stampalia, 196
Stanley, Comdr I., 178
Stass, 127, 132, 141, 206
Steele, Maj D., 9
Stirling, Col D., 2, 6, 8, 14–15, 18, 19, 20,
    23, 27, 30, 31, 33, 34, 35, 36, 38–42, 68
Stirling, Col W., 62, 65, 67
stress of battle, 70
Stormarella, 195
Sudan Defence Force, 10, 41
Sudh, 160, 203
sun compass, 10
Sutherland, Lt-Col D., 46, 47, 54, 56
'Swan', 79
Swindells, Cpl D., 150
Syracuse, 195

tactics and techniques, 7, 9, 12, 16, 28, 31,
    35, 40, 41, 43, 44, 50–5, 58, 68, 77, 84,
    86, 88, 89, 91, 94, 95, 104, 107, 108, 109,
    110, 114, 121, 134, 138, 141, 147, 149,
    170, 187 *see also* helicopters, jeeps,
    parachuting, weapons
air support, 144
camouflage, 13
deceptions, 47, 71, 74
defensive battles, 55
disguise, 23, 129, 166
'hearts and minds', 121, 138, 147
lead scout, 129
leg bags, 70
liaison with other units (Borneo), 140
logistics and rations, 3, 11, 42, 78, 97,
    111, 134, 150
low intensity operations, 113, 155
in LRDG routines, 13
minefield defences, 141, 167
original concepts, 6
patrols, 13, 74–102, 122–3, 129, 132–40,
    141, 166, 167, 180–6

tactics and techniques – *cont.*
  raids, 9, 12–17, 27, 67, 74–102, 121,
    193–208
  security, 114, 125
  Standard Operating Procedures,
    principle of, 116
  step up tactics, 128
  surprise, 12
  surveillance, 167
  vehicle recovery, 87
Tactical Investigation Committee, 104,
  114
Tait, Sgt, 3
Tamet, 14, 15, 18, 193
Tacqa, 155, 157
Taranto, 63, 195
Tasker, Sgt A., 145, 146
Tawai Atair, 203
Tebedu, 125, 132
Telok Anson, 111–13, 202
Termoli, 62–3, 67, 195
Terrorists, 105, 106, 109, 147, 173
Tewfik, schooner, 55, 196
Thesiger, Lt W., 42, 156
Thimory, 87, 88, 91
Thompson, Maj H., 11–12, 113, 125
Thompson, Maj Gen J. H. A., 174
Timbaki, 47, 54, 194
Timpson, Capt, 30
'Titanic' I, II, III and IV, 72, 74
Tmini, 3, 22
TNKU (Borneo), 119
Tobin, Cpl T. P. A., 163, 164
Tobruk, 3, 11, 21, 29, 41, 42
'Tombola', 67, 197
Tonkin, Maj J., 77, 78, 97
Tourneret, Cpl, 25
training and selection, 6, 61, 67–9, 70, 104,
    105, 113, 114, 115, 117, 119, 127, 152,
    160, 167
  in languages, 79, 116
  specialized courses, 115
  Training Wing, 116
Tripoli, 194
'Trueform', 72
Tunisia, 194
Turkey, 43, 58, 59
Turnbull, Brig D. J. T., 55, 56, 58, 59, 60,
  112

USA and US Forces, 74, 78, 87, 117
  Armies: First, 43; Seventh, 47; Fifteenth,
    98
  Corps: IV, 98
  Office of Strategic Services, 79

Vaculik, Cpl, 80
Vannes, 78, 198
Vendée, 199
Verney, Capt J., 46
Verrières, 77
Vosges, 199, 200
Vrees, 102

Walker, Capt R., 150
Walker, Maj Gen W., 119, 125, 126, 131, 132
'Wallace', 72, 79, 96
Walsh, Tpr K., 134, 135, 137
Warburton, Lt, 27
Warburton, Tpr J. N., 143
Watson, Lt, 87, 88, 89, 91
Watts, Maj Gen J., 150–1, 153, 155
weapons, 84, 85, 97, 170 *see also* Lewes
    bomb
  Armalite, 135, 157
  K-guns, 29, 35, 84, 90
  Mortars, 60
  XFS grenade, 170
Wedderburn, Lt, 66
'white-out', 177
White, Sgt F., 96
Wight, Capt A., 182, 185
Williams, Sgt Maj F., 126
Wilson, Tpr, 93
Wilson, Prime Minister H., 166
Wingate-Gray, Col, M., 133
'Wolsey', 72
Woodhouse, Lt-Col J. M., 107, 110, 113, 118
Woodiwise, Maj R., 134
Woodward, Rear Admiral, 'Sandy', 175

Yates, Sgt, 3, 6
Yedi Atalla, 58
Yemen and Yemeni, 142, 153, 159, 204–5
Yugoslavia, 56, 79

Zahidi, General, 45
Zara, 197
Zirnheld, Capt, 30, 38
Zliten, 194